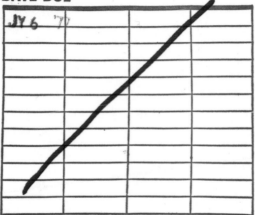

The Individual and Culture

THE DORSEY SERIES IN ANTHROPOLOGY AND SOCIOLOGY

EDITOR   ROBIN M. WILLIAMS, JR.   *Cornell University*

ANDERSON   *Sociological Essays and Research: Introductory Readings*

ANDERSON   *Toward a New Sociology: A Critical View*

BARNOUW   *Culture and Personality*

BARNOUW   *An Introduction to Anthropology*
 Volume I.   *Physical Anthropology and Archaeology*
 Volume II.   *Ethnology*

BELL   *Marriage and Family Interaction*   3d ed.

BELL   *Social Deviance: A Substantive Analysis*

BELL & STUB (eds.)   *The Sociology of Education: A Sourcebook*   rev. ed.

BREER & LOCKE   *Task Experience as a Source of Attitudes*

GAMSON   *Power and Discontent*

GEORGES (ed.)   *Studies on Mythology*

GOODMAN   *The Individual and Culture*

GORDEN   *Interviewing: Strategy, Techniques, and Tactics*

GOTTLIEB & RAMSEY   *The American Adolescent*

HAGEN   *On the Theory of Social Change: How Economic Growth Begins*

HSU (ed.)   *Psychological Anthropology: Approaches to Culture and Personality*

JACOBS   *Pattern in Cultural Anthropology*

JOHNSON   *Crime, Correction, and Society*   rev. ed.

KNUDTEN   *Crime in a Complex Society: An Introduction to Criminology*

KNUDTEN   *Crime, Criminology, and Contemporary Society*

KOHN   *Class and Conformity: A Study in Values*

LEMASTERS   *Parents in Modern America*

MARIS   *Social Forces in Urban Suicide*

SALISBURY   *Religion in American Culture: A Sociological Interpretation*

SHOSTAK (ed.)   *Sociology in Action: Case Studies in Social Problems and Di Social Change*

WARRINER   *The Emergence of Society*

WILSON   *Sociology: Rules, Roles, and Relationships*   rev. ed.

The

Individual and

Culture

MARY ELLEN GOODMAN

Professor of Anthropology and Sociology

Rice University, Houston, Texas

1967

THE DORSEY PRESS

Homewood, Illinois

First Printing, January, 1967
Second Printing, September, 1968
Third Printing, September, 1969
Fourth Printing, June, 1970
Fifth Printing, September, 1971

Library of Congress Catalog Card No. 66–29191

Printed in the United States of America

To the memory of Clyde Kluckhohn,
brilliant scholar,
patient and inspiring teacher.

Anthropologists are not willing to allow determinists to make of culture another absolute as autocratic as the God or Fate portrayed by some philosophies. Anthropological knowledge does not permit so easy an evasion of man's responsibility for his own destiny.

Clyde Kluckhohn

Preface

I am happy to acknowledge assistance and cooperation of a variety of kinds.

The manuscript for this book was read, at least in part, by Robin M. Williams, Jr., Morris E. Opler, William McCord, and Konstantin Kolenda. With their thoughtful questions and criticisms each has given me more help than he could know. I am most grateful.

Over the past three years my students have subjected the evolving manuscript to scrutiny and challenge. Their insistence on clarification, and their fresh outlook, have been greatly valued.

To the authors, editors, and publishers who have so kindly given permission to quote from their articles and books I offer my sincere thanks and appreciation.

Mrs. Deni Seinfeld, who has seen the manuscript through its several phases, has been unfailingly patient, efficient, and kind. She has my eternal gratitude. My thanks go also to Mrs. Marie Thomasen, Mrs. Dong J. Louie, and John Durham for their faithful assistance with preparation of the final manuscript.

MARY ELLEN GOODMAN

Houston, Texas
December, 1966

Table of Contents

CHAPTER   PAGE

INTRODUCTION   1

    Excerpt No. 1, Gordon W. Allport, *Becoming*   6

PART I

1. THE NATURE AND DEVELOPMENT OF THE INDIVIDUAL   13
    The Creative "I". Individual Psychology. Will and Creativity.
    Functional Autonomy; Intention; Tolerance. Altruism. Loving and
    Awareness. Individual's Positive Potentials; Superior Qualities and
    Types. Individual in Context—Basic Propositions.
    Excerpt No. 2, Philip L. Newman, "Wild Man Behavior in a New
    Guinea Highlands Community"   27

2. THE NATURE OF CULTURE   32
    Culture: Its Salient Features; Its Individualization. Patterns. Ideal
    and Behavioral Patterns. Symbols, Beliefs, and Values. Cultural
    Themes and World Views. Generic Features of Culture.
    Excerpt No. 3, H. G. Barnett, *Innovation. The Basis of Cultural
    Change*   50

3. THE INDIVIDUAL IN TOTAL CONTEXT   54
    Organism and Environment. Cultural Boundaries. Society and
    Culture. Physical Environment and Biological Factors. Individu-
    ality and Its Implications.
    Excerpt No. 4, Andrew Hunter Whiteford, *Two Cities of Latin
    America*   63
    Adaptation No. 1, Ethel M. Albert, "Women of Burundi: A Study
    of Social Values"   64

PART II

4. DEGREES OF CULTURAL COMPLEXITY: IMPLICATIONS FOR
    THE INDIVIDUAL   75
    Ethical-Moral Systems and "Primitive" vs. "Civilized" Peoples.
    The Simple-Complex Continuum. Technology. Literacy. Com-
    plexity: Its Advantages and Disadvantages for the Individual.
    Adaptation No. 2, C. S. Coon (ed.), *Reader in General Anthro-
    pology*   89
    Excerpt No. 5, Robert Redfield, "The Folk Society"   93
    Excerpt No. 6, H. G. Barnett, *Innovation, The Basis of Cultural
    Change*   96

CHAPTER   PAGE

Excerpt No. 7, John W. Bennett, "The Interpretation of Pueblo
Culture: A Question of Values"   97

5. PATTERNING OF INTERPERSONAL RELATIONSHIPS:
   IMPLICATIONS FOR THE INDIVIDUAL   101
   Attributes of Interpersonal Relationships in Preindustrial and in
   More Complex Contexts. Family Relationships and Personal Se-
   curity. Interpersonal Relations and the Individual: Basic Propo-
   sitions.
   Adaptation No. 3, Jules Henry, "The Personal Community and Its
   Invariant Properties"   118
   Excerpt No. 8, Dorothy R. Blitsten, *The World of the Family* ...   122

6. ENCULTURATION: IMPLICATIONS FOR THE INDIVIDUAL   128
   Tribalism and Individuation. Complexity and Enculturation. Vari-
   ability of Enculturation Content and of Patterned Concepts of
   Childhood. The Social Acuities of Young Children: Evidence from
   Japan and the United States. Child-Centered Enculturation. Child-
   Centeredness and Individualism. Enculturation and the Individual:
   Basic Propositions.
   Adaptation No. 4, Edward Norbeck, *Takashima*   146
   Adaptation No. 5, Verne F. Ray, *Primitive Pragmatists*   148
   Excerpt No. 9, Ernestine Friedl, *Vasilika: A Village In Modern
   Greece*   152
   Adaptation No. 6, John W. M. Whiting, *Becoming a Kwoma*   156
   Adaptation No. 7, John L. Fischer and Ann Fischer, "The New
   Englanders of Orchard Town, U.S.A."   162

PART III

7. THE PRESS AND PULL OF CULTURE   167
   The Protective and Regulatory Functions of Cultural Press. Regu-
   latory Patterns in Disorder, in Flexibility, and in Extreme Inte-
   gration. Mind and Psyche as Both Formation and Cause. Cultural
   Press and Pull: Some Basic Propositions.
   Excerpt No. 10, Symmes C. Oliver, "Individuality, Freedom of
   Choice, and Cultural Flexibility of the Kamba"   183
   Excerpt No. 11, E. O. Reischauer and J. K. Fairbank, *East Asia:
   The Great Tradition*   185
   Adaptation No. 8, Jessie Bernard, *American Community Behavior*   188

8. THE UNIQUENESS AND THRUST OF THE INDIVIDUAL   194
   Human Restlessness and Cultural Change. Individuality in Folk
   Societies. Individuality in Conformity. Individuality in Flexible,
   Permissive, and Supportive Contexts. Willful, Aggressive, Thrust-
   ful Individuals: Variable Incidence and Responses to Them.
   Thrustfulness in Relation to Supporting and Boundary Conditions.
   Excerpt No. 12, Alexander A. Goldenweiser, "Loose Ends of
   Theory ... "   208

CHAPTER   PAGE

Excerpt No. 13, Ruth Fulton Benedict, "Anthropology and the
Abnormal" 212

Excerpt No. 14, Jane Belo, "The Balinese Temper" 214

Excerpt No. 15, Robert B. Ekvall, "Law and the Individual among
the Tibetan Nomads" 216

9. THE NATURE AND CONDITIONS OF AUTONOMY 219

Autonomy and Individualism. Autonomy and Cultural Milieu.
Autonomy and Cultural Complexity. Autonomy within the Com-
plex Society. Autonomy and Values. The Autonomous Man.
Genesis of Autonomous Man. The Demand for Autonomy. The
Sense of Autonomy; Its Feedback. Cognitive Theory: The Com-
plexities of Decision Making. The Reality and Significance of
Autonomy.

Adaptation No. 9, A. H. Maslow, "Self-Actualizing People" 240

EPILOGUE

EPILOGUE 245

BIBLIOGRAPHY

BIBLIOGRAPHY 249

INDEX

INDEX 261

INTRODUCTION

> I have on my table a violin string. It is free. I twist one end of it and it responds. It is free. But it is not free to do what a violin string is supposed to do—to produce music. So I take it, fix it in my violin and tighten it until it is taut. Only then is it free to be a violin string.
>
> Sir Rabindranath Tagore

This book is addressed to an old question: to what extent can a man determine his own destiny?

To approach this ancient and perennially vital question anthropologically is the aim of this work. The anthropologist sees man-without-culture as like the violin string unmounted—a thing mute and inert. Man-plus-culture takes on the properties of the violin string mounted—it has now a voice and almost a soul. But the string, however marvelous its potential, can never wail or sing at will. It can have no autonomy; its destiny lies in the hand of novice or master. Is man-endowed-with-culture still no more than the mounted string, no freer, no more self-determining?

Behavioral scientists, anthropologists included, seldom face the question forthrightly. Much of what they say implies a low estimate of the individual's potential for self-determination. In extreme cases—e.g., radical behaviorists in psychology and radical cultural determinists in anthropology—even the possibility of autonomy is ruled out. B. F. Skinner tells us that when the individual feels himself to be exercising his freedom he is in fact enjoying an illusion. (Skinner, 1948 and 1953.) And Leslie White is sure that once culture came into existence the individual became permanently

1

the pawn of this irresistible force created by his forebears. (White, 1948.)

Unqualified determinisms of these sorts simply do not square with human experience or with judicious assessment of behavioral science data. Even in a science-dominated age some account should be taken of the subjective experience and there are scholars who do not regard it as stooping. Gordon W. Allport does not disdain the fruits of introspection. All the tricks of self-deception not withstanding, "if we look into ourselves," he says, we "know" a degree of personal integrity. "We know that we have selected, reshaped, and transcended" the ways of our world "to a marked degree." (Allport, 1955, p. 35.)

This sense of personal autonomy has been passed off lightly by academicians enamored of the objectifiable features of context and contemptuous of subjective experience. Data derived through study of the former are accepted respectfully however trivial they may be. But subjective experience has been regarded chiefly as grist for the psychoanalytic or some other interpretive mill. It has been assumed that the individual neither knows what he says nor says what he knows. The assumption reflects a remarkable arrogance on the part of the analyst, particularly in view of the shaky foundations on which it rests.

Clearly the raising of the autonomy question could lead us into a critical evaluation of types of data and of data-gathering methods. But this is not our purpose. Nor is it our purpose even to sketch the history of this question so long debated, and debated so often in terms of revelation or speculation only.

What is attempted here is a relatively modest task: an exploration of that literature in anthropology—a fair sampling of it—which bears on the question of individual autonomy. Not all the scholars whose works are cited are anthropologists. Where we examine the individual, his nature and development (Chapter 1), we naturally and properly draw upon the works of psychologists. But subsequently we draw mainly upon the works of anthropologists.

This book reflects two premises: (1) that the anthropological literature contains much that is highly pertinent, and (2) that this literature has not been mined for its resources relevant to the autonomy question. I mean at least to call attention to these underutilized resources, and to some principles they suggest. The anthropological resources are sampled in two ways: (1) by references and quotations incorporated in the text, and (2) by the attachment to appropriate chapters of substantial excerpts (or adaptations) from the literature.

This exploration has some novel features. It relates closely to culture-and-personality studies, and it should be classified as a variant form thereof. It differs from previous culture and personality studies in being oriented less toward psychology and more toward sociology and philosophy.

Apart from standard works in culture and personality (e.g., Victor Barnouw, 1963) this work claims as its nearest kin Douglas Haring's *Personal Character and Cultural Milieu* (1948; revised editions 1949 and 1956). An apparent kinship also exists with three recent books dealing with the individual and his freedom: Dorothy Lee's *Freedom and Culture* (1959); Herbert J. Muller's *Freedom in the Ancient World* (1964); Konstantin Kolenda's *The Freedom of Reason* (1964). The slants of philosopher (Kolenda), historian (Muller), and anthropologists (Haring and Lee) inevitably differ. But all seem to share with this writer in a quest for fresh and apt conceptualizations and data. All seem to share a conviction that the question of individual autonomy is both academically and practically central, crucial, simultaneously abstract and concrete, and at once ancient and contemporary.

In this work we examine autonomy as a matter primarily of relationships between individual and culture, as a drama of individual thrust and cultural press. But there are other forces acting upon the individual—the biological, the physical environmental, and the societal. Our concern with these three types of antecedent and influence is secondary to our concern with culture, but still lively. The press of culture, while analytically distinguishable from the other major forces, is one with them in the flow of events experienced by the individual. What he is and what he does must reflect not just heredity, physical setting, the nature of his society and of his culture, but these four sets of variables elaborately interacting and interinfluencing.

Nor is this all. For each individual these four sets of variables must be, in minute detail at least, unique, and their combination therefore unique. Necessarily, then, the person will be unique in this matter of antecedents and influences. But he must be unique for another reason too. It is that man, alone among the animals, inspects and reflects upon his situation and himself. As he perceives and reacts he will alter, at least minutely, his situation and himself. Being unique in nature and experience no two men can ever perceive and react in identical ways. Their uniqueness is cumulative and self-reinforcing.

To say that a man reacts should not be taken to mean that he merely responds to a stimulus. There are of course levels of simple reflex behavior. But with these levels we are not concerned here. We are concerned with the levels which involve complex cognitive functioning. It is at these levels that man becomes truly human, and his superiority over other animals unarguable. These are the levels of creativity, innovation, and autonomy. Lacking them, man the organism fails to reach his potential humanness. "The continuous expression of creative and assertive individuality . . . [is] essential for . . . survival and fulfillment as man." (Von Mering, 1961, p. 141.)

We know that individuals vary in capacity for cognitive functioning and creativity. It can be assumed that they vary in capacity for autonomy too, quite likely in close accord with their cognitive and creative capacities. Here we do not examine these intraindividual components in light of the current and relevant body of knowledge. We do not pretend to examine what underlies behavior but rather the behavior itself, or what people say about what underlies their behavior. We are concerned primarily with what is overt and at or near the level of consciousness.

It is the business of an anthropologist to observe and record behavior and to arrive, after accumulating quantities of such data, at generalizations. His generalizations about customary behavior in a particular society amount to a description of that society's culture. But he is not likely to let it go at that—a set of statements about how most of the people behave most of the time. His observations allow him to say much more.

The culture he observes is made up not only of modalities (what most of the people do, or believe they should do, most of the time) but also of alternatives and deviances. In even the best regulated and most orderly of societies, as in families, there will be less than perfect conformity. It may be merely a matter of imperfect reproduction of patterned roles. It may be defiant nonconformity or creative nonconformity. It may be deviance of sorts explicitly or implicitly invited by the very nature of the patterned values. But always individuality will find expression somehow, and whether it is rewarded or punished. The press of culture is uneven and never wholly adequate to suppress or sublimate the thrust of individuals.

Cultures vary with respect to press and with respect to pull as well. "Press" is conducive to modal behavior; "pull" is conducive to selection between alternatives, to creativity and innovation. A culture of the tribe or "folk" is homogeneous and modest as to total content (i.e., the sum of all that is known, practiced and believed by the people). A culture of an urbanized or "sophisticate" people is relatively or absolutely heterogeneous and it is bulky as to total content. Heterogeneity and bulk imply variety and a rich array of choices. There is "pull" in these potentialities, and it is enhanced where individualism is valued.

Individual thrustfulness is affected also by childhood experience. It is affected by the nature of the child's social world—his personal community—and by the ways in which the culture of his people is transmitted to him (the process of enculturation). Security short of stifling; clarity and firmness in the transmission of a coherent set of guidelines—these are conditions which enhance individual confidence and competence. The confident and competent man or woman is optimally prepared to explore and exploit the potentialities of his social and cultural universe. He is prepared to exercise his thrustfulness judiciously and not compulsively. His expression of individuality is likely to take the form of creative innovation rather than of hostile nonconformity.

The anthropological record suggests these views of man. In the following chapters we examine a sampling of the theory and data which support such views. In Part I we consider the major variables which establish limits as well as directions for human behavior—i.e., man's inherent nature and its developmental course; as well as the nature of culture and society. In Part II we examine the press of culture, and its pull, as they vary with cultural complexity. Part III is devoted to discussion of individual autonomy, and the extent to which it is affected by culture.

The following excerpt from Gordon Allport's *Becoming* states succinctly the case for a fresh approach to the question of personal autonomy.

EXCERPT NO. 1*

"The problem of freedom," which Allport describes as a source of "consternation for the scientific psychologist," is no less a persistent and sticky problem for other behavioral scientists. Allport's statement, if cast in slightly different language, could as well have been written by an anthropologist.

When we say that we [individuals] select from the available elements of culture, or that we act in accordance with our conscience, or that we refer our decisions to our schemata of values, we are skirting the problem of freedom. No other issue causes such consternation for the scientific psychologist. One may look through a hundred successive American books in psychology and find no mention of "will" or "freedom." It is customary for the psychologist, as for other scientists, to proceed within the framework of strict determinism, and to build barriers between himself and common sense lest common sense infect psychology with its belief in freedom. For the same reason barriers are erected against theology. But to our discomfort recent events have raised the issue all over again. Existentialism insists on freedom; much of the psychotherapy now in vogue presupposes it; psychology's new concern with values is at bottom a concern with choices, and therefore revives the problem of freedom. Up to now the tug of war between free will and determinism has been marked by naïveté. Just as we have learned with some success to transcend the monolithic oppositions between mind

---

* From Gordon W. Allport, *Becoming* (New Haven: Yale University Press, 1955), pp. 82–88 (italics added).

and body, nature and nurture, we should strive for better perspective in our view of freedom and determinism. The following considerations may help.

1.   In the first place, it is essential that we distinguish the viewpoint of the scientist from that of the acting person. The superior wisdom of the scientist may unfortunately blind him to the process of growth that is actually taking place. The scientist's frame of reference is like the frame of an omniscient being: to him all things have time, place, and determined orbits. But this frame is definitely not the frame of the acting person. The situation is much like that of the watcher from the hilltop who sees a single oarsman on the river below. From his vantage point the watcher notes that around the bend of the river, unknown as yet to the oarsman, there are dangerous rapids. What is present to the watcher's eye still lies in the future for the oarsman. The superior being predicts that soon the boatman will be portaging his skiff—a fact now wholly unknown to the boatman who is unfamiliar with the river's course. He will confront the obstacle when it comes, decide on his course of action, and surmount the difficulty. In short, *the actor is unable to view his deeds in a large space-time matrix* as does an all-wise God, or the less wise demigods of science. *From his point of view he is working within a frame of choice, not of destiny.* As psychologists we ought to know, and do know, *that the way a man defines his situation constitutes for him its reality.* Choice for him is a paramount fact; how matters appear to the watcher on the hill is irrelevant. It is because existentialism takes always the acting person's point of view that it insists so strongly upon the attribute of freedom in man's nature.

2.   Even when we take the view of the scientist we note that *certain conditions make for relatively more or less freedom for the individual. One of the conditions we are most sure of is self-insight.* A therapist of even the most deterministic persuasion assumes that a patient who achieves a high degree of self-objectification, who sees his personal equation clearly written out, is at last in a position to weigh his inclinations, comprehend his limitations, and follow with some success a self-chosen course of action. If this were not so every system of therapy would operate on false pretense. Psycho-

therapy gives hope that a corrected self-image, a more rational assessment of one's behavior, will reduce compulsions, induce order, and free channels of development to accord with chosen aims. Hence even a scientific psychology concedes that self-knowledge may lead to a relative freedom.

3.   *Similarly, relative freedom, we know, depends upon the individual's possession of multiple possibilities for behavior.* To state the point paradoxically, a person who harbors many determining tendencies in his neuropsychic system is freer than a person who harbors few. Thus a person having only one skill, knowing only one solution, has only one degree of freedom. On the other hand, a person widely experienced and knowing many courses of conduct has many more degrees of freedom. It is in this sense that the broadly educated man is freer than the man narrowly trained. Today we are witnessing the frightening things that political leaders with one-channeled minds can do. What alarms us is their simplicist view of social and political reality. They know only one solution; and this solution is totalitarian and spurious. Their lack of tolerance and fear of dissent reflect their own lack of freedom. One-channeled minds can never comprehend that truth may have many channels.

4.   Finally, psychology knows that there is relatively greater freedom in certain modes of choosing than in others. Man's effort is not particularly effective when he tries to meet an impulse head on, by cracking his knuckles and gritting his teeth. Centering attention upon an impulse often brings with it a strong desire to perform the impulsive act. "The evil I would not, that I do." This law of "reversed effort" is familiar to us all.[1] And at this level freedom often seems to be a cruel illusion.

But when I stop cracking my knuckles and become momentarily reflective, asking myself whether "on the whole" this is the course of action I want to take, the picture is changed. The very act of asking "on the whole" brings with it a lessened strain and opens new pathways of decision. This moment of reflection serves to set into activity the larger systems of propriate striving, and their activation

---

[1] Cf. William Brown, *Science and Personality* (New Haven: Yale University Press, 1929), pp. 150–52.

may blot out or absorb incompatible segmental systems and impulses, leaving the individual free to be himself.[2]

The psychologist knows that most of the specific acts we perform ordinarily proceed in accordance with superordinate systems of motivation. If the superordinate system involves, let us say, a loyalty, then the individual, by calling the system to mind, automatically gives it precedence. Under its dominance decisions follow. The weakness of the habit theory lies in assuming that all acts, by the principles of repetition and reward, are theoretically of equal importance in building the structure of personality. Habits appear and disappear not only in conformity with the principles of frequency and reward but also as subsidiary events in relation to a central or propriate structure. William James hastened to repair his doctrine of habits by affirming that the one ultimate act of freedom at man's disposal is his ability "to keep the selected idea uppermost," by which he meant that when we call upon our self-image we automatically reappraise, inhibit, steer, or activate subordinate courses of conduct. Higher-level systems determine the "go" of the lower, and it is for this reason that man is able to keep as closely as he does to his own major systems of value.

It sometimes happens that the very center of organization of a personality shifts suddenly and apparently without warning. Some impetus, coming perhaps from a bereavement, an illness, or a religious conversion, even from a teacher or book, may lead to a reorientation. In such cases of traumatic recentering it is undoubtedly true that the person had latent within him all of the capacities and sentiments that suddenly rise from a subordinate to

---

[2] The point at issue here is of considerable theoretical importance. According to psychoanalytic conceptions the defeated impulse is thought to be repressed, and to continue to plague the individual from the limbo of the unconscious. I am suggesting that under certain circumstances— especially when the comprehensive propriate motive holds sway—the incompatible impulses are not normally repressed; they simply evaporate. Freud himself made a similar observation, though he did not follow through its theoretical implications. In a too seldom quoted passage he writes that he has become "mindful of the distinction between the mere *repression* and the true *disappearance* of an old desire or impulse." (Italics added.) S. Freud, *The Problem of Anxiety* (New York: W. W. Norton, 1927), pp. 82 ff.

a superordinate position in his being. What he had once learned mechanically or incidentally may suddenly acquire heat and liveliness and motive power. What once seemed to him cold, "out there," "not mine" may change places and become hot and vital, "in here," "mine."

I mention this phenomenon of saltatory becoming, not because it is frequent or typical but because it illustrates the complexity and lability of the organizational process. Becoming is not a mere matter of forging links to a chain. It sometimes involves the shifting of dominance from segmental systems to comprehensive systems, or from one comprehensive system to another. Just why or how such shifts occur we cannot say. When they are better understood we can align them with our discussions of determinism and freedom.

These considerations fall short of solving the problem of freedom. They urge us, however, to forgo naïve solutions. That there are upper limits to the possibilities of growth in each life no one can deny. But it seems likely that these limits are movable by virtue of the capacities for reflection, for self-objectification, and to a degree by breadth of education, and by the effort an individual may put forth. From the ethical and theological points of view the stretching toward this limit, whatever it is, is as much of a triumph for a life of slight potential as for a life whose potentials are great.

PART I

CHAPTER 1

The Nature and Development of the Individual

> . . . Culture is indeed a major condition in becoming. Yet personal integration is always the more basic fact. . . . Some elements in our culture we reject altogether; many we adopt as mere opportunistic habits, and even those elements that we genuinely *appropriate* we refashion to fit our own personal style of life. Culture is a condition of becoming but it is not the full stencil.
>
> Gordon W. Allport

In this book the frame of reference is largely nonpsychological. Primarily we view the individual not as a bundle of psychic forces but as a unit of society and a bearer of culture. We view him as at once the creator and—to a degree—the creature of culture. For present purposes overt behavior is the primary datum, and human rationality and creativity are primary interests.

The long preoccupation of most scholars with other aspects of behavior—with the covert, irrational, unconscious, and morbid—has produced an inadequate model of man. Focus on personal pathology has led to one-sided interpretation of the pressures exerted by society and culture; man is seen as the hapless and helpless victim of these pressures, and the pressures themselves tend to be seen as mainly malign.

The behavioral sciences now reflect more of Sigmund Freud than of George Herbert Mead. This is to say that we have been made much more aware of repressions, frustrations, and anxieties—of the ways in which culture constrains and distorts the individual, than of rationality, creativity, and empathy—of the ways in which culture humanizes and liberates man and man shapes and re-shapes culture. Significant research or conceptualizations focused on the individual's potentials for psychic health, characterological strength, spontaneity and zest for life are few. There are not many beside George H. Mead (the creative "I"), Alfred Adler (individual psychology), Otto Rank (will-psychology; the creative capacity), Gordon W. Allport (functional autonomy; intention; tolerance), Pitirim Sorokin (altruism), Erich Fromm (loving and awareness), Abraham H. Maslow (the self-actualizing person).

The concepts of man's nature advanced by these few are of signal importance for our exploration of the individual-culture relationship. We shall review briefly their most significant and relevant contributions.

THE CREATIVE "I"

George Herbert Mead (1863–1931) was a brilliant pragmatist. With other conspicuously able men Mead created at the University of Chicago a great center of intellectual leadership from the 1890's to World War II. Today sociologists and social psychologists find Mead's concepts and interpretations still fresh and stimulating. But the Meadian views translated (e.g., by Talcott Parsons and Robert Merton) seem more static, negative, and deterministic than in the original.

It is . . . possible to maintain that sociologists, who tend principally to be social determinists, read Mead as if he too were a social determin-ist, although his reiteration of the potential influence of individuals upon society should have warned against any such interpretation. . . . The pragmatists, Mead included, emphasize the active role that men play in shaping their environments and destinies. . . . (Strauss, 1964, pp. xii, xiii and xxi.)

In his introduction to a collection of Mead's papers Anselm Strauss stresses also the philosopher's "continual emphasis upon emergence in social relations" (*ibid.*, p. xv). Interpersonal give-and-take were for Mead dynamic processes from which variety and change, perhaps only minor but sometimes major, must emerge. Though it is from contact with others and from observation of them that he learns the culture of his society and develops a concept of self, the individual is more than a mirror.

Seeing himself reflected in the reactions of others the child develops a "me." The "me" (society incorporated) is uncreative and static. It serves as personal monitor and policeman. But there is another part of the self—the "I." The "I" is inner; it is the private self in which the individual preserves a core of integrity. It is impulsive and creative. Individuals are, then, "somewhat freer agents than is allowed in the more usual sociological view: freer not only to find ways to circumvent norms and rules, but also freer to help change the social structures within which they find themselves." (*Ibid.*, p. xv.)

INDIVIDUAL PSYCHOLOGY

Alfred Adler (1870–1937), an Austrian psychiatrist, is perhaps best known for the concept of "inferiority complex." However, this famous complex originally figured only as an item in Adler's "individual psychology." His attention centered on "everything that concerns the individual, society, and their mutual relations." (Ganz, 1953, p. 3.)

Adler saw that from infancy people make vigorous efforts toward self-assertion, attention-getting, and acclaim-winning achievement. These are manifestations of individual will. Not infrequently they are a matter of compensation for perceived inferiorities (including physical inferiorities) in the self. The individual recognizes in himself some shortcoming, and the recognition spurs him to heightened activity. The activity may or may not be of a sort to win a greater measure of admiration or acclaim, but quite often it is. The inferiority complex need not be either a cause or a label for neurosis or psychic crippling.

Realistic self-appraisal, combined with a desire to meet the standards and expectations of his society, provides a powerful source of motivation. When the self-appraisal leads to recognition of personal inadequacies a certain anxiety about the self and dissatisfaction with it are probable. But these sensations, at moderate levels, are scarcely escapable for man in society. One must live in a dream, or he must be a rare paragon, if he fails to sense himself as often inadequate. What measures he uses will be very much a function of time and place—a function of his culture. But the prevalence of concern lest one not measure up must be a universal feature of individual response to society.

It must be universal, too, that in any society many individuals will act on this concern. They will strive to mold the self closer to approved standards which have become (by the learning of their culture) the ideals of the self. Recognition of personal "inferiority" often serves a positive purpose. Adler's "inferiority complex," and his concept of the "overcompensation" to which it may lead, have been widely interpreted as negative and undesirable. They are not, save in their neurotic or psychotic extremes. But these extremes are rarities in most, if not in all, societies. A mild case of "inferiority complex" can be realistic, healthy, and constructive.

In Adler's view of the individual his "present situation is the point of departure, but the goal is a better future." In Adler's diagnosis "The past is made to serve simply as a means of finding out the *style of life* that the individual is always and everywhere pursuing, and that only to assist in his education or re-education." (Ganz, *op. cit.*, p. 5.)

Freudian psychology, by contrast, tended to be preoccupied with the past and with analysis of cause and effect "to the exclusion of all freedom and spontaneous creation. That is the root of its pessimism." (*Ibid.*, p. 2.) Adler emphasized individual will (as contrasted with Freud's sexuality emphasis); his view was forward-looking, optimistic, and holistic (e.g., he did not consider dreams interpretable in terms of Freud's symbols or any other. Rather, he regarded dreams as expressions of the whole individual personality).

As a person Adler was, it seems, kind and wise, fervently democratic, and generous to a fault with his time and talents to help children, the poor, and the disturbed. He "stands far from the false cliché of the will-to-power and from the simple inferiority feeling-compensation paradigm that were at one time associated with his name."

Instead, he saw man, like all living creatures, as incessantly striving. The striving of man is toward some kind of individually conceived superiority, perfection, or success. When it is directed toward a narrow, self-centered goal, it provides the pre-condition for the various forms of failure in life. In the mentally healthy the focus is broad and shares in the "common sense;" . . . the superiority which is aimed for is not over other persons but over general difficulties, the overcoming of which will benefit others as well. (Ansbacher and Ansbacher, 1964, pp. viii–ix.)

WILL AND CREATIVITY

Otto Rank (1884–1939), Viennese psychoanalyst, practiced a therapy built on the concept of will and the individual's capacity to exercise it constructively. Rank's emphasis was also on the supposed "birth trauma" and its presumably persistent and—in some individuals, at least—its pathological results. In our present context his psychology is significant because of (1) his recognition of will as a force for self-direction and for creativity, and (2) his inclination, like Adler's, toward a holistic view of the individual.

Rank, unlike Freud and the proper Freudians, could conceive of a stubborn potential for strength and health surviving even in the weak and ill. His view departs from the gloom-and-doom model of man so vividly projected by Freud. G. W. Allport characterizes this model incisively when he comments on Freud's "refusal to see anything at all in the cooperative, socialized, affiliative, undertakings of mankind excepting goal-inhibited sexuality. To the sex drive he adds principally the impulses of aggression, destruction, and death." (Allport, 1950, p. 190.)

For Rank the individual was "a center of organized forces, not primarily an effect of any external influence but himself a moving effective cause, reacting upon parental pressures and social environment as truly as he is acted upon by them." Rank's view was of a dynamic individual, "in relation to birth, parents, sex and society, as opposite poles necessary for biological development

and psychic balancing." Jessie Taft, in the Introduction to a translation of Rank's *Will Therapy, and Truth and Reality*, continues:

> Every human being must needs represent in his internal organization
> not only the effect of these external influences, but a partial cause,
> a unique source of new energy which utilizes the outer for its own cre-
> ative needs. Freud has remained identified with the destructive over-
> whelming aspects of environmental influences, . . . and has put such
> creative energy into an effort to save the individual victims of life
> forces by means of a therapy of adaptation and adjustment that he has
> influenced the psychology of a whole world. Rank, with no minimizing
> of the environmental, has chosen instead to make a virtue of relativity
> and movement and to assign to the individual his full share in the
> dynamic. (Rank, 1945, pp. xx–xxi.)

Rank's interest in the creative force of the individual led him into
a full-scale study of *Art and Artist* (1932). The study treated the
arts as but one of the many forms through which creativity finds
expression. Rank wrote:

> . . . The human urge to create does not find expression in works
> of art alone: it also produces religion and mythology and the social
> institutions corresponding to these. In a word, it produces the whole
> culture. . . . (Rank, 1932, p. xiii.)

He spoke of an "autonomy of the spiritual," referring to a degree of independence from context which the creative individual
is able to maintain. But he was well aware of the importance and
influence of cultural context, and of the "*reciprocal action*" (italics
original) between individual and context. Rank was aware too that
creativity "manifests itself in such varied ways in the different ages
and cultures. . . ." (*Ibid.*, p. xvi.) Unfortunately he went far beyond this safe ground to wildly speculative reconstructions of
human prehistory and its psychology and philosophy.

Rank rejected what he saw as the psychoanalytic overemphasis
on infantile experience and underrecognition of the force of individual will. He held that the analysts were basically wrong in this,
but especially so in the case of strong-willed and creative individuals. "Childhood influences," he said, "do not build up the personality by themselves, and decidedly not the artistic type, which

. . . distinguishes itself very largely by its surmounting of everything traditional." (*Ibid.*, p. 422.)

FUNCTIONAL AUTONOMY; INTENTION; TOLERANCE

Among contemporary psychologists none takes a more balanced and sanguine view of man than Gordon W. Allport. It is a view based on thorough acquaintance with the research literature in psychology and related fields over the last forty years.

In his *Personality—A Psychological Interpretation* (1937), Allport introduced the concept of *functional autonomy* as a tool for understanding the dynamics of "the normal mature personality." (*Ibid.*, p. 191.) He wrote:

The dynamic psychology proposed here regards adult motives as infinitely varied, and as self-sustaining, *contemporary* systems, growing out of antecedent systems, but functionally independent of them. . . . Such a theory is obviously opposed to psychoanalysis and to all other genetic accounts that assume inflexibility in the root purposes and drives of life. (*Ibid.*, p. 194.)

The theory provides a key without which it is difficult to explain the evolution and the uniqueness of each individual's motives. It allows us to understand how the individual can be, and often is, his "own man" though rooted in his society and culture and constantly affecting and being affected by others.

In his more recent major work, *Pattern and Growth in Personality* (1961), Allport draws together and integrates the many strands of his complex theoretical system. Here he reiterates and clarifies his explanation of the functional autonomy of motives, and he underlines the relevance of such cognitive processes as planning, intentions, and interests.

Allport shows how the individual develops his own set of motives out of thought as well as will and emotion. Because man is capable of reflection and abstraction, of looking ahead as well as behind, he creates visions toward which he is then drawn. He plans; he formulates a set of intentions based on the goals and activities which interest him.

The intention, like all motivation, exists in the present, but has strong future orientation. Use of the concept helps us to trace the course of motivation as lives are actually lived—into the future and not, as most theories do, backward into the past. It tells us what sort of future a person is trying to bring about, and this is the most important question we can ask about any mortal. (*Ibid.*, p. 223.)

With his emphases on autonomy of motives, on cognition, on the mature and forward-looking aspects of man Allport has pioneered and continues to do so. He has created a model of man's nature which promises to survive the test of cross-cultural applicability. It is free of the crudities of earlier models which do not survive that test. As Allport says, "we are emerging from an epoch of extreme irrationalism when human motivation has been equated with blind will (Schopenhauer), with the struggle for survival (Darwin), with instincts (McDougall and others), with the steam boiler of the id (Freud). Under the powerful influence of these doctrines the role of 'the intellect' has been considered negligible." (*Ibid.*, p. 222.) This absurdity is now—and belatedly—quite generally abandoned.

Allport's interests center on normality, health, and maturity of personality. Yet he has written definitively on race prejudice, *The Nature of Prejudice* (1954). This work is focused on one of the more negative aspects of personality. But even with this focus Allport carries the discussion toward a facet of healthy maturity— i.e., the human capacity for tolerance and empathy.

Why is it that, although race, ethnic, and class prejudices are nearly universal aspects of cultures, they do not appear in some individuals? Allport reviews a variety of reasons:

Some [individuals] seem tender-hearted almost by nature. Others are apparently mirroring their early training. In some the aesthetic and social values are highly developed. Educational level plays a part; so too does a general liberal outlook on political issues. Self-insight has a place, likewise the ability to size up and deal with individuals (empathy). Above all, a basic security and ego-strength are present which counteract the tendency to repress, to blame others, and to seize upon institutional and authoritarian guarantees of personal safety. . . . Self-love is compatible with love of others. . . .

[The] tolerant orientation is possible because security has been experienced in the realistic handling of inner conflicts and social transactions. Unlike the prejudiced person, the tolerant person does not perceive the world as a jungle where men are basically evil and dangerous.
(*Ibid.*, p. 441.)

ALTRUISM

The human capacity and need for love of others, and concern for
them, has long been the central interest of sociologist Pitirim A.
Sorokin. From The Harvard Research Center in Altruistic Integration and Creativity, Sorokin has published extensively on love and
"ethical creativity."

The results of his feverish commitment and prolific writing are
disappointing. Hortatory rhetoric seems to have advanced knowledge but little. The problem to which Sorokin addressed himself
remains crucial, legitimate, and unsolved. In 1950, prefacing his
Altruistic Love, he stated the problem:

Strange as it may seem, we know little about the altruistic person.
We have studied the negative types of human beings sufficiently—the
criminal, the insane, the sinning, the stupid, and the selfish. But we
have neglected the investigation of positive types of Homo sapiens—
the creative genius, the saint, the "good neighbor." (Sorokin, 1950, p.
vi.)

Sorokin believes that some individuals—"the early-fortunate"—
are altruists from childhood. Others ("the late-matured" and "the
intermediary") become altruists after some experience of an eye-
opening kind. Albert Schweitzer, John Woolman, and Benjamin
Franklin are among his examples of the genuine article—the
early-fortunates. Their genesis he explains as a self-identification
phenomenon. Each has embraced, with his "heart" as well as his
mind and will, "the highest and sublimest values: God, Tao, Jen,
Logos, the Inner Light, etc., and always Love at its purest and
best." (Sorokin, 1954, p. 175.) Sorokin's analyses remain at this
level—"explanations" which merely restate an apparent phenomenon.

LOVING AND AWARENESS

The Art of Loving (1956) has also occupied the attention of psychoanalyst Erich Fromm. His discourse, while decidedly speculative, offers more than superficial description of persons who are alleged to be loving or altruistic.

Fromm shares Sorokin's premise that man is capable of love and of altruism. He shares Sorokin's convictions concerning the indispensability of lovingness if the individual is to live with zest and his society to be strengthened by his presence. Fromm goes on to deal with questions of genesis: how does the individual learn to be loving? Can the process be self-induced and self-developed?

Love is an art, says Fromm, which the individual is free to cultivate as he is free to acquire any other art or skill. "The process of learning an art can be divided conveniently into two parts: one, the mastery of the theory, the other, the mastery of the practice." (*Ibid.*, p. 5.)

Fully developed lovingness, like Sorokin's true altruism, is an attribute of the rare individual. It is "a capacity of the mature, productive character," and character development is heavily affected by culture. Contemporary Western civilization provides an unfavorable climate. Nevertheless, Fromm seems to be saying, it is possible for the Westerner to make himself into a mature and loving person. He can do so by studying the theory and practice set forth by Fromm, and by deliberately summoning up his personal resources in the way of self-discipline, patience, concentration, and reasoning powers. Loving and reasoning are not mutually exclusive; they are in fact complementary functions.

The individual can perform such prodigies of self-improvement because of those uniquely human capacities—high intelligence and self-awareness.

Fromm elucidates these views in discussion of "freedom, determinism, alternativism." He argues that there is an "essence of man" which is universal, transcending differences between cultures and surviving their "press" (our term, not Fromm's). This essence of man is not "a given quality or substance," like good or evil; it is rather "a *contradiction inherent in human existence.*" (Italics—Fromm's.)

This contradiction is to be found in two sets of facts: (1) Man is an animal, yet his instinctual equipment, in comparison with that of all other animals, is incomplete and not sufficient to insure his survival unless he produces the means to satisfy his material needs and develops speech and tools. (2) Man has intelligence, like other animals, which permits him to use thought processes for the attainment of immediate, practical aims; but man has another mental quality which the animal lacks. He is aware of himself, of his past and of his future, which is death; of his smallness and powerlessness, he is aware of others as others—as friends, enemies, or as strangers. Man transcends all other life because he is, for the first time, *life aware of itself.* (Fromm, 1964, pp. 116–17.)

It is in that ideal type—the "mature" individual—that man's inherent capacities for self-determination and freedom of choice are fully apparent. It is he who is in the strongest position to make choices between alternatives. Fromm's development of these points is arresting. He writes:

. . . We can use the concept "freedom" in two different senses: In one, freedom is an attitude, an orientation, part of the character structure of the mature, fully developed, productive person; in this sense I can speak of a "free" person as I can speak of a loving, productive, independent person. . . . In this sense the person who "is not free to choose evil" is the completely free person. The second meaning of freedom is the . . . capacity to make a choice between opposite alternatives. . . . The decisive factor in choosing the better rather than the worse lies in *awareness:* (1) awareness of what constitutes good or evil; (2) which action in the concrete situation is an appropriate means to the desired end; (3) awareness of the forces behind the apparent wish; that means the discovery of *unconscious* desires; (4) awareness of the real possibilities between which one can choose; (5) awareness of the consequences of the one choice as against the other; (6) awareness of the fact that awareness as such is not effective unless it is accompanied by the *will* to act, by the readiness to suffer the pain of frustration that necessarily results from an action contrary to one's passions. (*Ibid.*, pp. 132–33; italics in original.)

INDIVIDUAL'S POSITIVE POTENTIALS;
SUPERIOR QUALITIES AND TYPES

Each of the scholars upon whose works we have touched presents his ideas about personal health, strength, and goodness (psychically and characterologically speaking). Each recognizes and emphasizes, to a degree unusual among contemporary behavioral scientists, these positive aspects and potentials of man.

The recognition and emphasis are important for our purposes. In some of the thought we have reviewed there is explicit acceptance and development of the view that man is not automaton. In all of the works reviewed the discussion proceeds from the premise that individuals—some of them, some of the time, at least—can and do shape their own destinies.

Each of our scholars gives attention to the questions: which individuals? when? are in fact most inclined and most competent in this matter of self-determination. The answers, given by each scholar in his particular frame of reference, always resolve themselves into description of a superior human quality or type. Our authorities are not oriented strongly toward cultural comparisons, and they therefore do not develop their views as to the universality of these superiorities, either actually or potentially. They have little to say about the relevance of particular kinds and conditions of cultures. Exploration of this important matter falls in the anthropologists' frame of reference, and is a part of the business of this book.

Abraham H. Maslow has provided what is as yet probably the boldest, clearest statement concerning a superior human type. In addition he appears to be in process of evolving a pertinent method of study and a body of theory.

Far more than most behavioral scientists Maslow is a "rose-colored glasses" student of man's inherent and essential nature. Psychic health and strength seem to him but the "actualization" of that nature. Society and culture act upon the individual either to suppress or to draw out, but the growing occurs "from within rather than being shaped from without . . . Psychopathology in general results from the denial or the frustration or the twisting of man's essential nature." Whatever is conducive to "actualization of the inner nature of man . . . is good. . . ."

What this amounts to saying is that we may agree with Aristotle when he assumed that the good life consisted in living in accordance with the true nature of man, but we must add that he simply did not know enough about the true nature of man. . . . The only thing that Aristotle could do was to build a picture of the good man in his own culture and in that particular period of time. . . . We can now see not only what man is, but what he may become. . . . [And] we have learned . . . that self-realization cannot be attained by intellect or rationality alone. . . . We have learned . . . to respect equally rationality, emotionality, and the conative or wishing and driving side of our nature. Furthermore, from our empirical studies of the healthy man we have learned that these are definitely not at odds with each other. . . . (Maslow, 1954, pp. 340–42.)

Maslow's superior type becomes, then, the self-realized or self-actualized man. These individuals are rare, generally recognized and appreciated by their fellow men, and maximally productive as well as satisfied. They are independent (nonconformist) but by no means compulsively assertive. They are creative, not necessarily in the arts or sciences but in the sense that their thinking is not fettered by the big or little anxieties and dependences that hamper lesser men. They rise above the level of their contexts. Presumably (though Maslow does not make this point explicit) they thereby lead the way toward social and cultural change, and presumably too it would be change for the better. Maslow says:

. . . Research has established an important point in discovering that individuals can be healthier, even *much* healthier, than the culture in which they grow and live. This is possible primarily because of the ability of the healthy man to be detached from his surroundings, which is the same as saying that he lives by his inner laws rather than by outer pressures. (*Ibid.*, p. 351.)

One may join Maslow in celebrating the self-actualized man as a superior and an admirable human type. One may believe that the rich content of the world's total of culture owes much to such men. But one may part his company and refuse to follow when Maslow leads to the corollary propositions: (1) that men (all of them, by implication) would be superior if it were not for the social and cultural thwarting to which they are subjected, and especially that to which they are subjected in childhood; (2) that to produce a larger proportion of the superior sort it is necessary merely—or mainly—to cease and desist on "control, inhibition, discipline, training, shaping." What is required, if society is to reap a bounteous human crop, is only to provide a context for "spontaneity, release, naturalness, self-acceptance, impulse-awareness, gratification." (*Ibid.*, p. 352.) Permissiveness is at the heart of the matter.

Unfortunately, not all of the fruits of permissiveness are sweet. For this there is ample proof. Probably no one of us has failed to encounter a sample in the form of some little savage being reared entirely in accord with Maslow's prescription. The formula is too simple; the superior man does not simply unfold in the sunshine of love and permissiveness. It would be more apt to say that he is hammered out on the anvil of experience, much of it a matter of discipline, control, and training, though much of it is indeed a matter of affection, gratification, and acceptance.

It must be added that the "essential nature" with which the process begins appears to be highly variable. Some natures seem from the first to be so strongly inclined (e.g., toward creativity or crime) that no amount of either permissiveness or hammering significantly alters their course. The large majority, however, responds profoundly to the shaping.

INDIVIDUAL IN CONTEXT—BASIC PROPOSITIONS

We may conclude, after this sampling of relevant research and writing, that a balanced view of the individual in sociocultural context involves acceptance of these propositions:

1. The individual is endowed with will and creativity, as well as with intelligence and awareness; he is therefore creator and manipulator of culture, as well as receiver and reactor.

2. There is great variability between individuals within a given

context as well as between contexts, with some individuals showing themselves—from infancy or from later life periods—to be in some ways or quite generally superior in creativity, altruism, independence, or other specifics of personality and character.

3. The forces of society and culture acting on the individual may be, in terms of his personal well-being and development, either benign or malign; they are seldom so malign as Freudian psychology seems to assert, nor is the individual likely to be inherently so thoroughly benign as Maslow seems to suppose. Child rearing and other forms of sociocultural press provide enrichment and tools (knowledge, skills) as well as refinement of those inherent inclinations which are not consistent with personal satisfaction or a productive society. They can develop, for example, capacities for love, altruism, and empathy.

EXCERPT NO. 2*

In the following passages Newman discusses a distinctive type of behavior which occurs occasionally among the Gururumba of the New Guinea highlands. A man who goes "wild" departs radically from his previous behavior and from the norms. He seizes the property of others and forces himself violently and erratically upon others. He is impervious to persuasion to desist and indifferent to obligations and expectations he has previously honored.

Newman interprets "wild man" behavior as a culturally patterned escape hatch. The individual who makes use of it is in effect saying to his fellows: "I can no longer take the pressures of life; please let up." His fellows evaluate his performance for genuineness and appropriateness. If they judge that it meets both tests they do indeed "let up." Less is expected of this individual in the future.

The account illustrates a number of the points discussed in Chapter 1: individual variability; awareness of individual variability and sensitivity; empathy and tolerance; perception of personal "inferiority" and compensatory behavior (through abrogation rather than striving, however); the selection and manipulation of an aspect of culture in the interest of a personal need; responses to aspects of culture which for the responding individual have become malign.

---

* From Philip L. Newman, "Wild Man Behavior in a New Guinea Highlands Community," *American Anthropologist*, Vol. 66, No. 1 (February, 1964), pp. 16–19.

There are no recriminations against a wild man after he has gone wild, and no one in his clan or village will mention the episode to him. They do talk about it among themselves, however. It is evident from these conversations that after the wild man episode they do not think of him as the same kind of person he was formerly thought to be. Formerly he was thought of as a man with essentially the same capacities and capabilities as any other man. It is probably more accurate to say that formerly no one gave much thought to his capacities and capabilities, but that his actions as a wild man generate such thought. . . . The Gururumba are aware of the kinds of pressures social life imposes on them. When a man goes wild they also become aware of the fact that this particular individual is not as capable as others of withstanding those pressures. This awareness is reflected in their treatment of an individual after a wild man episode. Specifically, there is an observable reduction in the expectation others have of the degree he will participate in exchange transactions and a corresponding reduction in the intensity of demands made on him: He may still have debts, but repayment is not pressed aggressively; he still has obligations to affines (relatives through marriage), but others seldom attempt to further their own ends by encouraging their participation in the fulfillment of his obligations; he still contributes to group sponsored food distributions, but no attempt is made to extract a prior commitment from him as to how much he will contribute; he knows he can still call on his village-mates to help him in work projects, but his village-mates know that their compensation will be in the form of return labor rather than a share in a food distribution. The outcome of wild man behavior is thus a reduction of demands made without loss of social support. The wild man does not become an outcast or deviant in the eyes of others; he becomes a man now known to be incapable of, or unwilling to participate in, certain affairs with the same degree of intensity as others, but still a man who can participate to some degree.

This new assessment made by others is in accord with the way a wild man feels about himself. This can be seen in the way such an individual contrasts with two other kinds of persons. On the one hand, he contrasts with men who remain apart from the general life of the community. Such men are rare, but they exist. They live away from the village; they do not stay in the men's house, except occasionally; they seldom attend any village gathering; they only infrequently call upon others for aid. They do not appear rebellious but neither are they committed. On the other hand, the wild man contrasts with those individuals who will occasionally become so angry with some life circumstance that they give the appearance of renouncing all social ties. They threaten to leave the community or to withdraw their support by some other means. These outbursts are usually only temporary and such persons are mollified in most cases. Unlike the first kind of person, the wild man sees himself as committed to economic involvement but comes to realize that there must be limits to his commitment. Unlike the second kind of person, the wild man sees himself as one who cannot make clear to others the limits of his commitment by threatening an open breach when those limits have been taxed. All this suggests that the men who become wild see themselves as persons who will never succeed brilliantly but who also see themselves as doing better than failing miserably.

The real problem for such a man consists of letting others know what kind of person he is. In order to maintain the position he sees as congenial to himself, he must make others realize his willingness to "play the game" but with less intensity than others "play" it. This is difficult because he gives the appearance of being committed with the result that others press demands, and if demands are not met, others explain this in terms of his youth, his inexperience, or temporary situational difficulties. They assume he will eventually live up to expectations, but he thinks of the expectations as being too high. It is difficult to communicate this because he does not want to do or to say things that might indicate he is either "giving up the game" or issuing threats so the game will be made to run his way. Wild man behavior can be seen as a solution to the individual's problem of closing the gap between what he thinks of himself and what others think of him.

How is it that wild man behavior has this effect? The answer given here is speculative but, I feel, reasonable. The wild man is not directly presenting himself to those who view him; he is presenting his view of the way the everyday actions of others look to him. His aggressive collection of the belongings of others, his excessive valuation of objects having small worth, his refusal to hear objections to his acts, his refusal to speak about his acts, and his disregard for the way his acts may affect others (as in his destruction of their belongings or forced entry into their houses) are dramatic expressions of the way certain patterns of everyday life appear to him. Although Gururumba beliefs portray human nature as highly aggressive, people do not habitually act as if it mattered to them. By forcefully calling attention to this aggressiveness the performance of the wild man makes it clear that he is an individual who cannot fully accept it. What others know about this man—his current situation, his past performance, his character—is seen in a new light and given a new interpretation.

Revision of opinion by others occurs only in cases where the community can in fact review the individual's past life and find justification for believing this person is as he now presents himself to be. There are three kinds of situations where review does not occur. In them no revision of opinion is made nor is the individual allowed to carry out the wild man pattern. This occurs when young unmarried men attempt to present themselves as wild men. People laugh at them and accuse them of fakery or interpret the behavior as something other than wild man behavior. Being too young there is not enough in their life histories to warrant an assumption that they are different from others. It also occurs when a wild man wanders into the villages of other clans. In this situation he may be accused of faking, and his actions may be physically resisted. Being from another place these people are not as intimately acquainted with the details of the wild man's life as those who live in daily contact with him. Finally, it occurs in the case of the behavior called *afafaje*. . . . This looks, superficially, very much like wild man behavior except that it does not involve the taking of objects. It occurs, primarily, in older men and is brought to a swift conclusion by physically restraining the person and holding him over a smoking fire until he returns to normal. These older men are firmly established and there is no reason for the community to believe they are now any different than they have always appeared to be. The fact that a person can be accused of faking a wild man performance clearly indicates that a judgment of legitimacy is made by the community. If wild man behavior were simply a tension reduction mechanism, legitimacy would rest only on whether or not the performance remained within the bounds of the allowed pattern. In wild man behavior, however, legitimacy rests equally on the judgment that the performance reveals something about the performer. The performance can be seen as occasioning the reorganization of what people know about a person, but it must also be seen that the reorganization does not take place unless the community can find substantiation for it in the past behavior of the person.

CHAPTER 2

The Nature of Culture

Man has expressed his individuality in culture's many forms.
Morris E. Opler

In its simplest anthropological meaning *a culture* is the entire set of customs practiced by the members of a society. It is the particular way of life learned, shared, and transmitted by members of the society bearing that culture. A society is a considerable number of people who regard themselves, and are regarded by others, as a unit—a tribe or a nation internally organized and persisting through time. Each of the many such units past and present has developed its own distinctive culture—its way of life.

The fact of enormous cultural diversity around the world and through time has been thoroughly documented. In the course of the last century anthropologists have observed and recorded the life ways of hundreds of societies. They have extended their investigations, via spade and notebook, over all of man's time and most of the space he has occupied and now occupies. Prehistoric as well as historic and contemporary cultures have been studied. Even the complex urban-industrial cultures have become objects of anthropological investigation.

One of the results of these labors is an enormous reservoir of descriptive data demonstrating remarkable diversities in all aspects of human life. Making a living, raising children, dealing with the supernatural, keeping order both in the society and between it and other societies, communicating with one's fellows, in each of these and in other essentials and numerous nonessentials there is endless variation. The customary practices of many peoples appear bizarre or incredible when compared with customary practices in Western urban-industrial societies, yet in context they are seen as unremarkable and seldom questioned. Notable among cultural curiosities are certain arrangements for marriage and family living; for example:

In [traditional] China the males of a family are charged with responsibility for obtaining husbands for the daughters and even for the serving maids of the household. Non-marriage on the part of a woman disgraces the family. Hence Chinese often conclude that unmarried American lady missionaries have fled to China to escape the disgrace incurred by failure of their fathers or brothers to find a husband. (Haring, 1949, p. 33.)

To the American woman a system of plural wives seems "instinctively" abhorrent. She cannot understand how any woman can fail to be jealous and uncomfortable if she must share her husband with other women. She feels it "unnatural" to accept such a situation. On the other hand a Koryak woman of Siberia . . . would find it hard to understand how a woman could be so selfish and so undesirous of feminine companionship in the home as to wish to restrict her husband to one mate. (Kluckhohn, 1949, p. 18.)[1]

Among the Banaro of New Guinea the firstborn child must not be the offspring of the husband. The real father is a close friend of the bride's father. . . . Nevertheless the firstborn child inherits the name and possessions of the husband. An American would deem such a custom immoral, but the Banaro tribesmen would be equally shocked to discover that the firstborn child of an American couple is the offspring of the husband. (Haring, 1949, p. 33.)

Polyandry, of the type in which several brothers share one wife, is a popular form of marriage in Tibet. In one family we know, one lady presides over a committee of seven husbands. How a husband's right is to be apportioned among the claimants varies with each family. Some tacit understanding based on rotation always exists. This is especially true among the commoners; with them there are always some absentee

---

[1] From *Mirror for Man* by Clyde Kluckhohn. Copyright 1949. McGraw-Hill Book Company. Used by permission.

husbands out on pilgrimages or trading trips. Among the higher classes, precedence is automatically given to the most prosperous husband. . . . When a child is born, it is the most important spouse who gets the honor of being the father, the rest being mere uncles. (Shen and Liu, 1953, p. 142.)[2]

What has been called, irreverently, the "investigation of odd-ments by the eccentric" has produced rather more than an avalanche of such curiosa, however. It has laid an empirical foundation essential to formulation of reliable generalizations about human behavior. Some such generalizations are by now well validated and well enough known to be taken for granted by educated people. Others remain in the category of arguable and argued hypotheses.

Cultural determinism is among the argued generalizations. The question is: Does man simply become what he must, because of the cultural milieu in which he has his existence? Does he have no real choice, no real control over the destiny shaped by his culture? Cultural determinists answer in the affirmative.

But there are other views. Here we join with those who see culture as one of the several major factors which, taken together, constitute the individual's whole background and context. In this view culture is not *the determinant* of behavior. Culture is, rather, one of the foundations and boundary conditions upon and within which the individual and his potentialities develop. It is an indispensable condition of becoming human, and a powerful force inclining the individual toward humanness of a certain variety and within certain limits.

The foundation and boundary functions of culture are best understood in terms of example. Clearly, the man of letters or the nuclear physicist will not appear in the context of pre-literate and pre-scientific culture; the pacifist or the ascetic are near impossibilities in the context of aggression and sex-oriented cultures like those predominant in the New Guinea highlands.

However strong and unified the forces of his culture, the individual is always unique. Conventional theories of cultural determin-

---

[2] Reprinted with permission of the publishers from *Tibet and the Tibetans* by Tsung-Lien Shen and Shêng-Chi Liu (Stanford: Stanford University Press, 1953), p. 142.

ism do not fully or satisfactorily explain this uniqueness. A satisfactory theory must recognize individuality and take into account the factors which can explain it. Some of these factors—e.g., will, creativity, awareness—have been noted in earlier discussion of the individual (Chapter 1).

The theory of cultural determinism, in its unqualified or radical form, has waxed and waned in scientific and popular thought. It now enjoys a considerable vogue, and with results of a sometimes fantastic sort. As David Riesman observes:

> Social science has helped us become more aware of the extent to which individuals, great and little, are the creatures of their cultural conditioning. . . . Sometimes the point is pushed to the virtual denial of individuality: since we arise in society, it is assumed with a ferocious determinism that we can never transcend it. All such concepts are useful correctives of an earlier solipsism. But if they are extended to hold that conformity with society is not only a necessity but also a duty, they destroy that margin of freedom which gives life its savor and its endless possibility for advance. (Riesman, 1964, p. 38.)

Cultural theorists arguing for radical determinism tend to be selective with respect to the data they assemble in support of their position. Data demonstrating the undeniable force of culture, its apparent supraindividual power and persistence, are adduced. These data are quite true, but they are not all of the truth. Enthusiasts for cultural determinism vividly describe the forest: they are indifferent to its constituent trees.

> . . . Most cultural anthropologists overlook the individual event and actor in the attempt to delineate overall patterns and structures. . . . The failure to confront the meaningful particular is a reflection of academic pathology, of a falsely objective social science that seeks merely to report, or to build some theory which generalizes all human responsibility out of existence, and more seriously, in our presently complicated world, helps prevent us from understanding the critical and contingent nature of certain sequences of events. . . .
>
> The significance of the individual, and of the individual event in determining the course of history and thus the more abstract morphology of culture . . . can be readily established. . . . History is a thread of contingencies, woven by [individual] decisions into cultural forms. (Diamond, 1964, pp. 41–43.)

Here we shall examine human behavior from the perspective of individual in context. We are concerned especially with the potential and thrust of unique persons. We do not propose to ignore noncultural forces acting in and on the individual—the biological, physical environmental, and societal forces. But our principal concern is with the individual, with culture, and with the intricate reciprocities between.

What is culture? The minimal definition given at the beginning of this chapter now must be expanded and refined.

CULTURE: ITS SALIENT FEATURES; ITS INDIVIDUALIZATION

"Culture" has been defined and re-defined. In 1952, Alfred L. Kroeber and Clyde Kluckhohn published a work entitled *Culture—A Critical Review of Concepts and Definitions*. Their thorough search of anthropological literature to that date provided them with 164 definitions. From this array they culled the recurrent elements, and concluded that the central idea is now formulated by most social scientists approximately as follows:

Culture consists of patterns, explicit and implicit, of and for behavior acquired and transmitted by symbols, constituting the distinctive achievement of human groups, including their embodiments in artifacts; the essential core of culture consists of traditional (i.e., historically derived and selected) ideas and especially their attached values; culture systems may, on the one hand, be considered as products of action, on the other as conditioning elements of further action. (Kroeber and Kluckhohn, 1963, p. 357.)

This statement is not likely to be improved upon. It conveys the sense in which "culture" is used here. Kroeber and Kluckhohn continue:

All cultures are largely made up of overt, patterned ways of behaving, feeling, and reacting. But cultures likewise include a characteristic set of unstated premises and categories ("implicit culture") which vary greatly between societies. Thus one group unconsciously and habitually assumes that every chain of actions has a goal and that when this goal is reached tension will be reduced or disappear. To another group, thinking based upon this assumption is by no means automatic. They see life not primarily as a series of purposive sequences but more as made up of disparate experiences which may be satisfying in and of themselves, rather than as means to ends.

Culture not only markedly influences how individuals behave toward other individuals but equally what is expected from them. Any culture is a system of expectancies: what kinds of behavior the individual anticipates being rewarded or punished for; what constitute rewards and punishments; what types of activity are held to be inherently gratifying or frustrating. For this and for other reasons (e.g., the strongly affective nature of most cultural learning) the individual is seldom emotionally neutral to those sectors of his culture which touch him directly. Culture patterns are *felt*, emotionally adhered to or rejected.

As Harris has recently remarked, "The 'whole' culture is a composite of varying and overlapping sub-cultures." Sub-cultures may be regional, economic, status, occupational, clique groups—or varying combinations of these factors. Some sub-cultures seem to be primarily traceable to the temperamental similarities of the participating individuals. Each individual selects from and to greater or lesser degree systematizes what he experiences of the total culture in the course of this formal and informal education throughout life.

[Edward] Sapir [a leader in development of culture and personality studies] speaks of "the world of meanings which each one of these individuals may unconsciously abstract for himself from his participation in these interactions." . . . In some cases, as in social organization or linguistic usage and vocabulary, the individual carries out only a part of the socially observed pattern . . . , and we cannot say that his selection of behavior is the same as the social pattern. In other cases, as in grammatical structure, the individual's behavior is virtually the same as that which is described for the society as a whole. . . . Sapir shows how the speaker of a particular language uses the particular pattern of that language no matter what he is saying . . . the social pattern (i.e., the behavior of the other individuals in society) provides experience and a model which is available to each individual when he acts. Just how he will use this model depends on his history and situation: often enough he will simply imitate it, but not always. (*Ibid.*, pp. 308–09.)

Anthropologist Grace de Laguna comments on the individual as a kind of cultural microcosm, though in no simple sense. She says:

It is as if the basic pattern of the culture must be reflected in the internal structure of each individual person; as if the individual were in some sense a microcosm and the culture to which he belongs a macrocosm. Each individual, like a Leibnizian monad, "reflects" the culture of his world from his own point of view and with varying degrees of clearness and confusion. The experienced ethnologist is now able to reconstruct a considerable part of the culture system from any good informant, using not merely what the informant "knows," or can verbalize, but what he unwittingly reflects in his attitudes and modes of expressive response. . . . Observable differences are equally important and even more significant. The basic structure is rather to be found in the common ground of both their similarities and their differences, the trunk from which divergent personalities branch and by which they are all supported. (De Laguna, 1949, pp. 387–88.)

Three major propositions can be abstracted from the Kroeber and Kluckhohn and from the De Laguna statements. These propositions are:

1.   Overt patterns, implicit premises, systems of expectancies—all are salient features of a culture, and all may show some variant, i.e., subcultural, forms.

2.   These patterns, premises, and expectancies are among the cultural features and forms to which an individual is exposed as he grows up in his society, and from which he selects and synthesizes. The result is his own, an individualization which may or may not closely approximate what has served as a model.

3.   The individual "reflects" his culture, he does not precisely reproduce it.

Later (Chapter 8 particularly), we turn our attention to questions of individual variability and creativity, assertiveness and autonomy. But it should be emphasized here, at least in passing, that individualization of culture accounts for much of cultural change. Uniquely endowed, making his unique selection, interpretation and synthesis of cultural elements, the individual reproduces inexactly and thereby creates inadvertently if not deliberately. Margaret Mead provides an insight into one aspect of the process when she says:

. . . the simultaneous play of different kinds of imagery and different kinds of information in the individual human mind and between human minds is a principal setting for the birth of new ideas. (Mead, 1966, p. 68.)

PATTERNS

"Culture consists of patterns, explicit and implicit, of and for behavior. . . ." (Kroeber and Kluckhohn, *op. cit.*) It consists of other types of elements as well; some of these others we shall consider a little later in this chapter. The pattern element properly takes priority.

The term "pattern" is appropriate because the element in question serves the function of a physical pattern (e.g., a dress pattern; a mold for metal casting). The culture pattern, like the physical pattern, acts as a guide; it channels and establishes form, boundaries, and part relationships.

"Pattern" is an appropriate concept in culture for another reason as well. The term means not only a mold or guide but also an emergent design, e.g., "the tracing made by skate blades by a figure or dance step executed on ice; . . . the grouping made on a target by rifle or handgun bullets . . ." (Webster's Third New International Dictionary, 1965, p. 1657). Observe the behavior of a society's members, and you will see that it describes repetitive designs, like the skate blades, and that it shows clustering like the bullet holes around a target.

A culture pattern is, then, both mold and modality. It is a mold in functioning as a guide *for* behavior. It is a modality in that it is a central tendency (in the statistical sense) *of* behavior.

In either of these meanings pattern connotes standardization of behavior; it suggests that in a given society there are customary ways of doing most of the things that are done. It does not imply that all persons adhere to all of the customs all of the time. But there is adherence to the extent that modalities in behavior are evident to the observer, and many are persistent over time; they are customary behavior.

Kroeber and Kluckhohn note that patterns are both "explicit and implicit." Patterns are also both trivial and substantial. In the following passage Haring vividly illustrates the enormous range and variety of behaviors which are patterned:

Cultural behavior ranges from simple acts such as eating with a fork or with chopsticks, or tying a shoelace, to complex mathematical operations and philosophical speculation. A baseball game, an Iroquois game of lacrosse, the wearing of wooden sandals by Japanese, and a prayer meeting are cultural behavior of the participating individuals. The duties of the president and the techniques of safe-cracking, the forms of matrimony and the forms of parliamentary law—all are patterns of behavior learned individually by each person concerned. (Haring, *op. cit.*, pp. 25–26.)

Patterns of the explicit sort are not necessarily simple, though simple patterns are likely to be explicit. Those patterns which society's members are accustomed to put into words—e.g., as directives, specifications, contracts, constitutions, rules or codes—are of the explicit order. They are likely to be formal in the sense that they are well established, widely accepted, and important in the "system of expectancies" (Kroeber and Kluckhohn, *op. cit.*) familiar to members of a society.

Patterns of the implicit sort are likely to be complex, undefined, and largely a matter of "feeling." They are seldom brought forward to the light of rational inspection or even to be put into words. Premises—unstated and often unrealized by the very people who hold them—are the most important of these implicit patterns. Edward T. Hall conveys the nature of implicit patterns in his discussion of "informal learning." He writes:

Entire systems of behavior made up of hundreds of thousands of details are passed from generation to generation, and nobody can give the rules for what is happening. Only when the rules are broken do we realize they exist. . . . The principal agent is a *model* used for imitation. (Hall, 1959, pp. 93 and 92.)[3]

Members of a society do not have equal access to the entire stock of patterns. Even in a small and homogeneous society the culture is

---

[3] Edward T. Hall, *The Silent Language* (New York: Doubleday and Company, 1959). Used by permission.

to some extent parceled out, as it were. Different kinds of individuals—especially the sex and age kinds—will be expected to follow particular patterns regarded as appropriate to their kinds. The larger and more heterogeneous the society, and the greater the number of social kinds recognized, the more elaborate will be the system of linkage between social kind and pattern cluster. Some patterns will be for everyone; ordinarily this is true of language, for example. Others will have limited distribution in accord with (1) what is considered appropriate for given social kinds, and (2) what is in fact available to them. As Haring says:

> Some cultural behavior, as the wearing of clothes in conformance with fashion, is evident in the behavior of nearly everyone. Knowledge of a complex theorem in the calculus, however, becomes habitual in the activity of a minority only. Sins and crimes are cultural behavior, even though such activities are generally disapproved. (Haring, *op. cit.*, p. 26.)

We must take note of one more attribute of cultural patterning: i.e., the matter of range around central tendency.

We have said that a pattern is a modality, by which we mean that it is a central tendency with a range of variation around it. We must now note that the ranges of variation differ greatly as between patterns within a culture. A wide range may be tolerated in one aspect of culture though not in others. Moreover, wide ranges may be numerous and tolerated in Culture A but few and strongly disapproved in Culture B. American culture, for example, shows a much greater range of variation in respect to most types of behavior than does Tibetan. This contrast would hold for complex as against simpler cultures generally. Yet even within American culture the range of variation is much greater in the patterning of religious behavior or making a living than in food or clothing habits.

The individual learns to know the "leeway" areas of his culture, though he may not fully explore the range of behavior which is tolerated. He may, however, do that and more. He may push outward from the acceptable range and perhaps help to establish a new outer zone of the tolerated range. Much of this stretching-the-limits behavior occurs in urban-industrial cultures where change is already a commonplace. Little of it occurs in stable, traditional cultures.

IDEAL AND BEHAVIORAL PATTERNS

No aspect of pattern phenomena is more important than the distinction between ideal and behavioral patterns. It is a distinction between expectancies and actualities, between what people are expected to do and what they actually do.

Ideal patterns are modalities in the expectations or standards-for-behavior in which a given people believe. If we are told that Americans generally, or Americans of a certain age, sex, etc., *ought* to behave in certain ways under certain circumstances, and if we can observe that Americans believe in these standards because we see them react with some degree of shock or surprise to deviant behavior, then we have proof of the existence of ideal patterns. Behavioral patterns are modalities in the actual forms of behavior, and these actualities may depart little or much from the standards.

Some discrepancy between ideal and behavioral patterns seems to appear in every culture, but the degrees of discrepancy and the aspects of living to which they are related differ greatly. American culture shows a high frequency of quite glaring discrepancies. Among the most conspicuous of these is the discrepancy between what has been called the "American Creed" of equality and inalienable rights for all citizens regardless of race, religion, or national origins, and the actual modalities of prejudice and discrimination.

The distinction between ideal and behavioral patterns is somewhat like the popular notion of difference between theory and practice, but it does not represent a distinction between ideas and action. There are ideal patterns relating to ideas as well as to action, and similarly with behavioral patterns. Take for example the patterning of sexual behavior among Americans. In terms of traditional patterns one ought to be "pure" in both thought and deed (ideal idea and action patterns, respectively). On the behavioral level, if we accept the Kinsey Reports and much other evidence, action patterns depart notably from standards. We may safely assume that idea patterns necessarily do too (some ideas rather inevitably accompanying acts).

Ideal patterns may be described as explicit, formal, and primary, behavioral patterns as implicit or secondary. Ethel M. Albert states the distinction in these terms, and neatly establishes the functional relations between the two levels. She writes:

> Taken together, the explicit, primary norms and the implicit, secondary norms form the "active norms" of the society. By means of secondary norms, society can come to terms with the social and psychological impossibility of a perfect correspondence between the formal norms . . . invented by men in the interest of social order, and the actions of men confronted by the empirical realities of human existence.
>
> Each society has its own calculus of values by which it establishes its active norms, the norms to be respected verbally but understood to be neither practical nor practiced, and the rules of punishment which are to be taken seriously. . . .
>
> A society would be crushed by the weight of its own rules, if each infraction were punished strictly according to prescribed sanctions and if all formal norms were always respected. To be part of a society is to know which of its rules prescribe or prohibit absolutely or conditionally; whether a particular action which is not forbidden is nevertheless something that is simply "not done"; whether human beings, always imperfect, must in any particular case actually be punished or whether the offence should be blinked.
>
> Exceptions to the formal rules are not haphazard. Rather, they are ordered by . . . the implicit, or secondary or functional [i.e., behavioral] norms. These are as well known and as well established as norms which are explicit and formal [i.e., the ideal patterns or norms]. (Albert, 1963, p. 182.)

For any comprehensive understanding of a culture as a whole, or even of any important segment of it, knowledge of both ideal and behavioral levels, and in respect to both ideas and actions, is required. It is particularly necessary for any dynamic view of social situations—any estimates of trends, changes, and realities of the individual's life situation—that we know as much as we can about both ideal and behavioral patterns.

SYMBOLS, BELIEFS, AND VALUES

The survival of a human society and its way of life is heavily dependent upon interpersonal and intergenerational communication. Much of what men must communicate is highly abstract; it cannot be conveyed in the simple cries, postures, and imitable actions to which even man's nearest relatives are limited. Man's capacity for invention and manipulation of symbols is enough to require recognition of a vast difference between himself and all other creatures. Language is of course the prime example of patterned symbols, along with those concrete symbols with which we write. But the patterning of symbols extends to less obvious forms —to totems, family crests, religious and political insignia, and much more. Ideas and ideals, beliefs and values, are stated and conveyed by learned systems of connotation as well as through the more specific and denotative systems of language and writing.

Effective communication depends not only on shared systems for representing ideas but also on common understandings. Talcott Parsons (1951) has pointed out that it would be impossible for people to communicate consistently, intricately, and effectively had they not learned roughly the same sets of beliefs, and values as well as symbols, and much the same cues and canons for applying them in life situations. In a given situation all three types of patterning are likely to be involved, but with one of the three predominant.

The people of a given society or sub-society share beliefs of a great number of kinds. There are beliefs relating to empirical phenomena such as physical objects and nonhuman organisms, persons and/or personalities, social groups (collectivities), and cultural objects (i.e., man-made or man-altered objects). There are also beliefs relating to the nonempirical; these are matters of philosophy, ideology, the supernatural, and, in general, beliefs about nonobjective entities, attributes, and processes.

Such a matter as the Navaho belief in witchcraft, like most other locally important beliefs, involves subsidiary beliefs relating to a variety of both empirical and nonempirical phenomena. The kind of person and personality likely to be suspected of witchcraft, the objects the witch is likely to use, the processes of bewitching, the supernatural power upon which the witch can draw, all these and more form a set of related beliefs.

Patterns of expressive symbols also involve a wide variety of phenomena. Acts, qualities of personality or of the person, physical objects, or cultural patterns themselves may all become, by cultural definition, symbolic entities. The meaning of these is a matter of culture to the degree that they convey roughly the same messages to all or to certain categories of people in the society.

While the spoken and/or written language is perhaps the most obvious example of a system of expressive symbolism, there is in any culture a wealth of symbols of quite different sorts. Consider the "language" of gesture, facial expression, or posture, and how much can be communicated by a smile, a glance, a handclasp. Or think of the significance of such ubiquitous symbols as the flag, the national anthem, or national rituals such as the inauguration of the President or the proceedings in the Senate. Religious rituals have more explicit symbolic value, as do some of the more conventionalized art forms. The individual's clothing, house and other personal possessions speak more or less loudly to the initiated observer about the status of their owner. So, too, do his culturally patterned activities—his recreation at simple beer "joints" or fashionable restaurants, and, in the United States, his attendance at the Pentecostal Tabernacle or the Episcopal Church.

Value systems—standards of evaluation—are of crucial significance in social life. Society's members must constantly make choices between courses of action, between persons, and between things. They do so primarily in terms of learned systems of values, i.e., by measuring the possibilities against culturally standardized preference-rejection scales.

In addition to the more obviously patterned values which we ordinarily call ethics, morals, taste, standards, etc., there are patterned values basic to specific types of activity. There are "professional ethics," the "democratic way," the "free enterprise system," "good sportsmanship," and "the honor system." These are but a few of the more explicit codes embodying American values.

No culture, however limited its total content, is without its systems of symbols, beliefs, and values. In each society the individual must learn at least the rudiments of his culture in these aspects. The extent to which he may with impunity depart from the customary ideal or behavioral patterns will vary, as we have noted, between parts of a particular system as well as between cultures.

A man who knows the system—who can communicate with his fellows in terms they understand—is in a relatively strong position. He may deviate with deliberate and even with creative intent, like Maslow's self-actuating man. But he knows what he is doing. He can, if he wishes, explain and interpret his behavior in terms of the shared symbols, beliefs, and values. His position, vis-à-vis his fellows, and his power to extend the range of tolerated cultural variation, are enhanced because he commands the prime elements of the communication process. Like a skillful salesman, he may convince his fellows by manipulating their own patterned logic of beliefs and values couched in their familiar symbols.

The man who lacks this command of his culture is relatively vulnerable when he departs from the system of expectancies. His very departure may be a function of his ignorance. His reaction to social disapproval, censure, or punishment is likely to be disapproved too; he may strike out rather than manipulate.

A man of talent may come to play the role of leader or innovator. But the same talents might have been so used as to mark the man as deviant or even criminal. His character, the extent to which he holds to the patterned symbols, beliefs and values (or appears to do so) may tip the balance for or against him, for or against a constructive relation between the individual and his society.

CULTURAL THEMES AND WORLD VIEWS

Observers of human behavior long have been aware of what anthropologists are likely to label "theme," "ethos," or "world view." The labels identify those aspects of a culture which are implicit, highly diffuse and pervasive, and which strike the observer as encapsulating the distinctive "flavor" or "spirit" of a culture and a people. They are seldom recognized or stated by the bearers of a culture.

The subliminal quality of theme, ethos, or world view was described succinctly by Clyde Kluckhohn. He wrote:

> Cultures do not manifest themselves solely in observable customs
> and artifacts. No amount of questioning of any save the most articulate
> in the most self-conscious societies will bring out some of the basic
> attitudes common to the members of the group. This is because these
> basic assumptions are taken so for granted that they normally do not
> enter into consciousness. This part of the cultural map must be inferred
> by the observer on the basis of consistencies in thought and action.
> (Kluckhohn, 1949, p. 32.)[4]

Theme-ethos-world view are the very fundamental orientations
of a people, their basic and largely subconscious philosophical
viewpoints. They are likely to be evident (to the alert observer) in
many facets of the culture.

Following the lead of Morris Opler (1945), who defined "theme,"
Kluckhohn provided, from the Navaho culture he knew so well, an
excellent example.

> A factor implicit in a variety of diverse phenomena may be general-
> ized as an underlying cultural principle (theme). For example, the
> Navaho Indians always leave part of the design in a pot, a basket, or a
> blanket unfinished. When a medicine man instructs an apprentice he
> always leaves a little bit of the story untold. This "fear of closure" is
> a recurrent theme in Navaho culture. Its influence may be detected in
> many contexts that have no explicit connection. (*Ibid.*, p. 33.)[5]

The themes of a culture are not necessarily wholly congruent.
Neither in this aspect, in its patterning, nor in its belief and value
systems will a given culture exhibit a system of perfect internal
logic, harmony, and integration. This fact goes far to explain the
dilemmas in which the individual so often finds himself. He cannot
simultaneously operate in terms of wholly or even partly contradictory themes, expectations, or premises. It is true, as William
Graham Sumner long ago noted with respect to folkways and
mores, that there is a "strain toward consistency." (Sumner, 1907,

---

[4] Kluckhohn, *op. cit.*

[5] *Ibid.*

passim.) And, as Kluckhohn pointed out, this strain cannot be accounted for unless one grants a set of systematically interrelated implicit themes.

For example, in American culture the themes of "effort and optimism," "the common man," "technology," and "virtuous materialism" have a functional interdependence, the origin of which is historically known. However, the relationship between themes may be that of conflict. One may instance the competition between Jefferson's theory of democracy and Hamilton's "government by the rich, the wellborn, and the able." In other cases most themes may be integrated under a single dominant theme. In Negro cultures of West Africa the mainspring of social life is religion; in East Africa almost all cultural behavior seems to be oriented toward certain premises and categories centered on the cattle economy. If there be one master principle in the implicit culture, this is often called the "ethos" or *Zeitgeist*. (*Ibid.*, pp. 33–34.)[6]

GENERIC FEATURES OF CULTURE

Each culture will manifest all of the features we have discussed in this chapter—i.e., patterns, symbols, beliefs, values, themes and world views, and much more that we have not discussed. From the anthropologist's point of view every human society can be described in terms of its distinctive culture, and all human societies are "cultured." Putting the matter a little differently it can be said that *culture* is a universal phenomenon—a generic concept—and also that there are many *cultures*—specific examples of this generic phenomenon.

This conceptualization is basically simple enough. Parallel conceptualizations are common in the classificatory schemes of other disciplines. There is, for example, the biological usage of the concepts *mammal* and *mammals*. Biologists have demonstrated the existence of mammalia—of creatures having in common the capacity to bear their young alive, to nourish them via the secretions of the mammary glands, etc. But there are many mammals— creatures as unlike as whales and humans—who yet share mammalian attributes.

---

[6] *Ibid.*

It is similarly true that cultures, however varied, fall into one larger class of phenomena because all cultures show basic structural and functional similarities. There are today some 3,000 to 4,000 peoples whose cultures are sufficiently distinctive to be considered independent units, yet in every one of them there can be found a structure—a configuration—adequate to serve the universal needs of the human animal. Because these needs must be met if the society is to survive, all societies which are going concerns have developed comparable cultural structures which function toward comparable ends.

This abstract conceptualization about culture-generic and culture-specific is concretely symbolized by the existence of what are called the Human Relations Area Files (formerly known as the Cross-Cultural Survey) originally at Yale University. In the files are stored, under hundreds of topical and sub-topical headings, all of the known facts about more than 200 different cultures. The scholar wishing to study a particular type of patterning may find the relevant cross-cultural data readily accessible. There has been published, for example, a comparative study entitled *Patterns of Sexual Behavior*, by C. S. Ford and F. A. Beach (1951), in which are set forth many generalizations based upon data drawn from the Human Relations Files.

It is feasible to set up such a cross-cultural file, in which the topical headings represent the *universal inventory* (culture in the generic sense), because

the members of all human societies face some of the same unavoidable dilemmas, posed by biology and other facts of the human situation. This is why the basic categories of all cultures are so similar. Human culture without language is unthinkable. No culture fails to provide for aesthetic expression and aesthetic delight. Every culture supplies standardized orientations toward the deeper problems, such as death. Every culture is designed to perpetuate the group and its solidarity, to meet the demands of individuals for an orderly way of life and for satisfaction of biological needs. (Kluckhohn, 1949, pp. 24–25.)[7]

Culture in the generic sense has, however, still other features in addition to the universal inventory. From the study of large

---

[7] *Ibid.*

numbers of specific cultures there are beginning to emerge some reliable generalizations about cultural processes—about the physiology as well as the anatomy of culture, as it were. "We can recognize, behind the tremendous diversity of existing cultures and the innumerable episodes of history, certain basic principles of organization and growth. These are repeated again and again although the results will vary with the materials with which such principles operate." (Linton, 1945, p. 202.) Although the present knowledge of cultural processes does not allow of precise prediction, it long has been sufficient to have marked practical significance. Colonial administrators, Point Four and Technical Aid administrators, the U.S. Office of Indian Affairs, missionaries, and others who deal with practical problems involving cultural change have established this fact.

There are also beginning to emerge, from the study of large numbers of specific cultures, some reliable generalizations about individuals in cultural context. It is clear that each lifetime represents a drama of culture-learning (enculturation), culture-using, and culture-modifying. Each of these processes is highly variable in accord with the content of a specific culture, with noncultural factors (e.g., physical environment and its resources; population density and distribution), and with the inherent (genetically determined) capacities and inclinations of a particular individual. In the following chapter we turn our attention to the major categories of noncultural factors, their interrelations with one another and with culture, and their effects on the individual.

EXCERPT NO. 3*

It is no doubt true, as Morris Opler has said, that most individuals are "less unique, original, and daring than they suppose," and that "individuality occurs mostly in relation to minutiae." (Opler, 1946, p. 43.) Nevertheless, culture-modifying is, as we have noted, one of the universal features of the individual-culture relationship.

Lest this crucial fact be insufficiently appreciated we offer here an excerpt

---

* From *Innovation, The Basis of Cultural Change*, by H. G. Barnett, pp. 19–21. Copyright, 1953. McGraw-Hill Book Company. Used by permission.

from the work of an anthropologist who has explored in depth the innovative side of human behavior. Barnett, far more than most anthropologists, appreciates and emphasizes the ubiquitous fact of innovation ("every individual is basically innovative . . .") and its causes. But he is equally aware of individual differences with respect to inventiveness, and of the extent to which it is encouraged or discouraged in a specific culture.

Nothing is more common or certain than individual variability in concept and reaction. Such differentiation, moreover, is the only source of those aberrations that are chosen because of their social significance to merit the label of innovation. But giving them this name does not make them different from those variations which pass without a trace. Their fate is something apart from their origins, even though the latter might be provoked by ideas concerning the former. Change as such is a universal phenomenon. Human beings have an infinite capacity for responding divergently. . . . But in this ultimate sense of being deviant every individual is an innovator many times over.

Every individual is basically innovative for two reasons. No two stimuli to which he reacts are ever identical. They may be more or less alike, and it may require an expert analysis to detect the differences between them; but the variables which affect their presence and their organization inevitably make them distinct in some way. When an individual steps across the traditionally accepted boundaries of sameness and treats two different things as the same, he is displaying originality; and inevitably there are degrees of this as there are degrees of difference between the stimuli prompting him. The second reason for diversified reactions is that no one ever entirely or minutely duplicates his responses to what he regards as the same stimulus. Inevitably an organism is altered by its own responses; it is not the same after responding as it was before. This is so even when the reactions follow upon each other immediately; a person does not react to a second loud noise or drink of water as he did to the first. Changes in his reactions are even more evident when the passage of a long interval of time brings about physiological, emotional, and intellectual transformations in an individual. And responding differently to the same stimulus is also counted as original when it overrides the cultural dictates which make prescribed allowances for it. This dynamic situation is pregnant with novelty; and it is continually bearing strange fruit, as anyone may observe by close attention to his own behavior and that of his associates.

While it is true that novel reactions are routine phenomena in the experience of every man, it is at the same time undoubtedly true that individuals differ in their propensities and abilities to veer across the normal boundaries of acceptable deviation. It is a commonplace that some people are more inventive than others. Individuals differ in the frequency with which they depart from the norms of behavior, in the character of their preferences for doing so, and in the uniqueness of their divergent ideas. The characteristics of their immediate cultural setting have a great deal to do with this. . . . Opportunity differentials that are compounded of time and place factors in experience provide a partial explanation of individual variability in innovative potential. Equally important, however, are those individual peculiarities that are less directly and less certainly dependent upon the cultural background for their organizations. It is unnecessary to raise here the moot question concerning the extent to which these idiosyncrasies are biologically determined. It is sufficient to recognize that human beings, beyond the age of infancy at least, exhibit differences in what we call character and personality, and that these differences predispose some of them to a hesitant and retractile attitude toward experimentation with the new, while others are much more adventurous and intrepid. In short, some people, for whatever reason, are temperamentally more conservative than others. Some are more likely than others to think of something that will generally be regarded as new.

As far as innovation is concerned, individual differences are evident in the ability to conceive of something beyond the limits of the conventional range of routine variation. The ability is dependent upon a number of factors . . . among them are the capacity for meaningful observation, the ability to retain knowledge in memory, and, above all, the faculty to analyze the data of everyday experience and recombine them in new patterns. Innovative capacity is at times equally dependent upon attitudes toward existing modes. Individuals display different degrees of satisfaction with them, different degrees of tolerance of them under stress, and different degrees of detachment or emotional involvement with them, as well as different degrees of distrust of anything that might take their place.

In consequence of these factors individuals do react differently to the same situation, and some are certain to respond with greater originality than are others. Given any set of circumstances, some individuals will be constrained to the orbit of the customary more certainly and more securely than will others. Individual variability in this respect is unquestioned. At the same time, it is only a special aspect of the more general and universal phenomenon of idiosyncratic deviation. Within conventional limits individual deviation is inevitable; for excursions beyond those limits special conditions are necessary.

CHAPTER 3

The Individual in Total Context

> The organism and the environment—physical and social as well as cultural—have a kind of wholeness in the concrete, behavioral world. . . . The individual is an integrate in action.
>
> Clyde Kluckhohn and O. H. Mowrer

Viewed in total context and as "integrate in action" individuals assume some of the attributes of a series of pictures seen through a kaleidoscope. The picture elements are fixed in number and type, yet they recombine in what seem to be an endless variety of ways. Each has much in common with all of the others, yet each is unique. But here the analogy breaks down.

Man's sentience, emotion, and volition make mandatory that he play a part in his own becoming. The elements of which each of us is "made" are in themselves highly complex and variable and infinitely recombinable to produce infinite numbers of unique creatures. But even these are not all of the factors making for individual uniqueness. In each of us the rich tapestries of selfhood are woven as we grow in awareness and as we experiment with emotion and volition.

ORGANISM AND ENVIRONMENT

The "wholeness" of organism and environment Kluckhohn and Mowrer analytically divided into a number of major elements. There is the unique individual, who is not, however, totally unlike other individuals of his sex, age, tribe, or nation. And each of these unique individuals incorporates and reflects biological, physical environmental, social, and cultural antecedents and influences.

These various elements Kluckhohn and Mowrer represented in a sixteen-cell table of "personality determinants and components." (Kluckhohn and Mowrer, 1944.) We reproduce their table with modifications, so that it serves our purposes as a schematic representation of individual-in-context, and of levels of individuality. (See Figure 2.) But Figure 1 (Barbara Phillips, 1965) presents in graphic and simplified form the essential elements of the analytical scheme.

These diagrams analytically isolate and identify all that the unique individual—that integrate in action—*is*, along with the full scene of his action. Our individual—John Smith, let us say—*is* the whole of the four concentric circles of Figure 1. At his very core (Level 1) he is *idiosyncratic*—a creature unlike any other. But he is also a person whose individuality is definable in terms of *role* (Level 2), i.e., of age, sex, perhaps social class or caste, occupational or other status or function group. And John Smith is definable in more inclusive terms. His individuality incorporates *communal* elements (Level 3)—the features which mark him as a member of his subnational (or tribal) and national (or tribal) groups. Finally he is in some respects "everyman" (Level 4), clearly identifiable on the *universal* level as Homo sapiens.

Our man's individuality overall as well as level by level is compounded of four orders of antecedent-influence factors. Graphically we allocate to each a quadrant of our man (Figure 1). But this is a mere representational device. In fact, "the organism (quadrant A) and the environment—physical (quadrant B) and social (quadrant C) as well as cultural (quadrant D)—have a kind of wholeness in the concrete, behavioral world. . . ." (Kluckhohn and Mowrer, *op. cit.*, p. 28.)

John Smith as represented in Figure 2 appears to be a mosaic of sixteen aspects (1A through 4D). These sixteen cells do violence again to the "wholeness" of our man of context and in context. They must be understood as analytical conventions, and we must not lose sight of the constant and kaleidoscopic interplay of the

FIGURE 1

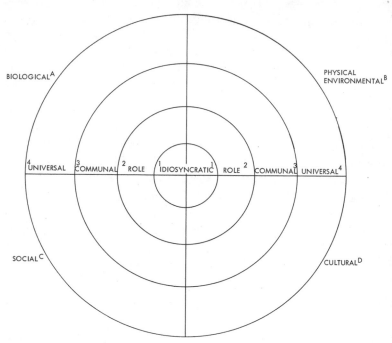

1, 2, 3, 4: Levels of individuality

A, B, C, D: Antecedents and influences

Source: From Barbara Phillips, "Critique" (student paper prepared for Anthropology 370, The Individual and Culture, Rice University, 1965).

several antecedent-influence orders at all levels of individuality.

There is another and more serious fault of these models: they fail to represent the sentient, affective, and volitional John Smith. They represent our man as though he were merely a product, though a complex product, of complex and interdependent forces. He is represented as a reaction, or at best as an involved set of inter-meshing cogs and wheels. But he is more; it is true that he reacts, but he also acts. That he acts within the boundary conditions estab-lished by his nature (1A to 4A) there can be no doubt. Nor can we doubt that the boundary conditions within which he acts are estab-lished also by his physical and sociocultural environments (1B through 4B; 1C and 1D through 4C and 4D).

FIGURE 2

Individual in Context*

LEVELS OF INDIVIDUALITY	ANTECEDENTS AND INFLUENCES			
	BIOLOGICAL[A]	PHYSICAL ENVIRONMENTAL[B]	SOCIAL[C]	CULTURAL[D]
UNIVERSAL[4]	4A Birth, death, hunger, thirst, elimination, etc.	4B Gravity, temperature, time, etc.	4C Infant care, group life, etc.	4D Symbolism, taboo on incest and in-group murder, etc.
COMMUNAL[3]	3A "Racial" traits, nutrition level, endemic diseases, etc.	3B Climate, topography, natural resources, etc.	3C Size, density, and distribution of population, etc.	3D Traditions, rules of conduct and manners, skills, knowledge, etc.
ROLE[2]	2A Age and sex differences, caste, etc.	2B Differential access to material goods, etc.	2C Cliques, "marginal" men, etc.	2D Culturally differentiated roles
IDIOSYNCRATIC[1]	1A Peculiarities of stature, physiognomy, glandular makeup, etc.	1B Unique events and "accidents" such as being hit by lightning, etc.	1C Social "accidents" such as death of a parent, being adopted, meeting particular people, etc.	1D Folklore about accidents and "fate," etc.

*Adapted from Clyde Kluckhohn and O. H. Mowrer, "Culture and Personality: A Conceptual Scheme," *American Anthropologist*, Vol. 46 (1944), pp. 1–27.

Note that items entered in the sixteen cells are only illustrative, and far from exhaustive.

But boundaries are not directives. Within the life space defined by his boundaries our man is at liberty. It is within this space that he exercises those faculties (discussed in Chapter 1) to which self-determination can be attributed. Moreover, the boundaries are potentially alterable. Fortuitous circumstances (e.g., meeting Jane Jones who has grown up in a very different society and culture) or a conscious choice (e.g., to spend his savings on travel) may significantly expand his life space. Man's potential for mastery of his conditions is, of course, limited, yet it is the less limited the more he becomes aware, thoughtful, and confident of his own powers.

CULTURAL BOUNDARIES

Much learned nonsense has been written in efforts to explain individual behavior as largely, even simply, a result of cultural conditioning. Among the most remarkable of such efforts there is the "swaddling hypothesis" (Gorer and Rickman, 1949), which ascribes some of the less endearing aspects of Russian national character to the practice of wrapping babies in yards of cloth until they look like bandaged logs. The babies are, allegedly, so deeply frustrated by this treatment that life for them becomes an exercise in retaliatory aggression against mankind.

This remarkably simplified theory of causality has been delightfully and deservedly lampooned. One Boris Shub (1950) produced a "review" of an alleged "monumental" book entitled *Childhood Rearing and the Neurotic-Aggressive American Personality*. Mr. Shub's fanciful author, the "illustrious Professor Ivan Pelionok," explains that, after five years of field studies in 450 U.S. communities, he can positively identify the source of American aggressiveness. It is, beyond the shadow of a doubt, "the commercial diaper service." The sterility, artificiality, and capitalistic exploitation inherent in the commercialization of diapers are subtly conveyed to the hapless infant. Along with his diapers, in their sterile wrappings, he gets the whole perverted essence of bourgeois decadence. It makes him neurotic and aggressive; so much for the sources of American national character.

In fact culture, even all of it, is not all in producing character either national or individual. The Russian, the American, the tribal New Guinean, the woman of Burundi (see Adaptation No. 1), or any other individual is a product of more than his culture. His type D antecedents and influences are ultimately inter-functioning with those of types A, B, and C.

SOCIETY AND CULTURE

Though they are intimately related, it is necessary to distinguish between the social and the cultural antecedent-influence categories. The differences are real and important. What is "social" is a matter of organisms and their positions, spatial or hierarchial, vis-à-vis one another. What is "cultural" is a matter of patterns, some of which heavily affect the distribution of individuals through ecological space *and* through the social system. A society is a cluster of positioned individuals. Their stations and movements through the social firmament are greatly influenced by a grand design—a plan, with associated standards and expectations, which is the associated culture.

The human animal is a gregarious creature. He very rarely lives alone and if he does he seldom appears to like it. Human populations cluster in groups, and the larger, more stable, and more self-sufficient of these we call societies. Every one of these societies can be described in terms of size, location, man-land adjustments, networks and frequencies of interactions between members, and other such attributes. Every society can also be described in terms of the distinctive lifeways learned, shared, and transmitted by its members. That is, it can be described in terms of its culture. The members of any given human society will be found to be the "practitioners" of a distinctive way of life—to be the bearers of a culture.

Kluckhohn (see Kroeber and Kluckhohn, 1963, pp. 254–56) differentiates between the "social environment," or "environment of interaction," and the "fourth" (the cultural) dimension. He comments on the "emergent" properties of both. Kroeber, in the passage below, provides a simile which should serve to clarify a complicated conceptualization. Kroeber suggests, too, that we approach the society-culture distinction by taking note of the fact that a society (nonhuman) without a culture (as man knows it) can and does exist. Kroeber writes:

The occurrence of cultureless true societies among the insects makes it clear that . . . society precedes and underlies culture, though in man the two always happen to come associated. At any rate, society is a simpler and more obvious concept to grasp than is culture. That is apparently why sociocultural phenomena—the phenomena of man's total history in the broadest sense, which necessarily contain both social facts and cultural facts—usually have their social aspects recognized first. The result has been that the social-plus-cultural combination came at first to be called merely "social," and in popular and general use still carries that ambiguous name.

For those who like their thinking concrete, it may help if they conceive the sociocultural total in man as similar to a sheet of carbon paper, of which the fabric side represents society and the coated side culture. It is obvious that to use carbon paper effectively, we must distinguish the sides. And yet the sheet is also a unit. Moreover, in certain respects, as when we are not concerned with manifolding but only with some operation like sorting, counting, or packing, a sheet of carbon paper is comparable to and is handled like a sheet of un-coated paper—which in turn would correspond to the cultureless animal societies. But if what we are interested in is the use of carbon paper, the impressions made by it, or if we wish to understand how it makes them, then it is the specific carbon coating that we must ex-amine, even though this comes only as a sort of dry-ink film carried by paper of more or less ordinary cellulose fabric and texture.

Like all similes, this one has its limitations. But it may be of help in extricating oneself from the confusing difficulty that the word "so-cial" has acquired a precise and limited meaning—society as distin-guishable from culture—in anthropology and sociology, while still having a shifting double meaning—society including or excluding cul-ture—in popular usage and in many general contexts. (Kroeber, 1948, pp. 9–10.)

A society, then, is conceptually distinguishable from the culture by which its members live.

In anthropological theory there is not what could be called close agreement on the definition of the concept of culture. But . . . three prominent keynotes of the discussion may be picked out: first, that culture is *transmitted*, it constitutes a heritage or a social tradition; secondly, that it is *learned*, it is not a manifestation, in particular con-tent, of man's generic constitution; and third, that it is *shared*. Culture, that is, is on the one hand the product of, and on the other hand a determinant of, systems of human social interaction.

The first point, transmissibility, serves as a most important criterion for distinguishing culture from the social system, because culture can be diffused from one social system to another. Relative to the particular social system it is a "pattern" element which is both analytically and empirically abstractable from that particular social system. (Parsons, 1951, p. 15.)

PHYSICAL ENVIRONMENT AND BIOLOGICAL FACTORS

The boundary functions of physical environment and biology are less subtle and difficult to grasp than are the societal and cultural boundary functions. Nevertheless we should take note of some instances and illustrations provided by Kluckhohn and Mowrer (1944).

The resources of the physical environment as exploited by the culturally available technology are the major determinants of vitamins, noxiants, and nutrition generally, and it is these which have patent consequences for corpulence, stature, and energy potential. . . . The physical environment imposes certain limitations upon the cultural forms which man creates or it constrains toward change and re-adjustment in the culture he brings into an ecological area. . . . On the other hand, a part of even the impersonal environment is man-made and cultural . . . (e.g., irrigation ditches, terraced hillsides; buildings and artifacts generally). . . . [Moreover] man's whole perception of the physical world [is affected by culture]. (*Ibid.*, pp. 11–12.)

Certain of the [role] categories are fundamentally biological. In every society the organism is differentially socialized according to sex. In every society different behavior is expected of individuals in different age groups, although where these lines are drawn and what behavioral variations are anticipated differs in different cultures. In all known caste societies physical criteria are to some extent involved, and class differentiations are often also tinged with appearance differences.

The correlation of the role and physical environmental . . . [factors] rests upon the fact that some categories of persons within a society have differential access to residential locations, house types, and material goods generally. . . .

[In sum], universal, communal, role, and idiosyncratic . . . [levels] all include biological, physical environmental, social, and cultural elements. . . . The old "problem" of "heredity *or* environment" is . . . essentially meaningless. The only pertinent question is: Which of various genetic potentialities will be actualized as a consequence of a particular series of life-events in a given physical, social, and cultural environment? (*Ibid.*, pp. 8–10.)

All men are born helpless; the external, impersonal world presents threats to survival; the human species would disappear completely if social life were abandoned. But the human adaptation to the external world depends not merely upon that mutual support which is social life; it also depends upon culture. (*Ibid.*, p. 5.)

. . . Biology sets the basic processes which determine *how* man learns, but culture, as the transmitted experiences of preceding generations [both technological and moral] very largely determines *what* man learns [as a member of a society rather than as an individual who has his own private experiences]. (*Ibid.*, p. 8.)

INDIVIDUALITY AND ITS IMPLICATIONS

Before leaving off discussion of the individual in total context it is important that we underscore several facts.

1.   The individual, though he has much in common with his fellow tribesmen or nationals (role and communal levels), and much in common with humanity at large (universal level), is also and everywhere unique (idiosyncratic level). ·

2.   The sources of his uniqueness are not entirely accounted for when we have cataloged what are certainly the principal antecedents and influences by which his development and his actions are affected. What these factors of heredity and environment represent are more accurately described as boundary conditions than as determinants.

3.   Certain boundary conditions are of course unyielding. No man can defy the genetic forces through which he is endowed with feet, not fins. The pull of gravity, the need for nurture in infancy, his restless mind—these are forces to which he is subject. He reacts to these forces. He reacts to the drives inherent in his biologically given nature and to those others learned so early that he feels them as equally, or almost equally, inherent.

4.   There is an immutable condition of life to which much of idiosyncrasy is traceable, that is, the impossibility of truly exact replications of behavior either by or between individuals. As we have noted earlier Barnett (see Excerpt No. 3) makes this point in his discussion of individual variability and innovation.

5.   Diverse though they are the individuals of a given society tend to cluster and to be classed. Social differentiation is inevitable because of individual diversity, and social differentiation is conducive to ranking and to social stratification. Once it has developed, a system of stratification becomes an antecedent-influence factor affecting new generations. Whiteford (Excerpt No. 4) states concisely the nature of the differentiation-ranking-stratification phenomenon. Albert's study of Burundi women (see Adaptation No. 1) provides a finely drawn illustration of this same phenomenon, of the interplay of antecedents-influences, and of the extent to which

individuals maximize or fail to maximize the potentialities of their life space.

EXCERPT NO. 4*

Because every society accepts certain culturally approved ways of doing things there always exist standards by which people and groups are judged. Broadly speaking the person who can best attain the goals valued by the society, who can achieve the kind of life which it recognizes as successful, it looked upon with favor, with admiration, with envy, and perhaps even with fear. Whatever the sentiment there is always the recognition that some people are better at attaining the goals than others. Success may be the result of hard work, personal brilliance, the backing of relatives, or the approval of the gods, but, whatever it is, some people get more of it than others. There are always inequality, differentiation, and distinction. And among men it is never sufficient simply to say "some are *different* from others"; it is always felt, suspected, implied or taken for granted that "some are better than others." Man is not only a taxonomist who thinks by separating things which are different and lumping things which are similar, he is also an "arranger" who invariably places them in some type of rank order leading from simple to complex, from low to high and from bad to good.

People who live in a small, simple community usually know each other so well that it is possible for them to place each person. Even here the problem of diversity may cause some to wonder whether or not a successful hunter should outrank a dangerous shaman but the problem is usually solved by custom. People know their place, and the places of others, in the prestige order even though the determinants may not be distinguishable to outsiders. In larger social groups, if the culture pattern is no more complex, the factors which lead to differentiation are very much the same. The chief difference is that there are enough people to make it possible for various

---

* From Andrew Hunter Whiteford, *Two Cities of Latin America* (Garden City, N.Y.: Anchor Book, Doubleday and Company, Inc., 1964), pp. 20–22.

individuals to be grouped. People who occupy similar or adjacent positions in the prestige hierarchy are associated together by others and they, in turn, recognize their mutual similarities and the differences which distinguish them as a group from the rest of the society. This identification and combination of groups of people who occupy similar positions in the social structure is one of the basic features of social class. People who occupy similar positions in the prestige system belong to the same social class. Outsiders tend to regard them as equal with each other, but the members are usually acutely aware of the subtle distinctions which define rank within the class.

When a community reaches the degree of complexity and heterogeneity which is associated with urbanization, the relative positions of the people in it become more difficult to determine.

ADAPTATION NO. 1 *

At the idiosyncratic level there occurs an elaborate interplay of forces and factors in unique combinations yielding unique results. Equipped with these distinctive attributes the individual makes his way through the social maze. The following selection from Albert's description of the Burundi women of tropical Africa provides an especially vivid illustration. Passages particularly pertinent to the foregoing discussion are italicized here (though not in the original). It should be noted that the fate of the individual Burundi woman is strongly affected by (1) biological-genetic factors (i.e., her sex, intelligence, physical strength and stamina), and (2) societal-cultural factors (i.e., the caste system, patriarchalism and patrilinealism). Though the life history of the individual is severely limited by such factors, Albert's account points up the extent to which individual women differ in utilization of their resources, and in their exploitation of life chances.

Success in realizing the central values of Rundi society is, for men and women alike, dependent on inherited caste position, intelligence and "luck." In this feudal, patriarchal society, the central values are political power and authority; wealth—especially cows and lands and, today, money and the goods and services it can

---

* From Ethel M. Albert, "Women of Burundi: A Study of Social Values," in *Women of Tropical Africa*, Denise Paulme (ed.) (Berkeley: University of California Press, 1963).

purchase; respect and love from one's dependents; and elegance of appearance, manners and material possessions. What is needed before all else for obtaining the good things of life, the Rundi say, is the favour of *Imana,* The Supreme Being or Providence. Divine favour is also requisite to the realization of such other important values as numerous children, protection against one's many enemies, and the retention of goods already obtained. *The chief terrestrial asset for realizing values is position in the social hierarchy.* The likelihood of happiness is greatest for the *mwami,* the king, and for the men and women of the royal and princely patrilineages. Opportunity and hope diminish progressively with decreasing status in the hierarchy, through the patrilineages of the Tutsi herders, the Hutu farmers and serfs, and, at the bottom, the Twa, potters and pariah.

Women, in so markedly patriarchal and patrilineal a society as that of Burundi, are by definition socially inferior to men. Political power, judicial rights, inheritance of cows and lands, and, indeed, the right to independent action outside the walls of the house, are traditionally accorded to men only. Yet, in point of fact, there are women who enjoy considerable authority and who own or control cows, lands and other forms of wealth. What a Rundikazi—a woman of Burundi—cannot do as a woman, she manages very well to do as a Rundi. *The life-history of an individual is limited but not fully determined by the formal structures of the society.* The dynamics of the social system make provision for political and economic mobility by which all but the most wretched Rundi know how to profit.

The social status of a Rundi is established by the caste and class inherited from the father. A woman is inferior to the men of her own social level and to her husband, but not to men of lower castes and classes than her own. The opportunities of a princess or of a woman of the aristocracy to acquire wealth are fewer than her father's or brother's but much greater than those of an ordinary herder or, certainly, of a poor farmer or serf. Moreover, women use the same techniques that make it possible for some farmers to own herds of cattle, or for some ordinary herders to become wealthier than some nobles. To advance from his official inherited status as far as possible toward happiness, a Rundi needs the favour of a superior in the social hierarchy. All good things come from the superior. The greater the power of the superior—whether the feudal master, the father, or the husband—the greater the ambition of the inferior—whether a herder, a serf or a woman. For the latter, it is sometimes enough to have a father who is impulsive and generous, or a husband who is docile or too stupid to distinguish the truth from a lie or true affection from flattery. Women attain their goals by means of men. There are always a good many of them available for use in projects both large and small.

Although caste and character rather than the simple fact of being male or female determine the lot of a Rundi, the mode of life and the behaviour patterns of women are decidedly different from those of men. Unlike a man, a Rundikazi in public does not speak, nor does she look you in the eyes. To each question, she answers: *Ndabizi?*—How should I know? In public, she lets it be thought that she knows nothing about politics, or where her husband is today, or even the wedding date of her daughter. She is the modest and obedient wife of her husband, the mother of her children, the conscientious mistress of her house, who is always working. Whatever she does, she does within the limits of her various feminine roles. However, the obligations of motherhood, of the household and of wifehood hardly prevent a woman from participating in other activities. Indeed, in Burundi, everyone is busy with politics—the large scale politics of the kingdom for the *abakuru*, the great ones, and the petty politics of daily life for the *abatoyi*, the humble folk. Women are not less interested in it than men, nor peasants less than princes. A peasant widow plays politics to obtain a length of cotton cloth or to protect against her enemies her rights to her little plot of cultivable land. A princess plays politics to obtain jewelry and cows and to decide a princely succession. A woman is sometimes driven by ambition for the sake of her son; sometimes it is to her advantage to help her husband; sometimes she enters the game entirely in her own interest. Peasant or princess, if a Rundikazi understands and desires happiness, if she knows how to dominate men in all subtlety, if she is clever and courageous, she may even defeat her own father or husband in the political game. The ambition of a Rundi or Rundikazi of inferior birth is seriously limited by the restrictive rules of the caste system. However, the ambition of a woman as such encounters only the sometimes purely apparent obstacle of a patriarchal, patrilineal system in which all the legitimate titles to wealth and power are for men. Women who are ambitious and intelligent do not seem to be at a disadvantage in having to function in politics by indirect means and in secret. These are, in any case, the preferred methods of men in the delicate business of increasing power and wealth.

Thus, in Burundi as elsewhere, one finds charming but formidable matriarchs who have considerable authority and who are perhaps more intimidating than the harshest of patriarchs. On the other hand, most of the women of Burundi never even approach realization of the central values of the society. They must work to the limit of their strength so that they will not die of hunger. This is because most Rundi are of the inferior castes, where men and women share the wretchedness of the poor. It would be vain to try to calculate the difference between the misery of a man and that of a woman, if both of them are of inferior birth, without relatives or a feudal protector, old, weak and not very bright.

Neither a Rundikazi who wields great political influence nor a man of low caste who has more political power and wealth than his social superior is regarded as an outlaw. On the contrary, they are looked upon as clever and lucky. *The social structure of Burundi, like that of other societies, does not describe behaviour. It only serves as a guide.*

The most direct route to happiness is conformity to the norms and rules of society. Most Rundi have some roles in which they are superior and others in which they are inferior and the accompanying obligations and compensations. A good wife of a generous and reasonable husband, a good mother of numerous and good children, a good mother-in-law of obedient and industrious daughters-in-law and of respectful sons-in-law, will be a happy woman. Unfortunately, it is necessary to take into account the ever-present and infamous "bad characters," the numberless misfortunes sent by *Imana* when he is in a bad humour, the truth that *Imana*—or, if one prefers, Nature, biology, or genetics—does not always pay attention to social norms. Thus, *it can happen that a man is not qualified for the role of patriarch, that he suffers all his life the oppression of a nagging shrew. It can happen that a woman is born too weak for manual labour.* If she does not find a kind husband who will carry the burden of the work of the household or a rich one who can provide her with workers, she will die very miserable and very young. *It can also happen that a woman is more intelligent and more enterprising than her father, her husband, or her son.* A woman of this kind is ordinarily encouraged to make use of her gifts—intelligence must not be wasted—but sometimes an energetic woman is tied to a husband who is cruel and stupid and can do nothing with her good-for-nothing sons. *In the social life of Burundi, the motto is, everyone for himself.* Each must do what he can with whatever *Imana* has given him.

If one road is closed, it is necessary to find another. If a husband is not generous, a woman will ask one of her brothers for gifts, or she will wait until her sons are grown. Yet again, if a man is muddled by drink, his wife or his vassal or someone who wants his favour will make a request of a gift in the presence of others; a promise given, drunk or sober, before witnesses must be respected at the risk of losing one's fair name. The rules of society provide only for a minimum of happiness. One must rely upon intelligence to point the way to supplementary means and to profit from every favourable circumstance.

Like any normal citizen of Burundi, a Rundikazi desires as much power and authority as possible, which is to say, numerous inferiors, including children, workers, feudal followers; wealth, which is to say, for women who can inherit nothing, many gifts from men and from wealthier women; respect and love, which amounts to having many inferiors; elegance, which is again to say many gifts, but also education in the home of a princess; many children, which depends on the will of *Imana*; protection against one's enemies, that is, against one's rivals and one's mother-in-law; and the good luck to retain what has been received from *Imana* and from human beings, which again depends on *Imana* and also on one's own intelligence, courage and strength of character. There is decidedly no psychological conflict in women of strong character, nor is there any conflict between feminine ambitions and social norms.

A woman starts very young to calculate what she needs in order to be happy. From her father she expects little more than that he will find her a husband who is wealthy and reasonable, or better yet, tractable; . . . From her husband, a woman expects to receive gifts in proportion to his wealth—clothing, copper bracelets, beads, cows, money. She also wishes workmen and servants, so that she will not have to perform the menial tasks of inferiors; so that she will have a great many inferiors to supervise; so that she will enjoy sufficient energy and leisure for the planning and plotting necessary to increase her wealth and her influence in family affairs, economic matters and politics. As her husband's business partner, an intelligent woman will be consulted at every turn or she may not even wait for her husband to ask her advice. She decides what must be done, and her decisions must be respected. A wife who is well-established will almost certainly be the preferred intermediary of those who seek the favour of her husband. As an intermediary, she receives gifts, particularly pots of beer, to persuade her to intervene with the superior. An intelligent woman who finds herself with more beer than she needs will send a servant to sell it and keep the money for herself. For women in the lower castes, there are various optional roles through which they can earn money. They may sell the excess baskets they weave; they may be midwives; they may be *bapfumu*, physician-pharmacists who sell medicines and amulets; they may be governesses or ladies-in-waiting for good families. A husband takes great pride in a wife who becomes wealthy. Her wealth advertises her cleverness and is at all events obtained at no cost to him. Some women, it is said, are so intelligent that a prince will make them *abashingantahe*, judges and councillors. Women who have this honoured position receive cows, clothing, jewelry and serfs. On occasion, a woman of this kind may be wealthier than her husband, but he has every reason to be pleased to have such a wife. A wealthy woman will keep some of her cows for herself for milk and butter. Others she will give to those who come and ask of her, and these will become her feudal followers who will work for her, respect her, and go about in quest of information for her.

The frequent absences of the husband are opportunities for a woman to show herself capable of managing the property. Work is for inferiors and is not a source of honour. It nevertheless establishes the realistic dependence of the superior upon his inferior, and it forms the solid basis, sometimes explicitly recognized, of the relationship between superior and inferior. A good manager is indispensable to a wealthy man, for he has many feudal vassals, serfs, cows and lands. A woman of a powerful and wealthy patrilineage can be of great assistance to her husband in the matter of forming useful political alliances. The wife will probably have considerable influence with her brothers and perhaps also with her father.

A woman is the inferior of her husband and of his distinguished visitors. To get what is wanted, an inferior must know how to please superiors, unfailingly displaying in public the respect and obedience due them. An intelligent woman makes herself liked or feared, according to the character of the men with whom she is dealing. Occasionally, it is said of a Rundi that "his house is burning," that is to say, despite the show of respect, his wife rules the roost. He is afraid of her, she nags him, she criticizes him, she wants to decide everything, and one fine day she will put poison in his beer, or she will calumniate him. However, a woman need not dominate her husband in so heavy-handed a fashion to earn her laurels as matriarch. She has her own inferiors to dominate, and there are other ways to become the *umutoni* of her husband and the other men. Apart from her ability as the mistress of her house and her generosity as a hostess, apart from all her obligations, a woman as an inferior is likely to understand very well the uses of flattery and subservience. She knows how to be an informant, to calumniate her superiors' enemies as well as her own hated rivals, to show herself always loyal and devoted, to make the welfare of her superior her primary concern. She also knows how to satisfy sexual desires, the need for alcohol, and other demands of the body and the spirit. Superiors, apart from their economic dependence upon inferiors, seem to seek them also for the satisfaction of what appear to be exceedingly urgent needs for love, respect, and loyalty and for entertainment that will take their minds off their troubles. It is to have these needs satisfied that they make presents, that they give what is asked of them. An intelligent woman busies herself with satisfying

the desires of her superiors and thereby making herself indispensable to their happiness. Neither the Sophists, nor Machiavelli, nor
the courtiers of Louis XIV have anything to teach the Rundi. An
intelligent Rundikazi, like any intelligent social inferior, knows that
to obtain happiness it is necessary only to say yes—to play along
with the internal weaknesses and needs by which the superior is en-
slaved.

PART II

CHAPTER **4**

Degrees of Cultural Complexity:
Implications for the Individual

> Put writing in your heart that you may protect yourself from hard labor of any kind and be a magistrate of high repute. The scribe is released from manual tasks; it is he who commands. . . . Do you not hold the scribe's palette? That is what makes the difference between you and the man who handles an oar.
>
> Paternal admonitions from a New Kingdom
> Egyptian document, V. Gordon Childe.

Organism and environment taken together constitute, as we have noted, an enormously complex system of inter-influences, -functions, and -dependences. Undeniably the destiny of the individual is bound up with the workings of this system. But, as preceding discussions suggest, that destiny appears to be no mere mechanical outcome of the workings of the system.

In this chapter we consider the question: to what extent must the destiny of the individual be altered in accord with the relative simplicity or complexity of the context in which he happens to live?

The discussion proceeds from these premises:

1. the world's cultures vary greatly with respect to complexity;

2. while complexity is not easily measured, there are some obvious and objective criteria;

3. technology and writing are probably primary among these

75

criteria, and there are important variables which cluster around each.

ETHICAL-MORAL SYSTEMS AND "PRIMITIVE" VS. "CIVILIZED" PEOPLES

Before we turn to consideration of these primary and objective criteria we shall digress to comment on a question which is likely to occur to the reader. He may suppose that technology and writing are of less importance, so far as individual destiny is concerned, than the cultural patterning of ethics and morals.

The reader may be under the impression that it is only in a "civilized" society, and indeed in a "truly civilized" society such as he sees our own to be, that the individual has really the possibility of shaping his own destiny. If he holds to this view the reader is likely to ascribe the "freedom of the individual" in our society to our religion-based ethical-moral beliefs and to our related political values (e.g., freedom, individualism, democracy). He may assume that these are the crucial variables, and that technology and writing are relatively unimportant.

The importance of ethical-moral systems and their relevance to individual decision-making and judgments are evident and unarguable but not a matter of "primitive" vs. "civilized." This we hope to make clear, and we shall discuss the not-so-evident facts about the fundamental and pervasive implications of technology and writing. To appreciate these facts requires that one take the long-range view of man.

An enduring contribution of anthropology is its data which extend our view of man through all of both time and space. Given this perspective the view of man here and now can no longer be provincial and ethnocentric. We of this present society are seen to be not in all respects at the pinnacle of human development to date. Indeed, one becomes cautious about identifying pinnacles.

In fact "primitive" cultures are often highly "democratic," respectful of the individual and his rights, and lofty as well as strict (even by our standards) in matters of ethics and morality. It is also true that both "primitive" and "civilized" cultures (our own included) incorporate patterns of quite opposite sorts (i.e., non-democratic, anti-individual, etc.).

Anthropologists repeatedly have documented the fact that "primitive" men do not lack ethical-moral systems, though the content thereof may be radically unlike what the contemporary "civilized" man regards as ethical and moral. Headhunting cannot be reconciled with the ethics and morality of urban-industrial cultures, though mass murder in warfare seems to be readily accepted (with appropriate supporting rationalizations). But headhunting, and other practices of the sort, generally reflect motives at least as noble as those underlying the Crusades.

Among the Ifugao, "an anarchistic tribe of head-hunting rice growers who live in northern Luzon in the Philippine Islands, . . . the taking of enemy heads is religiously and magically necessary." (Hoebel, 1958, pp. 159–60.)[1] This is by no means an unusual reason; it appears to be the motivation wherever headhunting is culturally patterned. Human sacrifice, too, reflects religious-magical beliefs. E. Adamson Hoebel says:

All head-hunting is tied up with supernaturalism and the belief that dead men's power can be taken with their heads. Polynesian wars were frequently undertaken to obtain sacrificial victims. Ashantis and other West Africans kept prisoners for sacrifice. The bloody religion of the Aztecs called for thousands of war prisoners for human sacrifice to the gods—a fact that proved their undoing when they came to grips with stout Cortez. The Aztecs fought to take prisoners; the Spaniards fought to kill. They baptized only survivors.

The essential difference between the religious warmaking motivations of civilized and primitive men is that the latter wage war to obtain victims for sacrifice, yet they have never sought to force their beliefs on others by means of war. (*Ibid.*, p. 516.)[2]

Ethical-moral systems, whether "primitive" or "civilized," are in fact riddled with internal inconsistencies. The headhunting Ifugao should not be written off as merely superstitious savages. Note the

---

[1] From *Man in the Primitive World* by E. Adamson Hoebel. 2nd ed., Copyright, 1958. McGraw-Hill Book Company. Used by permission.

[2] *Ibid.*

following list of "Ifugao basic postulates," and the "lofty" (by our own standards) ethical-moral values it incorporates:

Postulate I.   The bilateral kinship group is the primary social and legal unit, consisting of the dead, the living, and the yet unborn.

Corollary 1.   An individual's responsibility to his kinship group takes precedence over any self-interest.

Corollary 2.   The kinship group is responsible for the acts of its individual members.

Corollary 3.   The kinship group shall provide protection for its members and punish outside aggression against them.

Corollary 4.   The kinship group shall control all basic capital goods.

Corollary 4'.   Individual possession of rice lands and ritual heirlooms is limited to trust administration on behalf of the kin group.

Corollary 5.   Marriage imposes strict and limiting reciprocal obligations on husband and wife, but the obligations of each to his own kinship group take priority.

Corollary 5'.   Sex rights in marriage are exclusive between husband and wife.

Corollary 6.   Because children provide the continuity essential to the perpetuation of the kinship group, the small family exists primarily for its child members.

Postulate II.   *Men and women are of equal social and economic worth.*

Postulate III.   Supernatural forces control most activities, and the actions of human beings are either compatible or incompatible with the predilections of the supernaturals.

Corollary 1.   Compatibility should be determined for the most important activities by means of divination.

Corollary 2.   The supernaturals may be controlled to some extent by magic and influenced to a considerable degree by extensive sacrifice and appeasement.

Corollary 3.   The taking of enemy heads is religiously and magically necessary.

Corollary 3'.   A record of successful head-hunting gives a man (and his kinship group) power and social prestige.

Postulate IV.   Capital goods may be lent at interest.

Corollary 1.   Control of wealth gives power and social prestige: property is important.

Corollary 1'.   A debt never dies.

Postulate V.   Rice is the one good food.
Corollary 1.   Ownership of rice lands is the most important means
for control of wealth.
Corollary 2.   Since water is necessary for the growing of good rice,
control of water is essential to useful ownership of rice lands.

Postulate VI.   Propinquity of residence ameliorates the absoluteness
of the primacy of kinship ties and, conversely, outside the kinship
group responsibility to others diminishes with distance.
*Corollary 1.   People should avoid quarrels and quickly settle dis-
putes with nonrelated neighbors.*
Corollary 2.   A person may ordinarily kill a distant stranger on
sight. (Hoebel, 1958, pp. 160–61; italics added.)[3]

"Primitives" are, on the whole, less inclined than contemporary
Western man to regard religion as the major source and prop for
ethics and morals. But even this generalization admits of striking
exceptions. Reporting on his recent study of the Mapuche Indians of
southern Chile, L. C. Faron comments:

That religion is one of the forces most suited to mold the world
view of individuals is recognized both by the Mapuche and by Chilean
missionaries. The failure of the Christian ideal to take hold among
the Mapuche is testimony to the successful integration of Mapuche
society and its system of values, for religion provides the framework in
which the general inculcation of traditional values, attitudes, and procedures is accomplished. Four hundred years of missionary work,
economic imperialism, and even ultimate military defeat have failed
to crack the hard shell of Mapuche religious morality. (Faron, 1964, p.
205.)

It can be argued that it is "primitive" man whose life is dominated by a "moral order," while "civilized" man is dominated by a
"technical order." This was the view advanced by Robert Redfield,
who wrote:

. . . By a time seventy-five or fifty thousand years ago, the biological
evolution of mankind had reached a point at which the genetic qualities
necessary for the development of fully human life had been attained.
. . . For a period of time at least five times as long as the entire period

---

[3] *Ibid.*

of civilization man has had the capacity for a life governed by such moral orders as we see in primitive societies today. (Redfield, 1965, pp. 17–18.)[4]

In illustration of these contemporary moral orders Redfield cited "a tribe of western Australia, the Pitjendadjara; [who] today carry on a religious and moral life of great intensity," combined with an exceedingly meagre culture on the technical side. "Naked and wandering, with almost none of the material possessions and power which we associate with the development of humanity, . . . they follow a morality of personal relations with dignity and conscience." (*Ibid.*, pp. 16–17.)[5]

Margaret Read has emphasized the rigorous standards for personal character which were patterned in the traditional culture of the Nyasaland Ngoni. These cattle-keepers regarded themselves as greatly superior to neighboring tribes largely because of the dignity, efficiency, obedience, and courtesy to which they trained their children and held one another. These valued attributes of Ngoni character were linked with other qualities "emphasized in child training since they were expected of all Ngoni people in interpersonal relations." Read continues:

One was generosity in sharing anything a person had. It was a quality demanded of everyone. . . . The small child . . . was made to unclench his fist, in which he was hiding three ground-nuts, and give two of them to his fellows. . . . The big chief . . . [had the] duty at a feast . . . to see that everyone had enough and to send food from his own portion to anyone who looked hungry. (Read, 1960, p. 155.)

Other anthropologists have emphasized the extent to which the value systems of "primitives" are shaped by subsistence needs. Goldschmidt points to the widespread emphasis on "strength, stamina, perseverance, and self-control" because of their practical importance in hunting and warfare. For the same reason "skilled

---

[4] Robert Redfield, *The Primitive World and Its Transformation* (Ithaca, N. Y.: Cornell University Press). Copyright 1953, Cornell University. Used by permission of Cornell University Press.

[5] *Ibid.*

knowledge, whether practical or magical," is valued, along with maturity and industriousness. Generosity is universally, or nearly universally, valued by hunting and food-gathering peoples. It is a survival-enhancing value when applied to food and other necessities. But, as Walter Goldschmidt points out, it tends to become a generalized value and virtue:

> On the Andaman Islands a man is supposed to give away most of his kill to the people in his band, and the pattern of generosity extends to all the things he owns. . . . Among the Eskimos, food and possessions are freely borrowed and loaned, and the pattern of generosity extends even to a man's wives. (Goldschmidt, 1959, pp. 157–58.)

Clearly there is neither a morality of "primitive" nor of "civilized" peoples. Cultures can be ranged along a continuum from simple to complex, but their ethical-moral systems do not range correspondingly from bad to good.

Knowing only the position of his culture on the simple to complex continuum provides us with little basis for predicting the extent to which any individual, or individuals of particular age and sex, may be encouraged toward self-development, self-assertion, creativity, sensitivity to others and their needs, etc. However, it is true that among "primitives" men, and especially men of physical strength and men in their physical prime, are nearly always valued over women, children, and older and weaker men. The individual male of strength and maturity has an advantage over his fellows. Though that advantage is not limited to "primitive" societies it is likely to be more marked in such societies.

But among "primitives," as among ourselves, the individual of unusual intelligence, talents, personal beauty or personal charm is valued. He is likely to be accorded or to win easily recognition and power greater than the average man can attain. Standards for beauty and charm are culturally variable to a great extent; so is the reception accorded a man with talent for chicanery or bombast. Whatever the culturally valued endowments, the individual who possesses them is likely in any culture to make the most of them, and they are likely to be enhanced by use and deliberate cultivation.

THE SIMPLE-COMPLEX CONTINUUM

The phenomenon culture, and its Siamese twin, society, are universally characterized by certain features of (analogously speaking) "anatomy" and "physiology." The "anatomy" and "physiology" of culture and society present variable as well as constant features. The nuclear family is a constant; so is the primary group (Jules Henry's "personal community" discussed in Chapter 5). There is extreme variability with respect to number and complexity of patterned social units and relationships, and with respect to important specifics of culture content, e.g., writing, technological skills, scientific knowledge, elaboration in the arts.

Sociocultural "anatomy" and "physiology" may be simple, complex, or somewhere between, as is the case with organisms. In considering this continuum we are equating "simple" with "folk" and "complex" with "sophisticate." (See Figure 3.) Because the words "primitive" and "civilized" are so freighted with judgmental implications we propose to dispense with them entirely.

All known cultures could be ranged along a simple-to-complex continuum, if we knew enough about each. In fact, we do not. However, each specific culture which has been reasonably well described can be assigned an appropriate and approximate position along the continuum.

This is possible if one thinks of the continuum as a scale, or a set of related scales, on which certain points are marked off. (See Figure 3.)

In referring to a specific culture as "literate" or "nonliterate," which we often do, we are breaking the continuum at what is probably its most crucial mark. It is crucial because of the new variables which literacy brings in train. Robert Redfield, in describing the folk society (see Excerpt No. 5) has clarified the nature of variables associated with nonliteracy (e.g., homogeneity, isolation, solidarity) and with literacy.

Industrial technology is the second crucial mark. C. S. Coon has identified crucial variables associated with that segment of the scale which falls outside the range of industrial cultures. (See Coon,

Adaptation No. 2.) Coon's six "Levels" are based on size and complexity of social units and organizations ("institutions"), on amount of trade and functional specialization, and on the number and rankings of statuses available to individuals. It is questionable whether Coon's "Levels," even if they are as empirically clear cut as he seems to imply, coincide neatly with other crucial points, as Figure 3 suggests. But Coon makes clear he intended his "Levels" to be regarded as representing general hypotheses, and the whole of Figure 3 should be read in the same vein.

What is important, for the individual, is the extent to which his life is affected by the continuum location of his culture. Barnett (see Excerpt No. 6) emphasizes implications with respect to the individual as innovator. Whether on the hither or yon side of the literacy mark, or of the industrial technology mark, will inevitably make an enormous difference. The effect of these variables is overwhelmingly greater than of any others, because they are so fundamental and their implications so far-reaching. Each touches the

FIGURE 3

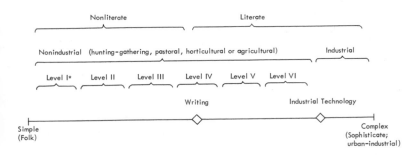

Level   I: Simple family bands (e.g., Reindeer Lapps)
Level II: Band contains several families (e.g., Andaman Islanders)
Level III: Rise of specialists and multiple institutions (e.g., Trobriand Islanders)
Level IV: Number of institutions per individual increases, and hierarchies begin (e.g., Ruwalla Bedouin)
Level V: Hierarchies and compound institutions (e.g., Aztecs)
Level VI: One complex political institution (e.g., Athenians)
(See Coon, 1948.)

° Refers to C. S. Coon's typology.

core of human life. Industrial technology is crucial because it radically alters man's relationship with the physical environment and his control over its resources and hence, indirectly, over his own destiny and the destinies of fellow men. Literacy is crucial because it radically alters man's relationships with other men, present and past, near and far, and his ability to command their knowledge and experience.

TECHNOLOGY

Though his focus was on culture history rather than on the individual in context, Ralph Linton stated very clearly the importance of technology. He wrote:

. . . Technologies set the limits within which all other aspects of a culture can develop and operate. I say "set the limits" since no technological system pins a society down to a single possible line of . . . cultural development. Any particular technological foundation is capable of supporting any one of several different cultural super-structures.

Thus a society which lives by hunting may develop either an elaborate clan or a simple family organization, it may be warlike or peaceful, worship a single great deity or a host of individual guardian spirits. However, it cannot develop a slave economy, or strong patterns of centralized political control, or even a class of skilled artisans who make their living by their crafts. . . .

The significant feature of the present period [with its efflorescence of complex cultures] is that the cultural changes which are in train are not only rapid and numerous but are also taking place in that very aspect of culture which is most fundamental [i.e., technology]. When men discovered how to produce power and how to apply the scientific method to the solution of technical problems, they dug a tunnel under the bars which have confined the . . . development of cultures throughout most of . . . [human] history. . . .

The fundamental changes [in technology] which have occurred in the course of human history have been surprisingly few. . . . In every case where such fundamental changes in technology have occurred, they have been followed by exceedingly rapid and far-reaching changes in other aspects of the culture. . . . There seem to have been only three of these fundamental *mutations* [analogously speaking] in human history. . . .

The first mutation . . . consisted in the development of tools and the use of fire. . . . Armed with tools and fire, man was able to push out into regions which he had been unable to occupy before and greatly to increase his numbers. . . . However, as long as men remained dependent upon the supply of wild foods, there were well-marked limits to the development of culture and . . . to the size of human populations.

The second basic mutation came with the invention of food raising. . . . In most regions food raising seems to have begun with the domestication of plants. Animals came later. . . . The ability to raise a balanced ration opened up a whole new range of possibilities. . . . Men could . . . settle down and live in the same place generation after generation. Nomads have to be jacks-of-all-trades since they can never tell when a particular skill will be needed or be sure that there will be a specialist at hand who knows it. . . . [In] the stable village . . . specialists of all sorts grew and multiplied, with a corresponding improvement in the various crafts. . . . In those areas where the soil was rich enough to support large populations and where adequate techniques of transportation had been developed, a new phenomenon appeared . . . the city. Here specialized manufacture and trade was centered, while the crowding together of great numbers of people set new problems of rule and organization. . . .

The third mutation . . . springs from two fundamental inventions . . . how to produce power [from fuels] and . . . the scientific method. . . . The tremendous productivity of modern industry and scientific agriculture . . . [provide] an enormous economic margin. . . . The present technological advance, like those of the past, has opened up a wide range of possibilities for social and cultural reorganization. . . . (Linton, 1945, pp. 210–20.)

The shift from preindustrial to industrial technology inevitably sets in motion a chain of extended consequences. In the process an entire culture undergoes radical and often highly disruptive changes. With the advent of work roles related to industry formal education becomes essential. New opportunities for personal achievement appear, and the traditional paths to recognition are likely to be eliminated or devalued. The patterning of family life, with its age and sex role expectations, is deeply affected. Customary family controls weaken; the individual finds himself with new and perhaps bewildering freedoms.

These extended implications of technological change are evident in all of the "developing" areas. Discussing the Moslem countries Dorothy Blitsten says:

The notion that children must be better than their parents is foreign to [traditional] Moslem families. Improvement is not conceived in individual terms. Bettering one's lot depends on improving the position of the whole family.

However, the improvement of family position is beginning to depend upon sending sons out of their households, often out of their countries, for a modern, secular education. It is even becoming important to provide daughters with formal training; if for no other reason than that educated men increasingly demand educated wives. Good marriages for traditionally reared girls are becoming difficult to arrange.

The development of Western industrial plants in Moslem countries, chiefly for oil and military installations, has provided technical training for lower-class youth. Individual enterprise is encouraged in the interest of maintaining secular states and modern technological economies . . .

These developments have brought the seeds of change to Moslem societies, but have sown them unevenly. (Blitsten, 1963, pp. 206–7.)

LITERACY

As for the impact of writing, it is difficult for literate people to appreciate fully the nature of life in a nonliterate culture or the profound changes literacy brings in train. Like advanced technology, literacy is a key which opens an incalculable range of possibilities. Primary among them are the accumulation and preservation of knowledge, and its dissemination through time and space.

No matter now meager its economic productivity, every socio-cultural system has offered a goodly number of opportunities for creativity: supernaturalism, humor, singing, dance, basketry perhaps, and doubtless many others. . . . [But] such inventiveness could not be cumulative and survive into modern times until the crucial invention of writing. . . . (Jacobs, 1964, p. 302.)

And elsewhere Melville Jacobs observes:

Scientific, technological, and cultural consequences of a script have everywhere been enormous in spite of its scant effects upon spoken language. Scientific work and fashioning of systems of scientific theory would be unthinkable without a tool of writing. (*Ibid.*, p. 128.)

Knowledge begets knowledge, and writing is essential to science.

It therefore appears that Linton's third mutation (how to produce power from fuels; the scientific method) was dependent upon literacy. Once literacy was well established technology lost some of its primacy, yet perhaps the balance has by now been again reversed.

Apparently writing and the early elements of science developed interactively and simultaneously in what was probably the first significant developmental center for both. Historian Ralph Turner comments on this conjunction in Mesopotamia, beginning about 3500 B.C.:

> Although by far the greater part of the early tablets in the Sumerian script are economic records that had only a temporary significance, certain of the tablets suggest that there was a slow accumulation of literacy and scientific materials . . .
>
> The learned traditions, like the writing system, were developed by the priests of the cults of the various cities. Schools for the study of writing were attached to the temples, and in them, it is fair to assume, literature and science developed. . . . Connected with the temples also were collections of tablets similar to modern libraries. . . . (Turner, 1941, p. 147.)

Writing frees man from dependence upon limited and fallible human memory and the distortions inherent in verbal communication.

> In Australia . . . it takes years for a man to learn all the tribal lore, which is largely historical. This he must pass on to younger men, who will memorize it in turn. As late as 800 A.D., in the Irish kingdoms, large colleges of druids, poets, and law-proclaimers spent as many as twenty years memorizing the complex system of Irish law and the vast body of Gaelic literature.
>
> Writing not only permits the accumulation of a much greater store of learning, but it is also a stabilizing influence. History, no matter how faithful the memory, tends to become mythical after being retold a few times. Ordinary events are soon miraculous, leaders soon become heroes, and before long deities. Writing retards this tendency and permits us to view past events and past personalities in a reasonably, if not wholly, accurate perspective . . .
>
> [Writing facilitates law and administration.] In Sumeria and Egypt it was most important to keep records of administrative details be-

cause of the complex irrigation system, large division of labor and the many far-flung trade operations of the merchant houses. . . .

Writing and its derivative technique, printing . . . [make] complex relationships of individuals possible, particularly those which involve highly synchronized actions of individuals widely separated in distant parts of the earth. . . . Without it, complex institutions of the type to which our economic and political institutions belong could not operate. . . . (Chapple and Coon, 1942, pp. 590–92.)

COMPLEXITY: ITS ADVANTAGES AND DISADVANTAGES FOR THE INDIVIDUAL

The advantages of literacy, advanced technology and other aspects of complex cultures are many. The innovator in a context rich in "cultural possessions" enjoys these advantages (Barnett, Excerpt No. 6). Nevertheless, complexity is a mixed blessing. As John W. Bennett points out (see Excerpt No. 7), American social scientists—Redfield conspicuous among them—have tended to contrast folk and sophisticate cultures with emphasis on the desirable features of the former. The scholar's own values are quite likely to affect his views in this matter or with respect to a given culture. This is apparent in the "organic" vs. "repression" theories of Pueblo culture.

Blitsten, in her analysis of "major types of family organization" (see Chapter 5, Excerpt No. 8), provides an admirably balanced evaluation. The autonomous nuclear family prototypical in the contemporary complex setting provides most for the freedom of the individual, least for his security. It is conducive to child-centering, a phenomenon by no means wholly advantageous for the individual, whether child or parent (see Chapter 6, pp. 140–45). Blitsten concludes that on the whole it is the bilateral extended family, rather than either the corporate or the autonomous nuclear, which best serves a considerable number of basic individual needs. Her argument is convincing, and it should warn against facile generalizations.

Life chances are not in all respects enhanced at the complex end of the continuum, but on average the individual's advantages at that end surely outweigh his disadvantages. A greatly extended life expectancy is in itself a great boon. The "primitive" man's expectancy of two and a half to three decades allows him little time either for development of his own potential or for exploitation of whatever potentialities his milieu may afford.

ADAPTATION NO. 2*

Coon's identification of preindustrial sociocultural types ("levels"), and his specification of the relevant criteria, is a valuable contribution to systematization along the complexity continuum. This contribution seems largely to have been overlooked and underutilized, as significant innovations scholarly and otherwise sometimes are. For example: Freeman and Winch (1957) report on their attempt to develop an empirical test of "societal complexity," but they make no reference to Coon's highly relevant work.

We recommend that the reader study carefully Coon's typology. He will then be prepared for the interesting experiment of testing it against ethnographic data. To classify a sociocultural system in terms of Coon's Levels is to arrive at a shorthand description of individual-in-context with emphasis on selected aspects of context (e.g., functional specialization, number of institutions to which an individual may belong).

What makes societies and cultures simple or complex is not any single trait or group of traits but the whole combination of technology and environment, including trade, as influenced by history. On this basis I have postulated, *very tentatively*, what appear to be six levels in contemporary and historically documented societies which have existed without the benefit of gunpowder, coal, and steam engines. I have based my judgment on combinations of four criteria: (*a*) The specialization of individuals, (*b*) Amount of consumer goods obtained by trade, (*c*) Number of institutions to which an individual may belong, (*d*) Complexity of institutions.

(a) The Specialization of Individuals

Level I.   Peoples living on the simplest institutional level have no full-time specialists. A number of men are part-time specialists in *healing*, i.e., shamans. Peoples whose institutional simplicity is

---

* From *A Reader in General Anthropology*, edited by Carlton S. Coon (Appendix, pp. 612–13). Copyright 1948, Holt, Rinehart and Winston, Inc. Used by permission of the publisher.

clearly environmental in cause, as the Lapps, may be all specialists, as in reindeer herding, and conduct stable if irregular trade relationships with other ethnic groups.

Level II. Shamans are specialists, usually part-time only. Older men may specialize in teaching and conducting ritual. A few men may be part-time specialists in work activities.

Level III. Shamans may become full-time, and specialists in the esthetic arts may arise. There may also be some specialization in processing and in trade. The political leader may be a full- or part-time specialist.

Level IV. Specialists become relatively numerous, in government, healing and ritual, the arts, processing, and trading. In some cultures specialization goes by hereditary castes.

Level V. Probably half of the population is engaged in some non-food-producing specialty, at least half of the time. Many traders, skilled craftsmen, boatmen, caravan men, soldiers, priests, diviners, etc.

Level VI. Nearly everyone is a specialist in some kind of activity, including farming.

(b) Amount of Trade

Level I. Usually very slight. People make their own tools, as a rule. In cases of environmentally enforced simplicity, trade may be great—Eskimos get soapstone for lamps from great distances, Lapps obtain all metal tools by trade. Among technologically primitive peoples at low levels the chief objects of trade are body-paint materials and other ritual or esthetic objects.

Level II. Moderate amount of trading, usually once or twice a year only, with paint, drugs, luxury objects predominant.

Level III. Trade increases; tool materials commonly exchanged as well as luxuries; some food may be exchanged.

Level IV. Probably one half of all consumer goods other than food are obtained by trade. Tool materials move long distances, through many hands.

Level V.   More than half the goods consumed, other than food, are obtained through trade. Special foods traded as well.

Level VI.   An almost complete exchange of products, with only rural communities producing majority of own food.

(c) Number of Institutions to Which an Individual May Belong

Level I.   One. His family band.

Level II.   Two. His family and the band or village. Membership in an age-grade, totemic association, etc., may take on characteristics of an institution and thus increase the number to perhaps a half dozen.

Level III.   Anywhere from two to a dozen. These include family, band, or village, shaman's clientele, ritual group, and trader's clientele.

Level IV.   About twice as many as on Level III.

Level V.   In extreme cases, as in India, between 60 and 100.

Level VI.   May go into the hundreds.

(d) Complexity of Institutions

Level I.   A simple institution consisting of a biological family, often with a few extra-familial dependents. Meetings with other families, even kin, are too infrequent or casual to establish stable relations or institutional structure as part of a larger group.

Level II.   An institution consisting of a number of biological families grouped into a band or village, often with age grading. Authority usually rests in a number of older men. Relations with other bands or villages may approach but not attain institutional status.

Level III.   Groups of bands or villages attain stability under a combined leadership, forming a compound institution. Individual leaders, with simple staffs, tend to take command as amount of political business increases. Religious institutions and associations may coexist with the political and simple economic institutions as well.

Level IV. Stable hierarchies appear in political or religious institutions, or both. Regional confederations may take on structure. Economic institutions increase in number, and regular markets may appear.

Level V. One or two institutions, political or religious, become departmentally complex. Economic institutions remain simple.

Level VI. The state is a complex institution with hierarchies and many interlocking departments, including religious and economic. Equilibrium is maintained by an elaborate system of interdepartmental control. Economic institutions are still simple owing to persistence of hand techniques in industry.

The conditions postulated for each of the six levels are approximated in these cultures:

Level I. *Simple family bands*
  Great Basin (desert) American Indians
  Canoe Indians of Tierra del Fuego
  Seal Eskimos (West of Hudson's Bay—Boothia
    Peninsula)
  Reindeer Lapps

Level II. *Band contains several families*
  Andaman Islanders
  Arunta of Central Australia

Level III. *Rise of specialists and multiple institutions*
  Northern Maidu (Indians of Sacramento Valley)
  Traders of the Trobriands
  Pygmies of the Ituri Forest (Congo)
  The Kurnai of Gippsland (southeast corner of
    Australia)

Level IV. *Number of institutions per individual increases, and
    hierarchies begin*
  Mano of Liberia
  Ruwalla Bedouin (desert nomads)

Level V. *Hierarchies and compound institutions*
        Vikings
        Aztecs
        India (early historic period and contemporary villages)
Level VI. *One complex political institution*
        Athenians
        Romans

EXCERPT NO. 5*

The reader should keep in mind that in these passages Redfield is describing what probably no longer exists—the small, the long- and wholly isolated, the homogeneous and solidary folk society. Perhaps in its pure or "ideal" type it never existed. Redfield himself hastily qualifies his statement concerning dead level uniformity as between the individual members of the ideal type folk society ("what one man knows and believes is the same as what all men know and believe"). However, the folk society is relatively if not absolutely as Redfield describes it.

Yet even in this "highly conventional" society the individual is not an automaton. He does not feel himself to be; he has "a sense of opportunity," and "the culture sets goals which stimulate action by giving great meaning to it." Nor does he treat others "thing-fashion." In the folk society relations with others are not only personal but familial in nature.

The people who make up a folk society are much alike. Having lived in long intimacy with one another, and with no others, they have come to form a single biological type. The somatic homogeneity of local, inbred populations has been noted and studied. Since the people communicate with one another and with no others, one man's learned ways of doing and thinking are the same as another's. Another way of putting this is to say that in the ideal folk society, what one man knows and believes is the same as what all men know and believe. Habits are the same as customs.

In real fact, of course, the differences among individuals in a

---

* From Robert Redfield, "The Folk Society," *American Journal of Sociology*, Vol. 52 (1947), pp. 293–308, by permission of the University of Chicago Press.

primitive group and the different chances of experience prevent this ideal state of things from coming about. Nevertheless, it is near enough to the truth for the student of a real folk society to report it fairly well by learning what goes on in the minds of a few of its members, and a primitive group has been presented, although sketchily, as learned about from a single member. The similarity among the members is found also as one generation is compared with its successor. Old people find young people doing, as they grow up, what the old people did at the same age, and what they have come to think right and proper. This is another way of saying that in such a society there is little change.

The members of the folk society have a strong sense of belonging together. Moreover, against such knowledge as they have of societies other than their own, they emphasize their own mutual likeness and value themselves as compared with others. They say of themselves "we" as against all others, who are "they."

We may characterize the folk society as small, isolated, nonliterate, and homogeneous, with a strong sense of group solidarity.

The foregoing characterizations amount, roughly, to saying that the folk society is a little world off by itself, a world in which the recurrent problems of life are met by all its members in much the same way. This statement, while correct enough, fails to emphasize an important, perhaps the important aspect of the folk society. The ways in which the members of the society meet the recurrent problems of life are conventionalized ways; they are the results of long intercommunication within the group in the face of these problems; and these conventionalized ways have become interrelated within one another so that they constitute a coherent and self-consistent system. Such a system is what we mean in saying that the folk society is characterized by "a culture." A culture is an organization or integration of conventional understandings. It is, as well, the acts and the objects, in so far as they represent the type characteristic of that society, which express and maintain these understandings.

Behavior in the folk society is highly conventional, custom fixes the rights and duties of individuals, and knowledge is not critically examined or objectively and systematically formulated; but it must not be supposed that primitive man is a sort of automaton in which custom is the mainspring. It would be as mistaken to think of primitive man as strongly aware that he is constrained by custom. Within the limits set by custom there is invitation to excel in performance. There is lively competition, a sense of opportunity, and a feeling that what the culture moves one to do is well worth doing. There is no drabness in such a life. It has about it all the allurements of personal experience, very much one's own, of competitive skill, of things well done. The interrelations and high degree of consistency among the elements of custom which are presented to the individual declare to him the importance of making his endeavors in the directions indicated by tradition. The culture sets goals which stimulate action by giving great meaning to it.

It has been said that the folk society is small and that its members have lived in long and intimate association with one another. It has also been said that in such societies there is little critical or abstract thinking.

These characteristics are related to yet another characteristic of the folk society; behavior is personal, not impersonal. A "person" may be defined as that social object which I feel to respond to situations as I do, with all the sentiments and interests which I feel to be my own; a person is myself in another form, his qualities and values are inherent within him, and his significance for me is not merely one of utility. A "thing," on the other hand, is a social object which has no claim upon my sympathies, which responds to me, as I conceive it, mechanically; its value for me exists in so far as it serves my end. In the folk society all human beings admitted to the society are treated as persons; one does not deal impersonally ("thing-fashion") with any other participant in the little world of that society. Moreover, in the folk society much besides human beings is treated personally.

In short, the personal and intimate life of the child in the family is extended, in the folk society, into the social world of the adult and even into inanimate objects. It is not merely that relations in such a society are personal; it is also that they are familial. The first contacts made as the infant becomes a person are with other persons, moreover, each of these persons, he comes to learn, has a particular kind of relation to him which is associated with that one's genealogical position. The individual finds himself fixed within a constellation of familial relationships.

EXCERPT NO. 6*

In this brief excerpt Barnett emphasizes the relation between "size and complexity of the cultural inventory" and the individual's innovative potential. In a context rich in "cultural possessions" the individual has an advantage "that is denied individuals in less well endowed societies." The innovator's forward leap is made from a platform supplied by his culture. Not even a genius can leap from a low platform and achieve the height a quite ordinary innovator may reach from a high platform. Platforms rise as a result of accumulation and preservation of knowledge in written records and through intercultural communication (diffusion and borrowing).

All cultural changes are initiated by individuals. . . . Conditions external to the individual have a marked effect upon his innovative potential and upon the potential of the group in which he lives. . . . For the most part these externals are not of a person's own making. . . . Most of any person's cultural environment falls in this category. Each of us is able to make some slight modifications in the cultural milieu in which we live, and some individuals make significant changes; but we all begin with a body of ideas and a range of things and behaviors that have been assembled and integrated by our predecessors long before we are able to comprehend them. The complexity and the orientations of this traditional inventory inevitably have a determinative effect upon the interests, the competencies, and the innovative potentials of the members of any society. . . .

The size and complexity of the cultural inventory that is available to an innovator establishes limits within which he must function. . . . A sizable inventory allows for more new combinations and permits more different avenues of approach in problem solution than does a small one.

---

* From *Innovation, The Basis of Cultural Change*, by H. G. Barnett, pp. 39–41. Copyright, 1953. McGraw-Hill Book Company. Used by permission.

Some societies are much richer than others in cultural possessions; hence their members have an initial advantage that is denied individuals in less well endowed societies. The Australian aborigines and the pygmies of Africa have a minimum of technological devices. It is not to be expected that a member of either group, regardless of his ability, would invent a photoelectric cell or evolve a theory of world government. The same may be said of our own ancestors of a few hundred years ago. Einstein could hardly have developed his theory of relativity had he lived in the Neolithic age, nor could the atomic bomb have been invented in the days of Newton. The cultural base must provide the materials for further development. If the necessary ingredients are not contained in the inventory that is available, a new idea involving them is obviously impossible.

Sometimes the question of availability of innovative resources relates to the intellectual perspective of the innovator. His cultural horizon may be limited to the knowledge that exists only within his own society, or it may extend beyond . . . to adjacent or remote groups in other parts of the world. . . . Facility and extent of communication influence the accumulation of ideas. With well-developed channels of communication there goes a greater possibility of building up intellectual resources. . . .

Accumulation [also] results from a building upon the past, not a discarding of it; and the amount of past development conditions the amount and variety of what can be done at present.

There are marked differences between societies in this matter of an interest in the past. To some extent it is correlated with the existence or non-existence of written records, but this is not the sole determiner.

EXCERPT NO. 7*

Bennett touches on a disturbing aspect of reporting and interpretation by anthropologists. To what extent have they been able to observe and analyze

---

* Edited from John W. Bennett, "The Interpretation of Pueblo Culture: A Question of Values," in Douglas G. Haring (ed.), *Personal Character and Cultural Milieu* (Syracuse, N. Y.: Syracuse University Press, 1956), pp. 205–6.

*objectively? Certain biases—for example, an inclination to value the homogeneity
and "wholeness" of the folk society above the "heterogeneity and diffusiveness
of modern civilization"—are apparent. Selecting from anthropological accounts
of lifeways among the Hopi, Bennett effectively illustrates his point.*

. . . [There is] a context of theory basic to much of anthropology
. . . which lays stress upon the organic wholeness of preliterate life
in contrast to the heterogeneity and diffusiveness of modern civilization. One may trace this emphasis from the earliest American ethnological writings to the various manifestations of the configurational
approach and to Redfield's formal theory of the "folk society." This
general viewpoint is in part an expectable outgrowth of the anthropological preoccupation with preliterate communities, in part traceable to certain perspectives in the culture of American social
science.

In the latter case I refer to a general *critical* attitude of the social
scientist toward the heterogeneity of modern life, and a fairly clear
attitude toward the organic character of preliterate life as preferable.
Some direct statements of this value position can be found. In
other cases one must perceive it more by the frequency of the choice
of and emphasis on problems which deal with it. In this paper I
wish to make the imputation by studying the general linguistic
atmosphere. For example:

[Here Bennett quotes from a well-known work in which Hopi culture is described in glowing terms. The description emphasizes the
author's impression that Hopi lifeways are smoothly integrated to
a remarkable degree. This integration is reported to be evident in
many ways, and to be expressed in aesthetics, in cognitive habits
and world view, and even in subsistence technology. In dealing
with their physical environment as well as with human society the
Hopi are said to show a fine and unifying sense of logic, of the
practical, and of the aesthetic.] (Anthropologist A.)

The choice of such words and phrases as "harmonious," "acute,"
"notable achievement," "logical," and "consummate skill" in this
passage is, I think, fairly good evidence of the possibility that the

author approves of the Hopi configuration. There is nothing to be condemned in such approval—one only asks perhaps for a more conscious recognition . . . [by the author] of the value orientation, plus some thought as to its probable influences on the analysis of . . . data.

As to what such influences *might* be, we can consider the following passage:

Actually the Hopi way . . . sets up ideal conditions (in terms of external and internal pressures toward a single goal) for the development of an integrated system of social control, which functions effectively with a minimum of physical coercion, by fastening its internalization within the individual in the form of a super-ego or conscience consistent with the social goal.

There are two things of importance here: (1) the statement that the Hopi configuration is imposed "with a minimum of physical coercion"; and (2) a generalized swallowing-down and obfuscation of the imposition of group will and authority upon the individual— "external and internal pressures," "fostering its internalization," "conscience consistent with the social goal," and so on. These can be viewed as circumlocutions of what the other approach calls "authority" and "totalitarianism."

Now my preliminary conclusion is as follows: In this first, or "organic" theory of Pueblo culture, there is an implicit value orientation toward solidified, homogeneous group life. At least in the case of . . . [Anthropologist A], it appears possible that this preference-position is inarticulate and may influence . . . conclusions in such a way as to render certain features of the Hopi social system and culture less clear to the reader.

The second, or "repression" theory of Pueblo culture stresses the very features which the "organic" viewpoint elides or ignores. In regard to "physical coercion," . . . [Anthropologist B] emphasizes the severe physical and mental tortures of Hopi child initiation and socialization, including long descriptions of the horror and rigor of these rites. To these are added a multitude of subtle techniques for coercing the child into the norms. Whereas . . . [Anthropologist A] views Hopi participation in work as an example of "harmonious" and spontaneous cooperative attitudes toward fulfillment of the universal plan of Nature, . . . [Anthropologist B] states,

Large-scale cooperation deriving primarily from the needs of irrigation is therefore vitally important to the life and well-being of the Pueblo community. It is no spontaneous expression of goodwill or sociability. What may seem "voluntary" to some is the end of a long process of conditioning, often persuasive, but frequently harsh, that commences in infancy and continues throughout adulthood.

CHAPTER 5

Patterning of Interpersonal Relationships: Implications for the Individual

> Within the Gorges there is no lack of men;
> They are people one meets, not people one cares for.
> At my front door guests also arrive;
> They are people one sits with, not people one knows.
>
> Po Chu-i

The individual lives with others, and his relations with these others are highly variable. There are people "one meets" and people "one cares for," "people one sits with" and "people one knows." J. S. Slotkin (1950) quotes these apt lines from a Chinese poet in illustration of polar types of social relations. In their essential nature these "secondary" vs. "primary" types are, as Slotkin says, "distant, aloof and impersonal" vs. "close, intimate, and personal." (*Ibid.*, p. 23.) "In simple societies social interaction is usually primary; in complex societies, secondary." (*Ibid.*, p. 37.)

It is in large cities that secondary relations are the predominant type; the disadvantages of this condition have been repeatedly emphasized by social scientists (as we have already noted). It has been acknowledged, however, as in the following passage by Louis Wirth, that there are some compensations as well as disadvantages:

Whereas [in cities] the individual gains, on the one hand, a certain degree of emancipation or freedom from the personal and emotional controls of intimate groups, he loses, on the other hand, the spontaneous self-expression, the morale, and the sense of participation that comes with living in an integrated society. This constitutes essentially the state of anomie [rulelessness] or the social void to which Durkheim alludes in attempting to account for the various forms of social disorganization in technological society. (Wirth, 1938, p. 13.)

Whatever the nature of his society the individual moves through a complicated web of interpersonal relationships. Each relationship involves communication and interdependence. Some relationships are important for personal security. An important part of enculturation (a process discussed in Chapter 6) is learning the patterned expectations associated with particular relationships. The neophyte must learn his duties and prerogatives, his rights and privileges, in each. All through his life he will be affected by other persons whom he encounters in patterned relationships, and he in turn will affect them.

Interpersonal relations are basic among the mechanisms through which the individual learns his culture, achieves his goals, and attains his security and satisfaction in living. An occasional "odd-ball" may minimize human contacts even to the point of reclusiveness. Few of us are ready to pay such a price for release from the inevitable frustrations and irritations which come with interpersonal contacts. We need one another for self-fulfillment as well as for survival; it is a law of human life.

ATTRIBUTES OF INTERPERSONAL RELATIONSHIPS IN PREINDUSTRIAL AND IN MORE COMPLEX CONTEXTS

Folk and preindustrial contexts sharply limit the number of an individual's relationships and extend the functions of each of them.

Recall Coon's criteria for his Levels I through VI, particularly "number of institutions to which an individual may belong," and "complexity of institutions." In Level I societies (e.g., the Seal Eskimos or Great Basin American Indians) there is no social membership unit larger than the "simple family band"—an extended family whose members move together. Only rarely will members of this group encounter the members of others. Only within the family band will relationships be sustained over time. Coon classifies as "Level II" those somewhat more complex systems (e.g., Andaman Islanders; Arunta of Central Australia) in which the "band contains several families." Between Levels I and II the differences are largely in numbers of persons involved and in the intra-band differentiations between families.

From Coon's Levels III through VI and beyond, along the complexity continuum, there is great expansion in several dimensions. There is expansion in both numbers of persons and in structural differentiation by subgroups. In addition a new dimension—specialization of function—appears and expands. Specialization is a by-product of growing technological sophistication, and its implications for interpersonal relations are very great. E. D. Chapple and C. S. Coon (1942) explain why and how specialization develops from a simple division of labor.

Some techniques which people practice require comparatively little skill. For example, anyone can easily learn to weave a basket, skin a deer, or ride a donkey. Any one person can learn to perform all three of these actions, and others as well; he does not need to specialize. But the making of a wheel-turned vase, tanning a hide, or driving a railroad engine are actions which require much more skill and a comparatively long period of training. In order to perform any of these techniques a certain amount of specialization is necessary; expert potters are seldom master-tanners or railroad engineers as well. The average individual can absorb only a certain amount of training, and can attain a high degree of skill at only a few techniques. If he is to do any one thing well, he must be a specialist. . . .

In some societies, as we have seen, there are no specialists, since all techniques are simple; in other societies, there are many specialists because of the complexity of the techniques. In our own society almost everyone is a specialist of some sort. Now a specialist can produce more goods or perform more services per unit of time spent than a nonspecialist, particularly in the more complex techniques. Hence the amount of goods produced and services rendered per capita by any group will vary largely in proportion to the number of specialists among them; the complexity of techniques used will vary similarly.

This does not mean that in a society of specialists, everyone performs elaborate techniques; on the contrary, many individuals may perform extremely simple actions, which are actually parts of a total technique of great complexity. . . .

All human beings, all social groups, have some kind of a division of labor. There are two forms which this takes among all peoples: the age division and the sex division. The age division is universal, because . . . the human infant is unable to take care of itself at birth, and, in fact, matures so slowly during a long conditioning period that it is usually dependent upon its parents for food, shelter, and the other necessities until the age of puberty or later. The activities of a child, therefore, differ from those of an adult in the prime of life. The adult's activities again differ from those of an old man or woman who has lost his or her earlier muscular vigor, and whose faculties of sensory perception and of coordination may have been impaired by senile decay. All peoples recognize these three stages in the human age progression, and all of them make some provision for each group to have suitable tasks. . . .

The sex division is also universal, for the equally biological reason that the women are the ones to bear children and nurse them. . . . Men usually perform the tasks which will take them away from home all day or for several days at a time, while women usually perform those which can or must be done in the camp or house, or will take them away for only a few hours at a time, or can be done while they are accompanied by young children. Men perform tasks which require rapid motion, silence, and skill; women are ordinarily unable to perform such tasks because of the hindering presence of their children. Thus the household tasks fall to their lot, and the number of these tasks prevents them as a rule from becoming full-time specialists in any one technique. Furthermore, the materials or goods which they acquire or produce by their techniques are usually limited in quantity by the simplicity of the techniques and the fact that they cannot practice any one of them very long at a time. They only take care of home consumption and occasionally have a small surplus. In some societies, women sell their surplus eggs, handmade pottery, vegetables, and the like in markets, but the volume of trade in such cases is usually small. (Chapple and Coon, 1942, pp. 251–52.)

As Chapple and Coon point out, some division of labor along lines of sex and age is universal. Interpersonal relations are inevitably affected by this division and the limiting associations and expectations it implies. But in the more complex sociocultural systems these criteria may recede in importance in favor of more individualized criteria such as personal interest and talent. This of course means, for the individual, a wider range of possibilities. In societies like our own one need not be old to qualify as learned, and to be admitted to the councils of the learned. One need not even be a man. Academic certification (the Ph.D., for example) will serve to get women and the relatively youthful past the guardians of the precincts in which the learned congregate and cogitate.

Specialization of function brings in train a set of factors all of which affect the nature of interpersonal relationships. They affect these relationships in the direction of making them more formal, contractual, and impersonal. Sociologists especially have studied and reported upon the variable nature of interpersonal relations and specified the differences between primary and secondary relationships (e.g., Cooley, 1909). The former are described as being charcteristically face-to-face, sustained, intimate, informal, highly personalized or "particularistic" (Talcott Parsons' widely used term), functionally diffuse, emotion- and sentiment-laden. They are more often ascribed than achieved. Secondary relationships are, by contrast, characteristically nonintimate, formal, impersonal, "universalistic" (Parsons), functionally specific, and nonaffective. Achieved relationships (e.g., in the workaday world) are likely to be of this secondary sort.

In social relations, an individual can be said to behave in a personal manner to the extent that his actions reflect his recognition of their implications for the person affected. Through animistic beliefs, objects may be endowed with personality and treated in a personal manner. At the other extreme, completely impersonal behavior toward an individual disregards all of his social roles and treats him as an object. (Miner, 1965, p. xv.)[1]

Anthropologists have provided data basic to and illustrative of these generalizations about interpersonal relations, and especially the generalizations concerning preindustrial and preliterate contexts. The following passage is an excellent example of relevant anthro-

---

[1] Horace Miner, *The Primitive City of Timbuctoo* (rev. ed.; New York: Doubleday & Co., Inc., 1965). Reprinted by permission of Princeton University Press.

pological reporting. It comes from a study (by Colin M. Turnbull) of Congo Pygmies whose lifeways fit Coon's Level III. Turnbull lived for three years with these remarkable little people, for whom he developed great respect and fondness. This passage points up the fact that though relations in a folk society may be primary, informal, etc., the respective rights and responsibilities of the persons involved are to them quite clear and well understood. In cases of lapses from proper behavior the offender will be brought back into line by his fellows.

Turnbull describes an episode in which a man named Cephu breaks the well-patterned rules governing cooperative hunting and is punished by his fellows. Turnbull writes:

I had never heard of this happening before, and it was obviously a serious offence. In a small and tightly knit hunting band, survival can be achieved only by the closest co-operation and by an elaborate system of reciprocal obligations which insures that everyone has some share in the day's catch. Some days one gets more than others, but nobody ever goes without. There is, as often as not, a great deal of squabbling over the division of the game, but that is expected, and nobody tries to take what is not his due. . . .

Cephu had committed what is probably one of the most heinous crimes in Pygmy eyes, and one that rarely occurs. Yet the case was settled simply and effectively, without any evident legal system being brought into force. It cannot be said that Cephu went unpunished, because for those few hours when nobody would speak to him he must have suffered the equivalent of as many days solitary confinement. . . . To have been refused a chair by a mere youth, not even one of the great hunters; to have been laughed at by women and children; to have been ignored by men—none of these things would be quickly forgotten. Without any formal process of law Cephu had been firmly put in his place, and it was unlikely he would do the same thing again in a hurry.

This was typical of all Pygmy life, on the surface at least. There was a confusing, seductive informality about everything they did. Whether it was a birth, a wedding, or a funeral, in a Pygmy hunting camp . . . there was always an unexpectedly casual, almost carefree attitude. There was, for instance, little apparent specialization; everyone took part in everything. Children had little or no voice in adult affairs, but the only adult activities from which they seemed to be rigidly excluded were certain songs and of course the molimo [the dance of death]. Between men and women there was also a certain degree of specialization, but little that could be called exclusive. (Turnbull, 1962, pp. 106 and 108.)

In his study of Timbuctoo (a preindustrial and largely un-westernized city) Miner has described social relations in this "in-between" kind of context. He shows the extent to which relationships are more functionally specific than in less urban settings, and the way in which this condition grows out of a "market economy" and is induced by contact with other societies and cultures. And Miner found the predictable: intra-family relationships remain least affected by urbanization (i.e., most thoroughly primary in nature). Miner writes:

> The city provides a social milieu in which economic success may be achieved with less regard for activities which are not primarily economic in nature. In the folk community, because of the close-knit functional organization of its culture, religious and family behavior have definite economic implications. In fact, it is exceedingly difficult, if not impossible, to say what is economic behavior and what is familial. In Timbuctoo it is often easy to make such a distinction. A market economy requires specialized and individualized activity. In these activities the market rewards secular and impersonal behavior. This fact, plus the inherent conflict between different traits of cultures in contact, results in interrelations of a nonfolk type. . . . Folk behavior appears to be most typical of family relationships. . . .
> There is a gradient in the degree of "folkness" which increases from the community unit to the family. (Miner, 1965, p. 293 and p. 297.)[2]

The primary/secondary distinction is not an all-or-none matter. Each type of relationship can be more or less informal, affect-laden, etc. But the attributes of relationships tend to cluster around the primary-secondary poles. And relationships of a secondary type are, for average individuals, much more numerous in sociocultural systems falling beyond the "writing" and especially the "industrial technology" points on the continuum. In such contexts primary relationships tend to be concentrated in the family.

---

[2] *Ibid.*

FAMILY RELATIONSHIPS AND PERSONAL SECURITY

The nuclear family (though not the *autonomous* nuclear family) is found in all societies. Whatever its form, the family may be the only social unit to which the individual belongs (Level I), or it may be one of many (often but not necessarily the case in the urban-industrial setting). In any event the family is likely to serve, particularly in the individual's preadult years, as his most important personal community.

The personal community is that group of people "on whom an individual can rely for support and/or approval" (Henry, 1958, p. 827). During the relatively helpless years of infancy and early childhood one's personal community is essential to his sheer physical survival. Later its functions are different, but no less essential. Few are able to live really alone; for most humans both security and a sense of satisfaction are heavily dependent upon close bonds with others, a few others at least.

Henry (*ibid.*) identifies what seem to be the critical and universal "properties" of the personal community: *reliance, number, constancy,* and *involvement* (see Adaptation No. 3). When these properties appear in high degree the sociocultural context is likely to be of the sort Wayne Dennis describes in *The Hopi Child*. He writes:

[A] guess which we hazard with respect to the Hopi child is that he has a strong feeling of social security. To be sure, individual homes are often in imminence of being broken, and we have cited several instances in which domestic discord has affected the child. But in case of separation of the parents, it is a foregone conclusion that the child will remain with the mother; there is no uncertainty about this. If the mother should die, there is a vast circle of relatives, all known to the child and living in close proximity to him who would accept responsibility for him. His is a world which he knows intimately, and which accepts him completely. A Hopi is never driven from his village; he is never an outcast; he never starves when others have food; he never lacks a place in which to sleep. While the child may learn early the unfriendliness of the climate and the danger of starvation which faces the entire village, he lives in a social world in which he has an indubitable place. He does not face an unknown vocation or an uncertain future, but looks forward to a life which even today is much the same as it was in the past. (Dennis, 1940, p. 190.)

It is Henry's thesis that urbanization and Westernization (i.e., movement to the complex end of the continuum) tend to alter significantly the properties of the personal community, and often in a direction disadvantageous to the individual. Reliance, especially in the modern bureaucratic or corporation nexus, tends to be low. The personal community is likely to be reduced in number. Constancy, measured by ratio of time-absent to time-present, is likely to be unfavorably affected. Involvements shift toward the formal, impersonal, and nonreciprocating.

Social scientists, in the West at least, have long accepted Henry's view of urbanization and Westernization. However, there is increasing evidence that it represents an oversimplification. Edward Bruner writes:

Contrary to the traditional theory (concerning effects of urbanization), we find in many Asian cities that society does not become isolated, kinship organizations do not break down, nor do social relationships in the urban environment become impersonal, superficial and utilitarian. (Bruner, 1961, p. 508.)

There can be no doubt that the properties Henry describes are real, variable in the general direction he indicates, and significant in relation to individual security and satisfaction. It is unlikely, however, that the statistical measures he proposes are adequate as measures of the personal satisfaction yielded by a relationship. Separations, resulting in a "low constancy ratio," do not automatically jeopardize personal bonds. The frequent absence of the father, or the working mother, from the American home need not generate "hostility" in the children and "guilt" in the parent, as Henry suggests. There is no evidence that the hostility-guilt formula operates in modern urban Japan, where the "salary man" is certainly as much away from home as is his American counterpart, the organization man (Vogel, 1963, *passim*; Norbeck, 1965, *passim*).

Two factors not identified in Henry's analysis are as important as time spent in actual proximity. They are: (1) level of expectation (what the individual expects of a relationship), and (2) *quality* of a relationship. Both are heavily dependent upon cultural patterning. To assume equivalence between quantity (hours spent in proximity) and quality in a personal relationship is to underestimate human flexibility and sensitivity.

Even the young child is flexible to a degree usually underrated in American psychologies and in American culture. Given what he senses as a genuine and abiding affection and concern for him he can accept, with only temporary anxiety or anger, the traumas of weaning, displacement by a younger sibling, parental preoccupations, death of a parent, or even a deliberate regime of physical or psychic hardening. Louis Nizer makes this point when he says:

> The scars left upon the child by an unhappy environment may be serious, or they may be overcome by a hardy personality. . . . [But] most children are as resilient as they are sensitive. Their capacity to recover from emotional trauma is as remarkable as that from physical injury. . . . Who has not observed a child, stunned by a parent's death, recover with almost disgraceful speed from the blow? The strongest water power in the world is a child's tears, but it also dries up fastest. Children divert themselves by new interests with far greater facility than adults. The process of growing is all-absorbing. (Nizer, 1961, p. 195.)[3]

The child's level of expectation becomes adjusted to what is current among the people around him. What might under some circumstances be felt as deprivation or personal injury is likely to be accepted matter-of-factly when it is a commonplace of the child's society.

There is great variation between cultures in the matter of patterned expectation for and of children, and equally great variation in their levels of acceptance.

In the Japanese village described by Edward Norbeck (see Adaptation No. 4), infancy is a period of indulgence. Yet the child of four or five has usually ceased to be the pampered center of attention. He has been subjected to discontinuity of a sort our psychologists often deplore, but there is no evidence that he has

---

[3] Louis Nizer, *My Life in Court* (New York: Doubleday and Company, 1961). Used by permission.

suffered psychic damage as a result. There is in fact no good empirical evidence to support the theory that he must.

An even more dramatic departure from approved American child rearing is illustrated in Ernestine Friedl's account of the hardening to which children are subjected in a modern Greek village (see Excerpt No. 9). Adult-child relationships are customarily marked by a great deal of teasing, ridiculing, and lying on the part of the adult. These practices, in their context, represent quite justifiable schooling for life in a society whose patterned arts and skills in interpersonal relations maximize guile and deception, at least within certain limits.

The Greek way of social hardening and sharpening is precisely parallel to the physical hardening and toughening to which children in hunting-warring cultures are often subjected. The Modoc practice of unexpectedly rousing a child, boy or girl, to bathe in an icy lake in the dead of a winter night, is a prime example (see Adaptation No. 5).

Discontinuities in child rearing, or what may look like harshness or cruelty by contemporary American standards, do not necessarily threaten the child's sense of security in his personal community. He expects the culturally approved treatment, and he accepts it. But he is extremely sensitive to the quality—the feeling tone, in relationships. Parental affection and concern for the welfare of their offspring is a universal and biologically rooted phenomenon. So too is the child's need for such affection and concern. His need can be satisfied from sources other than natural parents, and it often is. Grandparents, uncles and aunts, siblings, or still others who serve as participants in his personal community contribute to meet his need for a certain essential quality in relationships.

At the urban-sophisticate end of the complexity continuum, the child's personal community tends to be limited in number, as Henry says. The small nuclear family—Blitsten's "autonomous nuclear family" (see Excerpt No. 8)—constitutes the typical community. What, then, if this family is broken by death, divorce, or desertion? What if even this small community becomes commonly a frail or shaky unit? These are hazards widely discussed in the literature of the behavioral sciences, and quite rightly regarded as grave threats. However, some recent studies in complex cultures are re-assuring.

It may be that the vanishing nuclear family is more a phenomenon of urban mythology than of reality. A recent study of *Family Life in the Netherlands* by K. Ishwaran (1959) provides a notable example. Dr. S. Groenman, Professor of Sociology at the Universities of Leiden and Utrecht, comments in the foreword:

> The results of Dr. Ishwaran's study are indeed surprising to us. He comes to the conclusion that the Dutch family throughout a period of social dynamism has maintained its essential characteristics. . . . Perhaps we are reluctant to acknowledge the relative internal stability of the family and the relatively slight changes in [its] structure. (Ishwaran, 1959, p. vi.)

Ishwaran himself says that the Dutch family, considered as a "closed system" and with emphasis on the functioning of its members, "has not changed in its essentials during the process of social change from a pre-industrial to an industrial society." (*Ibid.*, p. 214.) Moreover, he sees no great differences between urban and rural families. In both he finds "familism"—a high degree of importance attached to the family life. Kin ties are strong, even when communication between kin is limited. Reunions for important events, such as weddings and funerals, will bring relatives from long distances. Sentimental ties survive and social, even economic, obligations are still honored. Ishwaran concludes:

> No substitute has yet been found for the ties of sentiment and emotion, and, in general, those ways in which only the family can satisfy certain longings of the human heart. (*Ibid.*, p. 220.)

American sociologist Kingsley Davis and others have believed that extended kinship ties, and immediate family functions, have been "sheared away." (Davis, 1949, p. 423.) It is assumed that in the American middle class, at any rate, the reduced family unit is about as unstable as it can be without collapsing. Ishwaran says that in Holland "the family, far from being unstable, is in a state of equilibrium, relative to modern conditions of life." And he continues:

In fact, we are impressed that the feelings are so strong [e.g., between first cousins, between uncles and aunts and their nephews and nieces] when residence is not in common, and distances between houses may be considerable. The secularization of modern life, with its attendant specialization of interests and activities, and the possibility of mobility, all tend to militate against this feeling for relatives, which nevertheless is strong and healthy. (Ishwaran, *op. cit.*, p. 220.)

Moreover in Holland there seems to have been no significant change in the concept of family as the major transmitter of cultural values from generation to generation. With respect to the U.S., Charles W. Hobart (1963) finds " a few shreds of evidence" that the American family remains primary among value transmitting agencies, though the values it transmits are changing. It is his view that they must change; Hobart argues:

. . . If an affluent society is to survive it must undergo a value revolution which will make . . . human values pre-eminent over production values. . . . The nature of contemporary urban society makes this increasingly necessary. . . . Earlier alternative bases of family solidarity are disappearing . . . commitment is an increasingly crucial bond. Increasingly, the family is the only security base available to man today. (Hobart, 1963, p. 412.)

It may be, then, that the crux of the security problem lies in values rather than in structures. Given a core of "sound values" strongly held and carefully transmitted, any type of family structure may meet children's needs. Clarity and firmness in the definition and teaching of values appear to be of prime importance.

Margaret Read (1960) provides an illustration in her analysis of traditional Ngoni (Nyasaland) child rearing and its results. The system was notable for extreme care in the teaching of patterns of interpersonal behavior. Restrictive rules of etiquette, deference, duty and the like were heavily emphasized. Discussing sources of the security she found characteristic of Ngoni children, Read says:

. . . An aspect of the security of Ngoni children . . . is the freedom conferred on a child because he learns early in life just how to speak and how to behave to other people. This may be an unusual view of the apparent restrictions placed on language, posture, attitude, actions, displayed by a child, particularly toward adults. Anyone who has brought up children however knows that they are unhappy with unlimited licence in behaviour, and is aware that the learning of etiquette and manners and obedience, apparently so tiresome in its early stages, does eventually eliminate a number of perplexing choices for children, and by regulating certain relationships confers freedom in other directions. That was my reading of the Ngoni children's reactions to the somewhat formal code of manners taught from their early years and strictly enforced. Ngoni good manners did not mean that the children were coerced and subdued. They were happy, busy, friendly, endlessly inventive and full of initiative. . . .

The seeming absence of frustration and overt rebellion in the years just after puberty was due to the social recognition by relatives and by the village community of the new stage reached by boys and girls, and to the increasing responsibility required of them for carrying out allotted tasks and for preparing for their future careers. (Read, 1960, pp. 169–70.)

Ngoni values were conveyed also in terms of personality ideals. The child was taught, from infancy, to admire and strive to be like persons in whom the ideals were realized, or approximately so. Read reports:

The positive virtue of being law-abiding was constantly emphasized in families, villages, and in the kingdom generally. Inherent in showing respect and being obedient and law-abiding was the much-stressed quality of self-control. Early travellers remarked on the restrained, dignified and courteous behaviour in Ngoni villages, which was my experience also, and especially in the vicinity of leading Ngoni families. This kind of self-control was taught . . . in a great variety of contexts, from avoiding greedy and noisy eating as young children to putting up with being ordered about in the boy's dormitory, and from the insistence on the decorous forms of greetings and thanks to the suppression of any overt fear or pain at the puberty ceremonies.

Two other qualities were emphasized in child training since they were expected of all Ngoni people in interpersonal relations. One was *generosity* in sharing anything that a person had. It was a quality demanded of everyone, from the small child who was made to unclench his fist in which he was hiding three ground-nuts and give two of them to his fellows, to the big chief whose duty at a feast was to see that everyone had enough and to send food from his own portion to anyone who looked hungry. A number of proverbs called attention to the value of generosity and to the social attitude toward meanness, which was felt to be despicable. . . .

The other quality was the conventional display of sympathy, especially at times of mourning for the dead, but also on occasions of severe loss, such as cattle dying, or illness or accident. . . . Visits and expressions of sympathy could not be omitted without grave social disapproval. . . . To assist in these condolences so that the speaker and the hearer would readily understand each other, proverbs were used such as: "If the pot is broken it is broken indeed," and, "When water is poured out it cannot be gathered up." . . .

All through the later stages of training children and young adults the importance of speaking well was emphasized. This at first referred to correct language and being audible but not noisy. Later . . . the art of speech was held up as a Ngoni characteristic. . . . When a person brought out clearly the point of an argument the listeners said, "You have rung a little bell"; and when after a prolonged discussion or the hearing of a case in the courts the audience accepted a decision as conclusive and just, they said, "The upper and the lower teeth meet together." . . .

The ideal personality of Ngoni women . . . had four main aspects: physical capacity and appearance, relationship to her husband and his relatives, competence in household management, and general reputation for justice and wisdom. (*Ibid.*, pp. 155–57.)

. . . The Ngoni . . . had a more or less distinct ideal personality rooted in their culture and answering the question: what kind of people are the Ngoni and how do they want others to regard them? This ideal personality was the goal of their child training. . . . (*Ibid.*, p. 171.)

The Ngoni belief system was positive and optimistic. The properly trained child would become an admirable man or woman, whose chances for a satisfying and worthwhile life would be excellent. The "true" Ngoni was proud, self-respecting, confident, industrious, capable of initiative and leadership. His tradition and bearing were, in the connotative sense, aristocratic.

Elsewhere there are patternings of an opposite sort. The Quechua of the central Andes (Peru) sustain a culture stressing negatives; pessimism assumes the proportions of a world view. The children are trained for glum submission and for a mute, plodding, struggle for survival. Subsistence skills are heavily emphasized. Personal satisfaction in life is not.

The *Quechua* child is taught to be submissive and to bow before authority, to distrust the outsider, to fear the Christian-pagan hierarchy of spirits and deities, and to struggle as best he can to gain a livelihood. Throughout his life, he remains hemmed in from all sides. His daily experiences together with subtle family indoctrination teach him that he has no weapon with which to defend himself and tend to produce the familiar *Quechua* personality—the sullen and resigned Indian . . .

But the *Quechua* also learns to be a good farmer, to carry on animal husbandry, and to work at the arts and crafts connected with his village and family. It is with these economic activities that the overt educative process is concerned. (Mishkin, 1963, p. 460.)

In the contrast between Ngoni and Quechua we have an illustration of the ways in which culturally patterned concepts affect adult-child relationships and the child's orientation toward life. The contrast does not lie in degree of control by adults; adults are firmly and unquestionably in command of both societies and in control of adult-child relationships. But in the one (Ngoni), these adults conceive of children as properly on their way to become confident, commanding, capable of initiative and leadership. In the other (Quechua), expectations are quite the reverse; it is taken for granted that sullen resignation will mark the character of the developing individual. Through interpersonal relationships culturally patterned concepts concerning the individual and his potential for autonomy can affect that potential. It is unlikely, however, to be extinguished in all individuals, even in so unfavoring a context as Quechua culture.

INTERPERSONAL RELATIONS AND THE INDIVIDUAL: BASIC PROPOSITIONS

In this chapter we have centered our attention upon the web of relationships which constitute, in all sociocultural contexts, a recurrent and essential feature of each individual's life. These relationships are basic among the mechanisms through which the individual learns his culture, achieves his goals, and attains security and satisfaction. Inevitably they bring him frustrations and obstacles as well.

Sociocultural contexts of the more folkish types provide limited numbers of relationships all of which are largely primary in nature. What the individual does, and with whom he does it, will be affected by his sex and age, as well as by his personal talents and interests. In more complex settings the functional specialization that is a by-product of technological sophistication opens new avenues for exercise of personal abilities and inclinations. This specialization facilitates secondary relationships. Intra-family relationships retain their primary quality, however.

The individual's family, whatever its nature and composition in his particular culture, is very likely to be also his most important personal community. His relationships within this community are important for his sense of security, particularly in childhood and youth. Many social scientists believe that urbanization and Westernization alter significantly the nature of these relationships, and that as a result personal security is seriously threatened. But there is reason to doubt that these effects necessarily follow.

Urbanization does not always weaken family bonds, nor are children so psychically fragile as to be necessarily damaged by certain common features of urban family life (e.g., recurrent absence of the working father from the home). The child must have affection and care; given these he can accept a wide range of conditions and meet a remarkable variety of expectations. He is more likely to feel secure if he is required to strive toward meeting clearly defined expectations.

What is most important about all this, in relation to the individual and his potential for autonomy, is the freedom conferred by security. Read states and illustrates this proposition in her report on Ngoni child-training and its results. Ngoni children, trained to meet clearly defined and sanguine expectations, were found to be "happy, busy, friendly, endlessly inventive and full of initiative." (Read, *op. cit.*, p. 170.) Interpersonal relationships—their nature and content, are important to the security and hence to the "freedom" of both children and adults.

ADAPTATION NO. 3*

Henry's analysis of "personal community" provides a useful framework for comparative studies. He isolates important properties of the personal community, and thereby facilitates cross-cultural comparisons in terms of these properties.

He says that under conditions of Westernization and urbanization the personal community decreases in size. There can be no doubt, as we have noted earlier, that when this occurs it means for the average individual a decrease in the number of primary relationships, i.e., relationships high in what Henry calls "reliance," "constancy," and "involvement."

To this extent we are in agreement with his views. We do not, however, agree that personal insecurity is a necessary concomitant of this process. With Henry we can "accept the fact that his personal community is the core of a man's security system." But we cannot accept the linked proposition: "it follows that changes in it will affect [adversely] his feelings of security." It is true that the process of change is in itself disturbing and likely to be conducive to at least transient anxiety. But it is our view that security, though certainly related, is not determined by the personal community, and that it is affected by numerous other variables as well.

An important function of social structure is to provide everyone with a personal community, a group of people on whom he can rely for support and approval.

In the first place, a personal community has a certain *number*, determined by counting those who most frequently contribute to an individual's welfare and approve his actions. In the second place, a personal community has a certain *constancy*, measured by the time spent by its members in direct interaction. Thus in our culture a mother has a higher constancy in the personal community of the child than does its father, and both have a higher constancy than a distant uncle. In the third place, the members of a personal community have a certain *involvement* in each other, that is to say, an obligation to give heed to and be swayed by each other's wishes. Involvement is the most complex of the properties of the personal community.

---

* From Jules Henry, "The Personal Community and Its Invariant Properties," *American Anthropologist*, Vol. 60, No. 5 (October, 1958), pp. 827–31.

A. The Personal Community

Ideally in our culture, a child's mother and father are persons with high reliance; but reliance in a modern bureaucracy or corporation is often notoriously low. It is quite clear that the coefficient of reliance becomes closely related to that feeling of being protected which, in our culture, is labeled "security."

In traditional India one could, by and large, rely heavily on one's joint family; nowadays the joint family is disappearing. The joint families of India and China, the rigid patrilineal systems of Africa, the matrilineal systems in the American Southwest, are examples of highly structured, rigid, tradition-determined personal communities aimed at achieving high reliance; the typical female American adolescent peer-group is an example at the other extreme, of a relatively unstructured, fluid personal community with low reliance. It can readily be guessed that problems of security are vastly different between the extremes.

B. Number

The number in the personal community is assumed to be important to cooperation and to feelings of security. Thus the child in an American family has an exceedingly small personal community, and so scans its members constantly and anxiously for signs of approval and affection, and as he grows older he attempts to expand his personal community beyond the kinship ties in order to increase his feelings of security. The large joint households of India and China, and other types of extended kin groups, provide much larger envelopes of security. However, even in extended kin groups the personal community is never coterminous with the lineage. Thus, for example, among the Hopi, in spite of extended matrilineal ties, it is the maternal household that is the core of the personal community. Number is one of the first properties of social structure that it attacked under conditions of urbanization and Westernization, for large numbers of persons often drop out of one's personal community. The undermining of social structures through death or out-migration is well known.

C. Constancy

Constancy is a property that is more central, more determining, more "biological," than any discussed here. Unless there is a certain constancy of presence in the human environment, the child fails to develop its capacity to respond. That is to say, particularly during the first year of life there is a certain necessary minimum of human interaction in the absence of which the organism will not develop normally.

At any rate, all social systems attempt to achieve some constancy among the members of the personal community. A person's constancy is measured by the ratio of the time he is absent to the time he is present. Thus, in the average American family, the mother is a relatively constant figure, the father is less so. The fact that the American father has such a low constancy ratio is one factor that may lead him to try to make himself attractive to his children in order to overcome their hostility and his guilt. There is little doubt that low constancy is biologically intolerable.

D. Involvement

This is the most variable property of the personal community. The great variety of human involvements is directly related to the absence in human beings of genetically determined mechanisms of social linkage. This has brought it about that human beings have set up a great variety of social structures depending on the way in which involvements are stipulated under varying cultural conditions. Thus, for example, whereas a kinship system is a structure predicated on biological involvement, modern corporations and governments are predicated on administrative involvements.

Other important types of involvement are: (1) External involvement, as in the relations between Indian castes, between the Mbaya and the Chane, where the Mbaya hunted for the agricultural Chane, or between the inland and the coastal Arapesh. The essential character of external involvements is that they rest upon the exchange of goods and services and that they generate pseudo-kinship ties. The Spanish *compadrazgo* relationship would be a special case of external involvement. (2) Ceremonial involvement is important in many parts of the world. The essential feature of ceremonial involvement is that within the structure of the ceremonial organization each individual is subject to its requirements. The Hopi ceremonial societies and the Plains Indians associations are examples.

The statistical problem in the analysis of involvement in any society is to determine the number of involvements in which each individual finds himself, the frequency of the demands for action arising out of each, and the power they are able to exert over behavior.

If number and constancy are affected by the involvements in which the individual finds himself, then to the extent that a person's feelings of security or anxiety are a function of his personal community, they cannot be understood in terms of number and constancy only but must be related also to the character of the involvements.

There are two considerations that affect all involvements: whether they are reciprocating or are characterized by relations of sub- and superordination.

If we accept the fact that his personal community is the core of a man's security system, it follows that changes in it will affect his feelings of security. Since, however, the personal community changes in terms of its properties, analysis of change in these helps us to understand changes in feelings of security. Thus, for example, under conditions of Westernization and urbanization the number of persons in a villager's personal community changes, and so does their constancy, for there often occur not only massive increases or decreases in the population, but in mobility also.

Most striking under conditions of Westernization (in India, for example) is the massive shift in types of involvement. The increasing importance of administrative—that is, governmental—involvements has many effects; there is no doubt that one of them is an increase in anxiety at the village level, though this is by no means uniformly the case. The Indian villager's anxiety in the presence of increasing administrative involvements stems not only from the fact that administrative powers are impersonal, non-reciprocating, and not subject to the same forces as are the linkages of intra-village involvements, but also that they can exert overwhelming power.

EXCERPT NO. 8*

"The world of the family" is in most societies the core of the personal community. Blitsten distinguishes, "on the basis of degree of autonomy exercised by their nuclear units," three major types of family organization: the corporate, the bilateral extended, and the autonomous nuclear. Each type tends "to be associated with particular combinations of general social and cultural conditions . . ." varying from advanced agrarian to modern urban. All three of these "ideal types" identified by Blitsten are therefore associated with moderately to highly complex sociocultural systems (probably Coon's Level V and beyond on the continuum).

The corporate family provides for the individual maximum security but significantly less freedom than the autonomous nuclear, in which the security-freedom balance is reversed. Blitsten adds to these evaluations the opinion that the bilateral extended family is a happy medium which provides "a good deal of individual freedom along with a fairly dependable base for security."

Like most social scientists Blitsten seems to regard the autonomous nuclear family as the predominant urban type, as highly unstable, and as largely responsible for both personal insecurity and the major urban social problems (e.g., delinquency, crime, addiction and mental illness). We believe she overstates her case and, like Henry, overestimates the effects of structural variables while underestimating the effects of patterned values and expectations. But Blitsten, again like Henry, provides an analytical framework useful for cross-cultural comparisons of individual-in-context variables.

Corporate families are correlated with predominantly agrarian societies in which land is the principal source of wealth. They are found in societies in which communications and transportation systems are little developed. Political control is usually authoritarian, but tends to be curtailed at the level of local regulation. Religious organizations are powerful and religious institutions relatively uniform for the population. Cultural levels are often high, but

---

* From Dorothy R. Blitsten, *The World of the Family* (New York: Random House, Inc., 1963), pp. 252–57. © Copyright 1963 by Dorothy R. Blitsten. Reprinted by permission of Random House, Inc.

only a small proportion of the populations of these societies have access to the cultural riches available. Those who do are most frequently the people who also control most of the material wealth.

Until modern times, these were the prevailing conditions in most societies. They still characterize societies in the Far and Middle East and Eastern Europe. In societies of this order, where the majority of the population is poor and the development of political, economic, and religious organizations is limited, corporate families fill the gaps in the chain of organizations necessary to maintain a society and provide for its population. Organization on the basis of kinship that guarantees extensive reciprocal aid for members is the only effective means for survival for most of the people, and political and religious formulations justify and reinforce the arrangements and powers of the families. Family authority tends to be dictatorial and absolute. Children are subordinate to parents, and women to men. Relationships both within the family and outside it are strictly hierarchical. The "great families" are important units in all spheres of life.

The extended families that are the chief operational units in corporate family organizations often exercise a great deal of autonomy. Their membership in a larger unit imposes some restrictions upon them, however, and units that are themselves powerful are not apt to contribute to the maintenance of a larger organization unless clear and immediate benefits are forthcoming from it. In societies in which physical survival is not particularly hazardous, means of communication are fairly well developed, and political organizations are capable of protecting the unity of the society from internal strife and external attack, the advantage of the corporate family is diminished. Furthermore, it interferes with the functions of organizations set up to provide for total populations. Under such conditions extended families begin to break away from former corporate organizations, or they do not combine to form them. When extended families do not require monolithic authority for their survival, but are still benefited by extensions of their control over economic resources or positions of power, mergers between the families of both spouses become desirable, and extended families develop into the autonomous bilateral *extended* type.

In the past, the *bilateral extended family* was associated with the ownership of land and with a distribution of power based on privilege established by birth and inheritance. Governments were chiefly monarchial and established churches powerful; however, there was some division between the organizations of church and state and important aspects of life were regulated by secular law. But the bilateral extended family is also found in modern, technologically advanced societies. Control over industrial plants or money replaces or supplements land ownership as the basis for their maintenance and power in their societies. Their nuclear units can enjoy a great deal of autonomy in personal matters and individuals can pursue many of their own interests without disrupting these families. The benefits of the pooling of some resources (principally economic) and the guarantee of access to others (such as education and occupations) are sufficient to keep individual members and nuclear families attached to extended families even in industrial and urban social settings. In modern societies some bilateral extended families are survivals from the past, but others are the result of special achievements by some of their members. The latter are found most frequently in the upper-middle and upper classes.

The emergence of the *autonomous nuclear family* as a fully developed family organization—not to be confused with small independent households among the poor and dispossessed that have always been numerous—is a relatively modern phenomenon. Autonomous nuclear families can be viewed as specialized family organizations in societies in which specialization is highly developed in all spheres of life. They are associated with clear divisions between political and religious organizations; the dominance of secular laws; secular education; advanced technology; the mechanization of agriculture, means of production, and even of housekeeping; the extensive development of lines of communication and transportation; and extensive urbanization. Since autonomous nuclear families have little control over the social and material resources necessary to their maintenance, their efficiency in the performance of family functions is far more dependent upon assistance from non-family sources than is that of corporate or extended families. Autonomous nuclear families are not important units in non-family organizations and have little power to command their support. This degree of dependence on the other organizations in their societies is one of the important sources of their relative instability. . . .

There are inherent assets and liabilities in the different forms of family organization that are relatively independent of the settings in which they operate. Autonomous nuclear families provide greater freedom for extensive and varied personal development, social relationships, activities, and physical mobility. But often they fail to provide security. Further, they demand great individual personal resources and effort on the part of the people who maintain them. In corporate families the assets and liabilities are reversed. They provide more security and less freedom. For the majority of family members, the range of personal cultivation is much curtailed. To a great extent the lives of women and young people are regulated by men and elders. The few heads of households frequently wield excessive power and monopolize a disproportionate share of the available benefits. On the other hand, these families control most of the social and material resources that they need and they are very efficient security systems for large numbers of people. Like large economic corporations in industrial societies today, they offer many "fringe" benefits to their members as the reward for loyal service. The special asset of the bilateral extended type of family organization is its ability to provide its member with a good deal of individual freedom along with a fairly dependable base for security. Extended families do not usually sacrifice one to the other.

These three basic forms of family organization also differ in their potential efficiency for meeting the needs of their members at different periods of their lives. The authoritarian nature of corporate families favors the aging and the old who are usually the administrators and executives of households and family enterprises. Children benefit from their collective significance as the guarantors of family continuity. They are welcome and, generally, well nurtured and cultivated. On the other hand, the need for many children to insure the survival of the clan tends to place emphasis on the child-bearing and child-rearing functions of women at the expense of their other potentialities. The lives of most women are highly restricted in corporate families. Finally, since age-grading is an important part of the exercise of authority in these families, young adults have to await the passage of years for opportunity to develop their own abilities. During this time, their personal lives are usually still supervised by their elders. Thus, what they gain in security is often achieved at the expense of their individual development and achievement.

Autonomous nuclear families tend to favor children and youths. Since children are generally viewed as sources of personal satisfaction and are often conceived as the result of a deliberate decision by their parents, the latter tend to feel deeply obligated to supply them with every possible material asset and personal opportunity. Autonomous nuclear families are frequently child-centered and their children are often greatly indulged. These families impose few specific restrictions on young adults and the middle-aged. The paths to personal cultivation and achievement are theoretically open, but they are often blocked by the heavy responsibilities of family life, which must be shouldered by only two people as a rule. Autonomous nuclear families are not felicitous for the aging, the old, the sick, or people handicapped in any way. They are too small and the resources they command are usually too limited for them to absorb inactive members without overburdening their own organization.

In general, the dependence of autonomous nuclear families on non-family organizations tends to weaken family ties. The members of these families scatter daily in pursuit of economic, . . . religious, and educational services. Non-family relationships compete with family relationships for the affection and loyalty of individuals. The limitation of the range of services that parents *can* provide their children in these families diminishes their authority over their young and seems to have all but eliminated filial responsibilities other than physical maintenance in cases of want. Siblings go their own ways and continuing reciprocities between them are voluntary. Since parents cease to be oriented toward their own parents, ties between grandparents and grandchildren lose institutional significance.

Consequently, autonomous nuclear families are often unreliable sources of personal help in the periods of strain or crisis that are almost inevitable in the life course of everyone. Young children may suffer from the dissolution of marital ties, adolescents may find themselves estranged from family support before they are able to establish the stable associations they need for their own maintenance, the middle-aged may be bereft of affection and respect from their children, and the aging and aged may be isolated and even exiled from family participation. The case histories behind mounting rates of delinquency, addiction, crime, neurotic disabilities, mental illness, and senility in societies in which autonomous nuclear families prevail suggest that frequent failure to develop enduring family ties is a serious inadequacy for both individuals and societies.

With respect to meeting the needs of different age levels, the bilateral extended family again seems to serve its members better. It accords neither children, nor young adults, nor the middle-aged, nor the old the degree of privilege that is awarded one or another of these categories by the corporate or the autonomous nuclear family. Each category has rights and obligations associated with its stage of life. The young are welcome, cared for, and cultivated, but they are taught concern for family welfare and are prepared to contribute to it. Adults are assisted to marriages and occupations and given help in times of need, but they are expected to maintain and augment family enterprises and give heed to the council of their elders. The aging and the old are usually guaranteed respect and care when they need it, but they are expected to direct their skill and wisdom to the enrichment of their family circles, to refrain from wasting family resources by drawing upon them needlessly, and to distribute their property fairly and efficiently among family members when they die. Bilateral extended families can and do take care of their dependent and handicapped members, but they demand active participation in their organizations by every member who is capable of it.

CHAPTER 6

Enculturation:
Implications for the Individual

> Every day society is submitted to a terrible invasion: within it
> a multitude of small barbarians are born. They would quickly over-
> throw the whole social order and all the institutions of society, if they
> were not well disciplined and educated.
>
> R. Pinot

The knowledge, beliefs, and practices involved in disciplining and educating each small barbarian are of great importance to him and to his society. The process of enculturating (transmitting a culture to the young) is highly variable from society to society and along the complexity continuum. The individual's self-concept, as well as his skills and goals, evolve as enculturation proceeds and are influenced by it. The individual child is not merely an empty vessel to be filled nor a largely passive receiver of culture. His individuality is apparent from birth.

Enculturation is one aspect—an important aspect—of the many ways in which individual and culture stand in dynamic relationship. Between individual and culture there exists through each lifetime an intricate set of reciprocal forces perpetually in shifting equilibrium. "In its ontological development . . . the human organism is faced with the problem of adapting itself on the one hand to the restrictions imposed by the particular cultural forms and on the other to achieving satisfaction for its instinctual impulses. . . . The maturational process, according to Gesell, exerts a regulatory function on the course of their interaction." (Hallowell, 1949, p. 318.)

TRIBALISM AND INDIVIDUATION

The course of individual development—of "becoming"—is described by G. W. Allport in terms of "two contrary forces at work"; there is "tribalism" on the one hand and "individuation" on the other.

[Tribalism] makes for a closed tribal being. It takes its start in the dependence of the child upon those who care for him. His gratifications and his security come from the outside; so too do all the first lessons he learns: the times of day when he may have meals, the activities for which he is punished and those that bring reward. He is coerced and cajoled into conformity but not, we note, with complete success. He shows a capacity even from birth to resist the impact of maternal and tribal demands. While to a certain degree his group shapes his course, at the same time it seems to antagonize him, as if he realized its threat to his integrity. (Allport, 1955, p. 35.)

While the child needs and wants love and security, he does not want them to interfere with his impulses, his freedom, or his preferred ways of acting. From the very start of his life he is resistant to the smothering effects of his social environment. Affiliation alone would make for slavish obedience to family or tribal living which provide the child with his early standards of conduct and with his definitions of the world around him. If these influences were the only ones acting upon him they would lead to conduct always conventional and stereotyped. It is a limitation of current theories of socialization that they do in fact deal only with the mirror-like character of the so-called superego, that they tend to define socialization exclusively in terms of conformity, and not also in terms of creative becoming. (*Ibid.*, p. 34.)

In his recognition of this "limitation of current theories of socialization" (or enculturation), Allport is not quite alone among contemporary psychologists. Martin Deutsch (1963) recognizes the inadequacy of the more usual views and quotes "some recent remarks of [William] Martin (1960)" as highly pertinent. Martin wrote:

. . . There is evidence from a variety of sources that there is in the making a cognitive theory of behavior and development. It would view the child not merely as a passive victim of either his environmental history or of his biological nature, but as one who strives to be the master of both his nature and his history. It will thus emphasize the unique characteristic which makes that mastery a possibility, namely, intelligence. . . . We seem to be rediscovering in our research and theory the mind of the child. . . . (Martin, 1960, p. 75.)

We know too little about the subtle, complex, and crucially important processes of enculturation, including the nature of the child's cognitive and other functions and their relation to what Allport so aptly labels "creative becoming." There is evidence, however, that each child reacts selectively to the array of cultural elements spread out before him or urged upon him.

The roots of this selectivity seem to lie in a "primary reaction pattern" characteristic of each child in infancy and persistent in each. Alexander Thomas *et al.* (1963) have reported this finding based on intensive studies of eighty children from birth to age two. This study documents both individual uniqueness and a high level of adaptability. The authors conclude that "whatever the child care practice, the children would, as a whole, be capable of adapting, as long as the particular mode of handling the child was compatible with life" (*Ibid.*, p. 87). Inherent uniqueness is soon overlaid with learned behavior, and the combination probably does as much to enhance the inherent range of variation between individuals as to induce similarities between them.

COMPLEXITY AND ENCULTURATION

The range of individual variation between children must be especially great in large societies bearing highly complex cultures. On the base of unique inherent capacities and aptitudes there is overlaid, in the complex context, an infinite variety of combinations of an enormous range of cultural items. Each child experiences an unique "cultural exposure" with distinctive content and conditions of learning. The Kluckhohn-Mowrer model (discussed in Chapter 3) accounts for the macrocategories of antecedents and influences relevant to both uniqueness and commonality.

The distinctive attributes of a society and its culture will inevitably affect both the process and the results of enculturation. Folkish cultures are as distinctive as are those at the sophisticate end of the range, and homogeneity at the individual level is characteristic of neither. Note, for example, Dennis' comment about Hopi children:

> Hopi children are like American children in exhibiting very distinct personalities. Some observers have professed to see but slight individual differences in communities which are culturally homogeneous. Hopi culture patterns are homogeneous but they do not stamp out individuality, and marked personal traits appear among both children and adults. (Dennis, 1940, p. 188.)

Redfield (1947) overstates individual homogeneity in the folk culture when he says: "one man's learned ways of doing and thinking are the same as another's." It is unquestionably true, however, that the range of antecedents and influences in the folk context is narrow as compared with the richness of the sophisticate setting.

As we have noted, this quantitative difference is paralleled by a qualitative difference which Redfield and others emphasize. In the folk society behavior is likely to be "personal," i.e., one does not deal "thing-fashion" with another participant in his society. In contemporary complex societies like that of the United States, by contrast, there is considerable evidence of "thing-fashion" response to fellow humans. The starkest evidence of this response—or lack of response—is spectator coldness, indifference, aloofness, or reluctance to become involved or to help a fellow who is in mortal danger. American values call for quite different behavior, but clearly these values are not always communicated in the process of enculturation. If they are, they remain on the ideal pattern level.

There is a societal variable involved. In a very large society the sheer number of people subtly suggests a thing-orientation. Only those few persons with whom one has communication through primary relationship become for him truly "persons." In the folk society, with its smallness and its largely face-to-face relationships, children learn early and easily to relate "person-fashion." The task of enculturation is in this respect different and more difficult in the sophisticate society.

But in the folk setting interpersonal callousness, and hostile-aggressive attitudes as well, may be culturally patterned. Among the eastern highlanders of New Guinea character ideals are such that

> The child most liked and admired by adults . . . is the one who commands attention by tantrums, by a dominating approach to his fellows, by bullying and swaggering, by carrying tales to his elders. These actions epitomize the characteristics so desirable in the "strong" man and woman. . . . They are the mark . . . of the fighter and warrior. . . . (Berndt, 1962, p. 92.)

Early enculturation is a matter of learning through imitation, informal training, and spasmodic guidance.

> Although there has been no systematic training for aggressive action associated with male dominance, the pressures have been such that most children are already oriented in this direction when more deliberate and organized training begins at initiation. (*Ibid.*, p. 93.)

During initiation ceremonies the boys are harangued at length. ". . . The formal verbal instructions or admonitions [are] repeated over and again, . . . phrased in an emphatic and categoric style" (*Ibid.*, p. 110).

Adult New Guineans are, on the whole, aggressive in the extreme. The enculturation process is highly effective. This feature of adult behavior is not a product of severity in child training, hence frustration, leading to aggression. The frustration-aggression hypothesis, though heartily endorsed by some anthropologists, is wholly inappropriate here. These people quite simply idealize aggressiveness, they demonstrate it more than amply before the children, they encourage and reward those who develop and demonstrate aggressiveness. Nor is aggressiveness here a manifestation of deviance; quite the contrary, as Ronald Berndt points out (*Ibid.*, p. 177). It is the mild and inoffensive person, child or adult, who is the deviant.

However folkish or sophisticated the culture, much enculturation goes on at levels not properly described as conscious, explicit, or formal. Much teaching, learning, and cultural transmission, especially in the realm of beliefs, ideas, and ideals, is subconscious, implicit, or informal. Adult expectations are transmitted mainly casually or in subtle ways. The process is largely a matter of "quiet coaching but with no sense of urgency." Robbins Burling conveys, in one paragraph about the Thai, an illustration of enculturation in the informal manner. He writes:

> Thai babies are constantly carried, cuddled, and fondled, and they are nursed whenever they show signs of hunger. The anthropologist Ruth Benedict suggested that Thai parents tend to leave the steps in maturation to nature and to the responsibility of the child himself. With quiet coaching, but with no sense of urgency, babies learn to walk. They wear nothing but a shirt, and nobody becomes upset when the baby soils the floor or someone's lap, for adults know that eventually the growing child himself will learn self-control. Nevertheless, children are expected to develop a kind of self-reliance that can be seen as anticipating the behavior of adults. Thai are often described as self-reliant; even their Buddhist religion emphasizes the personal quest for enlightenment and leaves its pursuit to the individual's own initiative. Nevertheless, older children can be vigorously punished when naughty, and although verbal threats are usually sufficient, they are spanked if necessary. Children may also be threatened with animals or spirits and in this way frightened into obedience. (Burling, 1965, p. 101.)

The realm of the conscious, explicit, and formal in enculturation expands greatly with increasing cultural complexity. Where the oncoming generation must learn much that is abstract and esoteric (e.g., the highly specialized knowledge of the physician or lawyer), enculturation can no longer be left to chance and to the adults of the child's personal community. The whole vast structure of formal education in contemporary urban-industrial societies rests on this elementary fact and its inherent logic.

What is commonly taught and learned during childhood in nonliterate cultures is

— knowledge, attitudes, and practices designed to protect the child from injury and illness, natural and supernatural;

— knowledge, skills, habits, and attitudes necessary if the child is to become an adult capable of coping with the environment and meeting the conditions for survival and necessary assistance to dependents;

— knowledge, attitudes, values, and practices intended to transform the ignorant and willful child into a "good citizen"—a person of admired character type—who has the admired qualities, who understands and respects others' rights, and who maintains the proprieties (e.g., in toilet habits and sex behavior).

John Whiting's pioneering Kwoma study of child rearing and the inter-generational transmission of culture fully illustrates these major categories (see Adaptation No. 6).

VARIABILITY OF ENCULTURATION CONTENT AND OF PATTERNED CONCEPTS OF CHILDHOOD

Content in the teaching-learning process is of course highly variable from culture to culture, whatever their locations on the complexity continuum. So too is the culturally patterned belief system having to do with the nature of the child. There are, as we have already noted, vast inter-society differences in child-rearing practices. On close inspection it can be seen that these differences rest mainly on the two variables: (1) cultural content—what is transmitted to children, and (2) cultural concepts—what is believed about the nature of the child and of childhood.

No adequate survey has yet been made of culturally patterned concepts about the nature, capacities, and proper roles of young children. But even a random sampling of "exotic cultures" will confirm that other peoples rarely dichotomize, as we do, between children and adults. Even fewer conceive, as we do, of a murky transitional phase—i.e., of adolescence.

The general inclination is to think of both children and adults as members of society. Society's members are seen as males and females individually differing in their knowledge, skills, and wisdom. It is taken for granted that there is correlation between age and these desirable attributes, which are understood to be to a large extent learned. Certain rigorous teaching and testing procedures may

precede ceremonies signaling that the individual has "passed"—
that he is now ready for full responsibility as a member of his
society.

Even when children and adults are thought of as belonging to
two different social spheres they may interact largely in but one.
We are told (by an anthropologist who is himself a member of the
society) that among the Igbo of southeast Nigeria the child "shares
two worlds." Victor Uchendu writes:

> Unlike American children, who are often confined to their own
> world, Igbo children grow up and participate in two worlds—the world
> of children and the world of adults. Igbo children take an active part
> in their parents' social and economic activities. They are literally every-
> where. They are taken to the market, to the family or village tribunal,
> to funerals, to a feast, to the farm, and to religious ceremonies. They
> help entertain their parents' guests. There are no children's parties
> which they are encouraged to dominate, nor are there parents' parties
> from which they are excluded. If there is a social or ritual ceremony
> going on in an Igbo village, everybody is welcome. Igbo children do
> not have private sleeping rooms. . . . Children take an active and impor-
> tant part in the work of the compound and the village. (Uchendu, 1965,
> p. 61 and p. 62.)

The cross-cultural record also fails to support the Western idea
that children are like "primitives" in thinking animistically—in en-
dowing the inanimate world with spirits. Indeed there is evidence
that animistic thinking is characteristic of adults and not of children—as among the Manus of the Admiralty Islands, for example
(Mead, 1932). It is therefore a learned and not a naïve or "inherent"
mode of thought.

The Western concept of the child as a creature of emotions,
psychically fragile and easily damaged, is almost without parallel.
The traditional Chinese, a sophisticated and learned people, did
not hesitate to expose their children to full acquaintance with the
world of adults. Little boys accompanied their fathers on business
errands. Children were not shielded from the facts of family mis-
fortune—loss of money or prestige, sickness or death.

Likewise, the concealment of sexual facts from children in Western civilization is a specific cultural pattern. The argument sometimes advanced that the "child mind" is not prepared for such revelations . . . [is] a patent rationalization of our practices. In other societies no such restrictions in knowledge may be found. . . .

Cultural factors as well as physical and mental immaturity must be considered as determinants in the differentiation of the child's world from that of adults in different societies. (Hallowell, 1949, p. 321.)

Our concepts lead us to "age grade" rigorously, attempting to control at each age level what the child does and learns or even attempts to do and learn. Among so-called "primitives" (e.g., Mead's Manus) the child is not likely to be told that he is "too little" or "not old enough" for what he asks to know or tries to do.

Peculiarities of the Western cultural approach to children stem from the extraordinary value we place on childhood and youth, hence on the child and the adolescent, as well as from our inclination to underestimate the social adaptability and acuity of children. Their capacities along this line seem to be as much taken for granted by most peoples as they are doubted by ourselves. This writer's studies of children in Japan and in the United States have helped to document the nature and extent of social awareness in children, and, hopefully, to dispel some of the mythology prevalent in the United States.

THE SOCIAL ACUITIES OF YOUNG CHILDREN: EVIDENCE FROM JAPAN AND THE UNITED STATES

Young children in any society, if observed closely and carefully, will demonstrate a remarkable grasp of that society's basics in social structure and culture.

In Japan the writer, with the assistance of four young Japanese scholars, studied intensively 300 urban, middle-class five-year-olds. (Goodman, *et al.*, 1956.) Our basic questions had to do with social awareness. We wanted to know: when these children look out at the social universe around them, what do they see, what do they think, what do they feel? Each child was interviewed four times. In each interview he was led to talk about the social world.

We found that among them the 300 children can name some 60

social categories; e.g., kinship categories, sex, age, and occupational categories. Usually they can add conceptualizations about what people of a given status or category do, wear, own, etc.; i.e., they can provide a considerable range of concepts associated in their minds with a particular social status or category.

Identification along the lines of age or sex is the commonest of a number of systematizing principles implicit in the subjects' social classifications. To these young children sex is the more apparent and unambiguous variable. Their concepts of the female role-personality suggest the traditional expectations—i.e., that the Japanese female be mild, kindly, and gentle.

Second only to age and sex, our subjects are given to identification in terms of kin or kin-type statuses. We use the designation "kin-type" to refer to the prevalent Japanese practice—seen in our subjects as well as in adults—of extending kin terms for use in reference or address to persons conceived as kinlike.

Among kin or kin-type identifications, own or pseudoparents, elder siblings and grandparents, uncles, and aunts are frequent in the order named. That younger siblings are seldom commented upon is probably a reflection of the facts that the terms for these statuses are not used in extension by either Japanese adults or by our subjects, that elder siblings are important parent surrogates, and that the subjects look to their elder siblings as persons of prestige and authority, as elder siblings are traditionally seen in Japan.

The interesting Japanese concept of nonkin status (*yoso no*—) appears quite frequently in the perceptual systems of our five-year-olds, who are aware of a considerable variety of specific statuses of this sort (e.g., mother of another's house/family).

The children are aware of a great variety of occupations, of which shopkeepers as a general category and doctors as a specific status are pre-eminent. The urban nature of the subjects' social milieu, with its wide range of occupational specialties, is clearly reflected in their social percepts and concepts. So, too, are statuses having to do with the educational system, but religion—to judge from the children's comments—is an incidental in urban Japanese life.

What we have called "locality," "individual attribute," and "romantic-literary" principles are seen in identifications in terms of spatial referents, of such personal evaluations as good/bad, rich/poor, etc., of historical or fictional characters. Of these the rich/poor dichotomy is particularly conspicuous, a fact which suggests the pecuniary awareness likely to characterize urbanites. The subjects' occasional perceptions of burglars and of beggars also suggest conditions of urban living, as do references to the "company" or "company person."

The children perceive foreigners as such as well as a variety of specific foreign types. Of these the American is by far the most conspicuous for them, though Americans presently are very few in the cities in which the subjects live. Conversely Koreans, though many, are relatively infrequently identified, showing clearly how little the present demographic situation need have to do with the social awareness of young children.

It should be noted that throughout the interviews self-reference was rare, and so, too, was the possessive (e.g., "my—" sister, friend, etc.). Moreover, our subjects infrequently identified in terms of personal names. Both of the above observations suggest the traditional Japanese nonindividualism—or even anti-individualism—with its etiquette of public reference to others rather than the self, and of reference to others via status labels rather than personal names (e.g., one speaks of or to "*Sensei*—," using the status label proper for the teacher, doctor, or other "learned person," and avoids the use of his name).

This thumbnail sketch of major findings will at least suggest the richness of social percept-concept systems in Japanese children, and the results of a mere five years of life in modern, urban Japan.

Studies of race awareness in young American children (e.g., Goodman, 1964) of their citizenship concepts (Goodman and Cockrell, 1958) and a vast amount of data from other studies and from observation support the conclusion that early social acuity is the rule in this country, too (excepting only children in severely "disadvantaged" or "culture of poverty" homes and neighborhoods). Yet in this country experts and parents alike have tended to underestimate the importance of learning in early childhood. Benjamin

Bloom comments on this fact in his report on research showing the significance of the child's early years. He writes:

> The prolongation of the period of dependency for youth in the Western cultures has undoubtedly been a factor in desensitizing parents, school workers, and behavioral scientists to the full importance of the very early environmental and experiential influences. . . .
>
> There appears to be an implicit assumption running through the culture that change in behavior and personality can take place at any age or stage in development and that the developments at one age or stage are no more significant than those which take place at another.
>
> A central finding in this work is that for selected characteristics [height, general intelligence, aggressiveness in males, dependence in females, intellectuality in males and females, general school achievement] there is a negatively accelerated curve of development which reaches its midpoint before age 5. We have reasoned that the environment would have its greatest effect on a characteristic during the period of its most rapid development.
>
> These findings and reasoning are supported by the results of [twelve major] selected studies. . . .
>
> . . . Another way of viewing the importance of the early environment has to do with the sequential nature of much of human development. Each characteristic is built on a base of that same characteristic at an earlier time or on the base of other characteristics which precede it in development. . . .
>
> A third reason for the crucial importance of the early environment and early experiences stems from learning theory. It is much easier to learn something new than it is to stamp out one set of learned behaviors and replace them by a new set. . . . (Bloom, 1964, pp. 214–15.)

To each child the environment presents unique experiences which he meets in his unique ways. If we knew enough about each child we could spell out the significant terms in his personal equation. In intensive case studies one can come close. The writer, in her investigation of race awareness in four-year-olds, attempted to do so. The conclusion was:

> There is no *single* key to the how and why of race awareness and race orientation in our children. There are at least six major *kinds* of keys, each of which has its own varieties. . . . In each case there is an interplay—an interdependence—between the several terms in each personal equation. . . . The significant terms are: individual attributes,

individual situation, models, needs and interests, values, and characteristic action-ways, feeling-ways, and thought-ways. . . . The process by which the patterned race attitudes characteristic of adult America get across even to very young children . . . [is] extremely complex. . . . This process is perhaps less a matter of *transmission* than of *regeneration*. This is to say that there begins early and proceeds gradually, in each individual, a process much more complex than the sheer *learning* of someone else's attitudes. It is rather that the individual *generates* his own attitudes, out of the personal, social, and cultural materials which happen to be his. In view of the fact that the variety of such materials is finite—that in a given country and community certain conditions and experiences are common and rarely to be avoided—our individuals tend to get hold of rather similar materials and hence eventually to generate rather similar attitudes. (Goodman, 1964, pp. 200–203 and p. 246.)

These generalizations, if they are true for the development of race awareness and race attitudes, should hold for social awareness, attitudes, values and concepts generally.

Each society conveys its "idea systems." Daniel Levinson points out that these idea systems

are presented to growing children . . . by a variety of formal and informal indoctrination agencies. The collectivity provides, as it were, an ideological environment . . . that facilitates certain ideational learnings and impedes others. . . . [But] *every individual forms his own idea systems, utilizing passively or creatively the viewpoints available in his social environment.* (Levinson, 1964, p. 298; italics added.)

CHILD-CENTERED ENCULTURATION

Field studies have provided a great deal of information about enculturation content—about what adults teach to children. Studies have provided very little about cultural concepts concerning children and childhood. No doubt this is because much of the content resides in overt and readily observable patterns. Much of the concept system, on the other hand, is covert and not readily observable. However, it is certain to represent an important segment of the belief and value systems.

John and Ann Fischer (see Adaptation No. 7) have provided, in their study of child rearing in a United States community, excellent and unusual data relating to the concept system. The Fischers' study is of particular importance also because it casts light on an enculturation phenomenon associated with Western urban-industrial cultures. There can be no doubt that the phenomenon in question—child-centered enculturation—has very great implications for both individuals affected by it and for their society.

In child-centered cultures adults tolerate, and even encourage, unusual degrees and types of self-assertiveness in children. And highly child-centered cultures do not occur at or near the folk end of the complexity continuum. Cultures at or near the sophisticate end are by no means uniformly or universally child-centered. However, there are in the complex context factors conducive to child-centeredness. For example:

1. In the urban setting, which is typically the home of complex culture, close interpersonal bonds are (as we have noted) relatively few in number. These few tend to become peculiarly precious. Under the circumstances children, who are as a rule precious to their parents the world around, become doubly so. They become the objects of unceasing solicitous attention, and much anxiety. The smallest details of their growth and development assume great significance.

2. There is likely to be ample time and energy for extravagant attention to one's children. Except for the folk society located in an Eden environment—and this is a rarity—the folk have little leisure after meeting survival needs and insistent social obligations. Under conditions of peace and prosperity in the urban-complex setting men and women, the latter especially, can well afford sustained attention to their children.

3. In the urban-complex setting a human life has meaning largely while it lasts. Only the few whose fame survives them are likely to be long remembered, unless by their children. The intensity of concern for one's children, and for their "happiness," may be in part an expression of anxiety lest one not be cherished by them, both while alive and after death.

4. Perhaps most significant of all is what might be called the vacuum effect. Child-rearing customs, which are so relatively clear and simple among the folk, are likely to become confused and contradictory as complexity increases. The more confused and con-

tradictory, the more paralyzed (by uncertainty or anxiety) the parents. Where parents do not assume the active, controlling role, children do. In this case the home becomes child-centered by parental default; the child moves into the power vacuum left by the parents' abdication.

All these are societal factors affecting child-centeredness. There are relevant cultural factors too.

Child-centering, as a patterned phenomenon, is a feature of cultures in the "Western"—the European—tradition. It appears in non-Western contexts roughly in proportion to the extent of their Westernization.

Francis L. K. Hsu, commenting on cultural differences in this matter of child-centering, observes:

> It is no exaggeration to say that while the Chinese glorify their ancestors and the Hindus glorify their gods, the Americans glorify their children. (Hsu, 1963, p. 195.)

Since patterns in culture are interdependent and interinfluencing, these several "glorification" patterns must have important correlates. And they do. Later (Chapter 9) we shall examine value systems as they affect individual autonomy. The patterning of values affects enculturation, also. Effects are both direct—a matter of specific·values taught and learned, and indirect—a matter of the conditions of teaching and learning.

Where childhood as well as children, youth as well as the young, are enormously valued, it is predictable that people will "glorify their children." But where interest and energy are focused heavily on ancestors or on gods children recede in relative importance.

The child's social concepts, and his behavior too, are affected by his perception of his status as a child. Hsu comments:

> The American family [by its glorification of the children] . . . fosters an over-whelming sense of self-importance in the growing child, and it correspondingly minimizes the importance of the older people who are responsible for bringing them up. (*Ibid.*, p. 195.)

A sense of self-importance is conducive to assertiveness, to attention-demanding, and to undervaluing of the importance of others.

It may be also conducive to boldness, assurance, and to a sense of autonomy. Armed with a highly developed sense of one's own importance, it is relatively easy to feel genuinely indifferent toward mores or laws, and toward authorities. The self-important child is likely to develop little social sensitivity, "for his environment is sensitive to *him*. In the Chinese scene the child . . . is obliged to be sensitive to his *environment*" (Hsu, 1953, p. 79).

In folkish, and even in most of the fairly sophisticate cultures, children develop early a realistic sense of their own relative status. They know themselves to be loved and valued, but they know too that in the status-ranking system adults and older children take precedence. This fact is expressed explicitly in patterns of etiquette and of dominance. Jane Belo says of Balinese children:

On occasions . . . when the strictest etiquette must be observed the children are not much in evidence, so quiet are they. . . . The hierarchy of age recognized in any family group . . . [is such that] every child knows that he is allowed to "speak down to," scold, and order about his younger brothers and cousins, just as he himself is spoken down to and ordered about by brothers and all relatives older than he. (Belo, 1935, pp. 129 and 130.)

Thai children learn early to accept and relate to a social world that is very clearly and hierarchically ordered, and in which a child must take his modest and proper place. Burling writes:

Whether through indulgence or strict discipline—or, more likely, through a subtle combination of the two—Thai children do learn to be courteous and respectful at a remarkably early age. A child soon learns the differences in status among the people around him. His parents will press his palms together and hold them to his forehead to show respect for the monks, and he soon learns to raise them to his face for his parents. Just as men are ritually superior to women, so older people are superior to younger, and a child must learn the ceremonious respect due his elders. Later he will also learn to grant the formal respect due to government officials and, above them, to royalty. Thai do not expect to associate with others as equals; everyone is seen as either superior or inferior. One cannot even speak the Thai language without indicating something about one's status, for pronouns vary with the rank of the speaker and that of the person to whom he speaks. To some extent status is determined by birth, but because one's status at birth is attributed to the accumulation of merit in former existences, it has, in a sense, been earned. All men can look forward to the increase in status. (Burling, *op. cit.*, p. 101.)

CHILD-CENTEREDNESS AND INDIVIDUALISM

In the stream of Western culture there is, beside child-centering, another pattern intimately related to child-centering: it is the celebrated Western individualism. This dominant aspect of the Western tradition is unusual, taking world cultures as a whole. It is as unusual as is the pattern of monogamous marriage exclusively (if serially). And the two are related.

Romantic love, with its emphasis on chance attachment, exclusive possession of the loved object, and complete ecstasy, is as much in harmony with the American individual-centered approach to life as it is out of tune with the Chinese situation-centered orientation, . . . in which individual feelings must be subordinated to the requirements of the group. . . . (Hsu, 1953, p. 39.)

To the Westerner the very idea of subordination is repugnant. He believes that under such a system the individual must be miserable, that he suffers outrageous curtailment of "inalienable" rights, and that his unique potentialities will remain undeveloped and unexpressed. The Westerner is learning, however, that there is another face to individualism—aloneness. The ties that bind individual to group may be sometimes irksome but they are also the anchors to windward. They ensure that one's trouble can be shared and that someone will help and care.

Individualism is manifest in physical arrangements for living. Western custom calls for maximum individual privacy with respect to space and possessions. The traditional Chinese home provides for family privacy—the house walled off from the street and other homes—but not for privacy of the individual.

The lack of privacy . . . finds its extreme expression in many well-to-do families of North China. Here the rooms are arranged in rows like the cars of a train. But instead of each room having a separate entrance, all the rooms are arranged in sequence, one leading into another. (*Ibid.*, p. 69.)

Privacy reduces surveillance, hence control. It promotes independence. Parents operating in the Confucian tradition were, according to that tradition, "always right." The culture in this pattern supported their control. Of perhaps equal importance as a control device was the lack of privacy available to children. Their physical world lacked separateness, and their social world too. Chinese parents kept their children with them in business, religious, or social gatherings. They expected a complete "community of interests" (*ibid.*, p. 80), and apparently their expectations generally were met.

ENCULTURATION AND THE INDIVIDUAL: BASIC PROPOSITIONS

Enculturation is no more a matter of "tribalism" than of "individuation." It is both. The child, in learning the culture of his society, conforms in response to pressures of a more or less insistent and forceful sort. But he also resists, evades, selects, and experiments. He becomes a member of his society, but the process is a "creative becoming."

It results in individuals, each of them unique though easily recognizable as Hopi, Kwoma, Ngoni, Japanese, American, or some other "tribe." Each begins life uniquely endowed as to "primary reaction pattern," and becomes both more and less like his fellows with time and experience (experience both shared and idiosyncratic).

What is taught and how it is taught are functions of necessity and of tradition. The minimum essentials of what is taught are matters of survival and of social know-how. The content of culture even in these essentials, and even at the folk end of the continuum, is impressively large. But children learn with remarkable speed, the absence of formal enculturation methods notwithstanding. Even in complex cultures a large proportion of the child's learning is informal and early.

In folkish settings, and in some highly sophisticate settings too, children share much of the world of their elders. In these contexts much is learned by observation, imitation, and participation.

In contemporary Western culture, and in its American variant particularly, an unusual view of children has appeared. It incorporates the idea that children are quite unlike adults; they are believed to be psychically fragile creatures. This concept supports segregation by age, a practice conducive to the weakening of adult-child relationships and to reducing the functions of the adult as model and security source. The Western view greatly underestimates the young child's social acuities—his awareness of his world of people and their ways. Early learning is for most children in any society both rapid and important as the base for later learning.

The child does more than learn the idea systems of his society (as represented especially in the members of his personal community). He also "forms his own idea systems, utilizing passively or creatively the viewpoints available in his social environment." (Levinson, *op. cit.*, p. 298.) The process is "more complex than the sheer *learning* of someone else's attitudes. It is rather that the individual *generates* his own attitudes. . . ." (Goodman, *op. cit.*, p. 246.)

The American middle-class variant of Western urban culture is child-centered to an unusual degree. Children and youth, childhood and youthfulness, are "glorified" (Hsu). The child's self-concept is thereby affected; assertiveness and attention-seeking are encouraged.

The patterning of enculturation—what is taught to children, how and when, is no more important than the patterned concepts of child nature which underlie enculturation. Both affect importantly the child's potential for "individuation" and "creative becoming" (Allport). The process is affected by culture, but its locus is person and its nature is in significant part cognitive.

ADAPTATION NO. 4*

Norbeck reports on a fairly representative Japanese fishing village of the early 1950's. His account shows that the children growing up in this village were subjected to discontinuities and to other child-rearing "errors" (e.g., ridicule), such as our psychologists believe to be productive of poor mental

---

* From Edward Norbeck, *Takashima* (Salt Lake City: University of Utah Press, 1954).

health. Yet the account gives no evidence of any unusual incidence of such problems. On the contrary, the community seems to have been remarkably healthy and orderly.

Infancy is a period of indulgence and great attention until a child is succeeded by a new baby. But even if younger children are added to the household the first years of life are a period of indulgence. Two- and three-year old children frequently strike their parents (especially the less-strict mother) with their fists. This behavior is to be expected and is usually laughed at. Discipline is most commonly in the form of reprimand, and less frequently, by punishment or threats of punishment.

Physical punishment, while far from unknown, is usually avoided. Forms of physical punishment include pinching, the application of *moxa* (burning a powdered herb on the skin), the pricking of mischievous fingers with a needle, and striking or spanking. Striking or slapping is not in favor. There is an old saying that if a mother strikes a child, the child will strike others. Physical punishment for quarreling or other misbehavior usually ceases entirely before a child is ten and is replaced by admonition and the much more powerful force of ridicule.

Grandparents are usually extremely indulgent with children. Boys are more likely to be spoiled than girls; the only temper tantrums witnessed by the author were among male children.

Children past earliest infancy, and especially those old enough to walk, are frequently turned over for short intervals to the care of older sisters, and occasionally to older brothers, so that mothers may do their work unimpeded. Very young children are carried on the back where their small heads wobble about perilously as their older sisters or brothers play games.

Toilet training usually commences at the age of about six months, but it may be delayed if the child reaches that age during the cold of the winter months. The mother partially undresses the child and holds it over a receptacle or in a corner of the yard several times throughout the day. After this practice has been continued for a number of weeks children usually begin to understand what is expected of them. Training is fairly complete by about age two. There is said to be no punishment for errors except that children old enough to understand are told they must inform their mothers on such occasions and are sometimes scolded. There is no shaking or physical punishment which might induce the psychological trauma about which much has been made regarding the toilet training of Japanese children (e.g., by G. Gorer and by W. LaBarre).

Weaning is usually done when a child is about two years of age. The mother rubs her nipples with fresh, broken chili peppers. Weaning by this method is said to be dramatically rapid—and might well be traumatic. Children are, however, accustomed to solid food long before weaning time. Rice gruel and tangerine juice are usually the first introductions, at the age of five or six months. Other soft foods are gradually added and the child, sitting on its mother's lap, joins the household at the table for meals by the end of its first year of life.

.   .   .   .

Personal qualities are important status determinants. Industry, thrift, and intelligence are respected. The unbossy man with whom all relations are smooth is the ideal. Affability to the point of self-effacement is undesirable, but one must never be pushing or contradicting.

Direct action in matters of importance—arranging a marriage, for example—is untraditional, embarrassing, and confusing. Actions or transactions without precedent leave the average person at a loss and are avoided as much as possible. In any situation in which there is a possibility of direct discord, the usual course of action is avoidance. It is sometimes convenient to fail to see the other person.

Other than petty theft, crime is virtually unknown on Takashima. The method of combatting petty theft is to remove the opportunity. Police aid is never called.

ADAPTATION NO. 5*

The Modoc Indians of Northern California are described as "primitive pragmatists." They were aggressive, utilitarian, democratic. They were brave hunters

---

* From Verne F. Ray, *Primitive Pragmatists* (Seattle: University of Washington Press, 1963), *passim*.

and warriors whose society and culture met defeat at last in the Modoc War of 1872–73.

How were children trained and prepared to perpetuate this unusual culture? The data in Dr. Ray's account are insufficient to provide a comprehensive answer. They do, however, provide important insights. The most significant factors appear to have been those summarized (one through six) below.

1. Strong parental feelings; parental self-sacrifice to ensure safety and well being of the infant and young child.

Deep parental affection for children was shown in many ways. When the first child was born it was not unusual for the parents to alternate in sitting up with the infant throughout the night. Being well aware of the high infant mortality they feared the child would become ill and not receive prompt enough attention. Even though the child slept well the vigil might be kept for the first weeks at least. In winter one of the objects was to keep the fire burning so that there would be no danger of illness from exposure.

Fathers often cared for the children in the absence of the mother, even though others were available for the task. A father might sit for hours at a time beside an ailing son or daughter. The physical care of the older and apparently healthy child was often neglected, however.

2. Considerable freedom accorded children and few chores or accomplishments expected of them.

Children were never summoned for meals. This was not a mark of neglect but rather a recognition of the child's individuality and prerogatives. It was assumed that he would come at the proper hour if hungry. At any hour he was privileged to come to the house for any food available without preparation.

Older children were expected to supervise the activities of the younger ones. The object was to free the mother for other efforts rather than to acquaint the child with adult responsibilities. Few formal tasks were assigned to the young child. Formal training in economic activities such as hunting and basket making was not begun before adolescence.

Early efforts of children (e.g., in making baskets or bows and arrows) were abundantly praised by parents. The praise reflected true pride in the child's achievement; it was not a mechanism for stimulation. One informant said: "My parents were proud of me, and the prouder they were of me the more I wanted to work hard and the better I felt. So I was never lazy."

3.   Children were subjected to physical hardening and toughening experiences; this kind of training was not heavily emphasized, however.

Boys and girls were occasionally required to bathe in cold lakes or streams, even in winter, in order that they might become strong and brave. A child might be aroused in the middle of the night, without previous warning, and be taken or sent to a nearby body of water. But upon return home the child was permitted to warm himself by the fire.

4.   Boy's games were many and they developed physical endurance and skills.

An informant recalls: "We [several boys] went swimming in the lake. We had races to see who could swim farthest under water, or stay under longest. I played this game often when I was young.

"Every boy had bows and arrows that his father had made for him. We shot fish, frogs, and watersnakes. I was afraid of the watersnakes but I shot at them just the same."

The informant describes numerous games requiring skills in shooting and throwing (with bow, blowpipe, sling, or javelin), dodging, racing, jumping, and climbing mountains.

5.   Children were carefully trained in ethics and proper interpersonal behavior; obedience was demanded and discipline was sometimes severe.

Though there was no pressure on children to perform useful labor or to develop technical skills, they were conscientiously trained from earliest infancy in ethics, behavior, and tradition. Myths and anecdotes were told to them directly, or to the family group with the children as the significant auditors. Advice was frequently given respecting relations with other children and proper attitudes toward adults. Respect and obedience to adults were strongly emphasized. Lying was not tolerated. Older children were forbidden to punish younger ones left in their care.

"A child that talked back to its elders got a good whipping. Children were very obedient to all adults, whether they were relatives or strangers.

"If a boy were 'mean' his parents would try to whip it out of him. If a girl were mean she would be whipped in the same way.

"Sometimes children were punished by being given very little to eat.

"At other times a child was put in a sweat house for punishment. The entrance was closed and the child couldn't get out. It certainly was hot when they did that to me! I had been disobedient and I thought I was going to die in that sweat house.

"We were told: 'These mountains, these rivers hear what you say and if you are mean they will punish you.' As little children we used to hear the old people talk about what the earth did to them."

Young children were scolded or lightly punished—the pulling of an ear or switching on the legs—when they disobeyed, falsified, or caused damage in the home.

Children above six or seven years of age were expected to know the rules of proper behavior. They were no longer punished for minor transgressions but were more severely handled for serious infractions. Severe fighting with other children was the most frequent offense. Whipping over the back and legs with a heavy willow withe was the usual penalty. Either the mother or the father did the whipping, commonly the latter. Other relatives were not privileged to do so although grandparents did not hesitate to give advice.

6. Clear-cut personality ideals were held up to children.

A woman should above all else be industrious. The ability and willingness to spend long days at root digging was the best criterion of industry. It was said that a girl who was efficient at root digging was always beautiful. The girl should be quiet, retiring, and serious.

The qualities sought in a man were strength of character, bravery, and wit. He should also be a reasonably capable participant in the economic pursuits of men.

EXCERPT NO. 9*

Friedl's report on a Greek village points up vividly the extent to which children can adjust to trauma-laden relationships in the personal community. In Vasilika deliberate teasing, frightening, frustrating, lying, and even hurting are culturally patterned aspects of these relationships. But such experiences are appropriate schooling for the relationships of adulthood in the village. In this society "the constant vigilance necessary to avert becoming a dupe is certainly one of the sources of tension in the conduct of human relations. . . . [But] these strains [do not] have the same effect on Vasilika's inhabitants that they would have [presumably] on middle-class Americans. . . ."

There are . . . the ordinary physical hazards of life in a village like Vasilika. Children are kept from getting too close to the fires, to the oven, to other peoples' dogs; they are protected from the harsh effects of the weather. In addition, however, there are the hazards created by the behavior of other human beings. A woman suckling her infant, for example, may let the baby almost start to suck, then pull herself away, then let the child start again, then pull herself away. She may repeat these actions three or four times, talking and laughing as she does so, finally permitting the baby to suckle contentedly only after it has exhibited some discomfort by whimpering or squirming within its swaddling bands.

Such action is the beginning of a long series of similar teasing incidents in early childhood, sometimes connected with food, sometimes with other matters. A father of a two-year-old boy may call him over to have some of the sweet preserve that is being served to guests. The child runs eagerly to his father's knee. The father touches the spoonful of sweet to the child's mouth and as the boy opens his mouth to take the food, the father snatches the spoon away. He may repeat this several times until the child starts to cry. Then he lets the child eat, and hugs and pats him telling him he is a good boy.

In a different kind of situation, several boys of eighteen or nine-

---

* From *Vasilika, A Village in Modern Greece*, by Ernestine Friedl, pp. 78–81. Copyright © 1962 by Holt, Rinehart and Winston, Inc. Used with permission of the publishers.

teen encouraged the three-year-old brother of one of them to start a physical fight with his equally small cousin. The older boys shouted encouragement and made them intensify the pummelling of each other to the point where the children were knocking each other down and bruising themselves on the stones and rough earth of the yard. The little boys started to cry; the older boys laughed and then, still laughing, took the children into their arms and hugged and kissed them calling them by endearing names. On one occasion, when a government agricultural extension agent was in the village injecting chickens against Newcastle's disease, a father lifted his little two-year-old son into the air, turned him upside down with the child's back facing the agent, and laughingly told the child that he would have the agent inject him just as if he were a chicken. The child started to cry, and after two or three minutes, his father righted the child and comforted him.

Sometimes adults use similar methods to discipline a child. On one occasion, a group of women were discussing the coming Easter festivities, and the two-year-old niece of one of them kept climbing on and off her aunt's lap. The child was told several times to sit still but ignored the request. Finally, her aunt laid the child on its back across her knees and laughingly told her they would kill her like the Easter lamb. The woman ran the edge of her hand over the child's throat to demonstrate the slitting of the lamb's throat. The others laughed and added vivid details. The child's eyes showed panic; she struggled up out of her aunt's lap and sat quietly on a stool for about fifteen minutes until they both left. We heard the aunt speaking gently and endearingly to the child as they departed.

As the foregoing examples indicate, when adults deliberately frighten children or even stimulate milder forms of distress, they do not abandon the child to his misery but try to relieve the anxiety by physical affection and soothing words. In spite of this, however, a three-year-old child will often try to hit a parent or elder brother or sister who is causing distress. He is laughed at for his futile efforts by those watching the scene. Four- and five-year-old children respond to the teasing by walking away or by maintaining stolid expressions. Once they do this, the severity and frequency of the teasing by elders decreases, and the pattern continues mostly among the children themselves in their relations with each other. Practical jokes continue into adolescence. From the adults' point of view, the teasing is no longer amusing or valuable for discipline because the child has gained enough knowledge, enough intelligence to know that the process is a kind of game and has acquired the skill with which to handle his side of it. Mentally retarded individuals never learn, and they are baited and teased for the amusement of the watchers all their lives. From the child's point of view, the constant reassurance he receives after the pain may teach him that there is no real or permanent danger in the adult actions except that of ridicule, and that is what he learns to try to avoid.

Just as the teasing leads to a recognition that other people's actions and words should not be taken at face value, so does another common pattern of dealing with children—the pattern of deliberately lying to them. Usually, parents or older brothers and sisters lie to a child to get him to do what he does not want to do. For example, a three-year-old child may be asked to go into another room to fetch something. The child does not respond to several requests; his mother then tells him his father is in the other room and will give him candy if he goes. The child thinks he remembers that his father left for the fields early in the morning, and therefore is not likely to be in the next room; he makes a comment to this effect; his mother seriously reassures him that his father is really in the next room; he becomes uncertain and, finally, cautiously goes to the door, opens it slowly and looks inside. At this point his mother and anyone else around laugh at his look of chagrin.

Lying to children as a kind of palliative occurs in less dramatic ways as well. On one occasion, a mother was washing the legs of her two-year-old daughter. The child was standing on a table to be nearer the small water container hanging on the wall. When her mother finished, the girl did not want to come down off the table. She resisted, stamping her feet and calling for more water to play with. Her mother told her in a mild tone that there was no more water. This did not satisfy the child; she resisted further and finally the mother turned the spigot on and let her play with the water, of which there was quite a supply, for a few more minutes until the girl herself was ready to stop.

In both these instances the child easily detected the deceit of his elders. However, since there are occasions on which his father actually is in the next room and does give him candy, and other occasions when the water actually has run out, a child cannot know in advance when he is being deceived and when he is not. Inconsistency in the actions of elders results in a wariness in accepting or rejecting the statements of others, even within the family. Children may learn to love and respect their elders, but it is not required that they trust them completely.

Lying to children is one aspect of the general attitude toward truth and falsity characteristic of the village's adults. In the village the word for lies, *psemata*, is used much more freely, with less emotional intensity, and with a milder pejorative connotation than Americans use the English word. "Let's tell a few more lies and then go home," a man once remarked jovially near the end of a social evening. To accuse someone of mendacity is not the gross insult it is in the United States; it may be meant as a statement of fact in a situation in which, in village expectation, it would not be unusual for a person to attempt some deception. As in the training of children, some form of deception as a means of achieving a particular good is acceptable as a technique for conducting one's affairs in the village or with outsiders. Each man and woman expects to develop skills both in the art of guilefulness and in the art of detecting guilefulness in others. Vasilika's villagers are not humiliated because someone tries to deceive them; they become angry only if the deception succeeds. In other words, if a person is gullible enough to have been misled, he gets angry at the deceiver for having made a fool of him, and this results in accusations and counteraccusations. The standard phrase for deceptions means literally "He has made a laughing stock of me," "*Me yelase.*" Older children who have learned to turn table on their parents and try to deceive them are admired even as they are scolded. Certainly, any child who, in mild ways, learns to take advantage of a neighbor or another villager is privately approved of by his parents as "*ponyiros,*" "cleverly bad," although the neighbors use less ambivalent epithets.

The constant vigilance necessary to avert becoming a dupe is certainly one of the sources of tension in the conduct of human relations in the village. An American must not make the mistake of assuming, however, that these strains have the same effect on Vasilika's inhabitants that they would have on middle-class Americans whose training has included a stress on consistency and truthfulness. In Vasilika, the expectation of, and conditioning for, deceit does not eliminate the objective, realistic discomforts of living with somewhat unpredictable human beings, but the cultural expectation does seem to eliminate some of the intensity generated by the conflict.

The total situation does not result in an inability to predict the behavior of others to the point of chaos in human relationships, but rather in an expectation on the part of the villagers of a wide range of alternative actions and responses by others. There is uncertainty within set limits, but there is also an enjoyment of, and a taste for, the unpredictable. In a sense, when the villagers know each other so well that they can predict reactions with some precision, they are bored and look for other diversions.

ADAPTATION NO. 6*

In his pioneering study of child rearing Whiting reports in detail on the teaching and learning of Kwoma culture. What is presented here is inadequate to convey the richness of the documentation. It may serve, however, to illustrate how much must be learned by children even in relatively simple cultures, and to suggest that enculturation in such a setting is by no means haphazard, although it is largely informal.

PERSONAL SAFETY

When weaning has been accomplished parents tell the boy that he has become a little man. He now turns to the play group and spends his time playing games with other children, roaming in the

---

* From John W. M. Whiting, *Becoming a Kwoma* (New Haven: Yale University Press, 1941), *passim*.

forest, and participating to some extent in adult activities.

As his environmental horizon widens so do its hazards. He learns to avoid dangers with which he cannot hope to cope (e.g., large snakes, crocodiles, wild pigs, nettles and thorns, being out in heavy storms). His parents and older siblings help him avoid these dangers by warning him. He is not, however, permitted to show excessive fear of his environment. An overanxious child is usually called a "baby" in a derogatory manner.

The warnings of parents and older siblings include supernatural dangers. Ghost lore is taught during childhood. The spirits of the dead may be dangerous and the child is told not to go near a burial platform.

The widening of a boy's contact with the environment necessitates new discriminations about the edibility of things. The parents warn the child about the objects that are poisonous. Older children probably teach younger ones. The training is very effective; Kwoma children show a remarkable knowledge of the local flora and fauna. Parents provide a general formula to keep the children from eating harmful food. The formula is: if you do not know a thing is good to eat, do not try it.

A Kwoma child learns that, in addition to things naturally inedible, there are also foods which are made poisonous by sorcerers. Since relatives rarely sorcerize one another one may eat in their houses, but children are warned not to eat elsewhere. Non-relatives are not to be trusted.

One's blood is material which must be kept from sorcerers. The child is taught to take care to catch or wipe up blood from a scratch or cut, and to burn or hide all that has been lost.

A child does not have to be warned frequently about the dangers of sorcery because his parents show such fear of it. *Emotional attitudes as well as overt habits are subject to imitation.*

PROPERTY RIGHTS AND SHARING

In addition to learning that he may not eat things naturally poisonous nor food contaminated by sorcery, the child is conditioned against eating food which belongs to someone else. He comes face to face with the property concepts of the culture, and must learn to respect them.

A Kwoma child learns that he must not eat just any food he sees. He may eat only after his property rights have been determined. The principle holds also for the use of tools or toys, but these are scarce. It is in connection with food that property rights are primarily learned.

After considerable trial and error, and after explanations and examples from parents and older siblings, the child learns. He understands that all the vegetables which come from a certain plot in the garden, and the produce of certain trees, belong to him. He learns that he can take and eat this food without interference, except that he must contribute his share to the family soup when his mother asks for it, and must share with his brothers and sisters when requested, if he expects them to reciprocate. He learns that others in the household are usually willing to share their food with him if he asks permission.

Children also develop techniques of thieving. They discover that if they take food secretly and then deny that they have done so they can often escape punishment. If they are caught stealing, however, they will be even more severely punished by the owner than if they openly took the food. Despite the greater punishment, most children develop the art of thieving.

WORK

However adept the child may become in begging and stealing, he must learn that as an adult he cannot live by this means alone. He must acquire prescribed work habits if he is to be able to support himself and his dependents. Even in childhood he begins to participate in the hunting, gardening, and collecting occupations of his parents, and in the preparation and cooking of food (e.g., carrying water and firewood, fetching implements and utensils).

Children of both sexes participate in the work of gardening by helping to clear the site. It is their duty, together with the women and old men, to clear the ground of underbrush while the adult men are in the treetops lopping off the branches. Children are expected to help with this land-clearing work and are scolded by their parents and older siblings if they do not. Toward the end of childhood the boys are allowed to climb some of the smaller trees and try their hand at "man's" work. Girls sometimes help the women with weeding, which is woman's responsibility. However, any such help given by the children is voluntary. They may go off to play when they tire of the work.

When yams are harvested the children render more effective assistance. The boys pick up the yams that have been dug. The girls carry the harvest home.

Kwoma parents develop their children's interest in the work of gardening by setting aside a section of garden for each of them. The section is carefully marked off with bamboo poles laid end to end on the ground. Its produce is put in a separate bin in the family storehouse as the child's private property.

Hunting is restricted entirely to men. However, boys begin to learn hunting skills from early childhood. It is not until adulthood that a Kwoma may become a hunter of big game.

Kwoma children participate in caring for the family's domesticated animals and they assume full responsibility for their own pets.

Fishing is considered a sport rather than a serious activity. Girls participate in what little is done, often simply scooping fish from a swamp pool or mountain stream with their hands.

Children watch their parents make tools but do little such work themselves. Boys sometimes help their parents by fetching materials for various utensils, and girls begin netting before they reach adolescence. Otherwise toolmaking is restricted to older persons.

The Kwoma child discovers, little by little, that it is necessary to work to get food and other necessities. He learns, by both observation and participation, the techniques that have been developed in the culture for producing the necessities. He is forced to assume responsibility for some of this work, is allowed to help with other tasks if he wishes, and is definitely debarred from still others. Coercion to work consists in scolding or beating the child for not doing the tasks expected of him, and in warning him of the dire consequences which may result from doing the wrong thing.

CLEANLINESS

Usually cleanliness (toilet) habits have already been established by the time a boy or girl enters childhood. The Kwoma say that if a slip occurs it is the child's own business except that he is forced to clean up after himself and he may be laughed at. When a child of eight made a puddle on the floor in a house she was visiting the people said it was the act of an infant and that she was old enough to know better.

SEX

Sexual conditioning begins in earnest during childhood. A boy is punished for looking at the genitals of any female. He is scolded and may even be beaten. The person at whom he has looked usually does the punishing. She tells him that he should not look at her genitals because they are her own private property. The act is put in the context of offenses against ownership and property rights.

The sexual response for which a boy is most severely punished during childhood is that of tumescence in public. Boys will tease, shame, and warn one another. Older sisters, hearing of such an occurrence, will scold and threaten to beat the boy and try to shame him: "What are you, a baby? You should be old enough to control yourself." A boy is also restricted from fingering his genitals. Anyone who observes a child touching his penis scolds him for it.

Girls are not restricted from looking at the genitals of the opposite sex. They are, however, punished for masturbating, and they are scolded by parents and older siblings for exposing themselves unduly. When a girl has been immodest she is punished much less severely than is a boy. She is rarely more than scolded.

INTER-PERSONAL RELATIONS AND ETIQUETTE

A child is often aggressive toward younger siblings and sometimes aggressive even toward his parents (though usually only covertly). He is generally very polite toward his relatives who live in other hamlets. He learns to behave properly toward his mother's brother and sister, his father's sister, and their children. His parents teach him to greet these persons and to address each of them by the appropriate kinship term. Although these relatives seldom command the child, he is expected to obey them when they do.

Not only is the child punished by his parents if he is rude to one of these relatives, but he is warned that unless he behaves nicely toward them they will "break relationship" with him. They will then be like non-relatives, and he may no longer visit them with the expectation of a warm welcome.

A child also learns to behave appropriately (i.e., to be polite and friendly, not aggressive) to the children of his father's friends. His parents teach him that these children are his friends. He can visit and play with them without fear of sorcery, and he should be nice to them when they come to visit him.

Non-relatives, the child learns, are to be feared and avoided. They might do harm and they can not be expected to help or protect. A boy learns the names of non-relatives, and if he meets one he may exchange a brief greeting and gossip for a moment. Still, he is reserved and anxious, as he would not be in a meeting with a relative. His views and feelings about non-relatives the child learns from both parental warnings and from observation. There are many object lessons in the bitter exchange of insults and threats of violence between the adults of the hamlet and those not related to them.

But the child learns too that there are limits to the dangers presented by non-relatives who are members of his own sub-tribe. They and his relatives have a considerable community of interest. They will stand together against aggression from outside, they participate jointly in ceremonies and court meetings, and a complicated web of kinship bonds interlaces the whole sub-tribe and holds it together. It is the members of other sub-tribes (if they are not relatives by marriage) who represent the greatest menace. The child learns that these "foreigners" will sorcerize without shame and that they have little respect for his life or limb. He is told stories of head-hunting raids, and most Kwoma children actually experience a raid in which some acquaintance or relative is killed and decapitated by a group of foreigners seeking prestige.

ADAPTATION NO. 7*

The Fischers have documented, as have few others, a set of culturally patterned concepts concerning the nature of the child and its development. They show how these concepts underlie and shape child rearing and the expectations held by adults. The study provides a model for investigation of an important and neglected aspect of enculturation.

The community's conception of the nature of the child has important implications for the whole system of child training. This conception of the child's nature is based on ideas about how the child learns and how he develops. The philosophy behind the socialization process in this community is constant for all families. It allows, however, for a wide variety of training techniques and of goals for individual children and families.

Community people are not entirely aware of their own view of the child. However, evidence of their concepts is abundant in their conversation and in public speeches.

In Orchard Town, the newborn infant is thought of as a "potential," the various features thereof having been largely inherited. This concept of the child involves belief about the inheritance of characteristics, about the influence of parental training, about the influence of the social environment and education, and beliefs about stages and norms.

The infant as a potential is thought to be a bundle of largely inherited latent traits of emotional expression and abilities for achieving goals. The latent traits in the potential are thought of as (1) fluid, (2) partially concealed, (3) being both good and bad, and (4) being more or less subject to influence from without. The child's abilities can be realized only gradually as he develops. It is thought that children may have high or low potential for the de-

---

* From John L. Fischer and Ann Fischer, "The New Englanders of Orchard Town, U.S.A.," in Beatrice Whiting (ed.), *Six Cultures: Studies of Child Rearing* (New York, John Wiley & Sons, Inc., 1963), pp. 873–1010.

velopment of certain skills or personality traits. The combination of high potential and the best environmental influences is thought to be essential to the greatest success in achieving the goals available to adults.

Keeping the potential as fluid as possible is important for allowing the child to reach an ideal maturity. Fluidity is retained by non-interference. *It is felt that adult pressure may arrest development and set the child in a mold which is not the ideal expression of his potential.*

The belief that the potential is in part concealed leads to great emphasis on techniques for the discovery and disclosure of the child's potential. The potential can be better developed if it is known or divined in advance. Divining is highly developed; there are formal tests for intelligence, personality and achievement; there are also more subtle techniques such as informal questioning of the child or observing his behavior for clues. Clues include such things as the child showing a special interest in something (e.g., sports or animals), or doing something particularly well (e.g., dancing, drawing, various school subjects.)

Since both good and bad features are in the child's potential, he may momentarily exhibit either kind of quality. He is thought more likely to exhibit his bad features if he is physically tired or has had "too much" excitement. Some people are chiefly concerned with curbing the bad aspects of the child's nature. Others stress developing the good aspects.

It is believed that some traits are more susceptible to environmental influence than others. Sex, for example, is a rigid trait and one can only try to influence development of traits appropriate to the child's sex.

There are two bad traits presumed to be present in the child at birth or shortly thereafter. These are cruelty and indifference to time. It is the parents' responsibility to see that these traits are under control by the time the child becomes an adult.

Development is thought to occur through a progression of stages. These stages are seen as more or less inevitable and relatively inaccessible to influence.

The parent must avoid hampering the process of natural unfolding, at whatever cost to personal convenience. He should not impose his own standards upon the child any more than is necessary to curb bad aspects until the child can evaluate parental standards in terms of his own nature. A church guide advises: "Enjoy your child; do not push him into development." *Ideally, the parent acts as a kind of pleased observer who watches the child unfold.*

Irreparable damage is thought to occur if the child's potentialities do not unfold at the right time. Parents must therefore have some knowledge of norms, of what the child should have accomplished at a certain age. Books or observation of other children provide guidance with respect to norms.

Parental mistreatment is seen as the probable cause if the child is spoiled, lazy, nervous, or rebellious, if he presents a discipline problem or an eating problem. Lack of discipline causes both spoiling and laziness. Forcing the child develops nervousness, rebellion, discipline problems, and lack of appetite. Parents must try to be good "models."

It is also believed that this town in some way influences its children differently than do other places.

Education is felt to be a very important influence on development of the potential. No one believes that even excellent potential can be realized if the child does not acquire skills through education.

Parents often react to their children, whose potential they are expected to develop, as they do to other responsibilities. Responsibility for children weighs heavily on the two parents; it is not spread over an extended family, as it is in many societies.

Perhaps because of the concealed nature of the child's potential, the parent is never quite certain whether he is doing his best for the child. He is anxious, and he becomes more anxious if he meets with lack of success in training his child. Anxiety may lead to attempts to force the child into certain channels of development. Since forcing is contrary to the belief system, this often leads to further anxiety. The ideas of stages, norms, and the inheritance of characteristics act as convenient guideposts to the parents and as comfortable explanations for the behavior of the child.

PART III

CHAPTER 7

The Press and Pull of Culture

... The "press" of culture is such that the average individual is stamped with ways of perceiving, thinking, and acting which are characteristic of his society and predictable.

John Gillin

The smaller the area of choice, the smaller the temptation to take thought.

George Orwell

The anthropological studies we have sampled and discussed illustrate that culture is to the individual at once a potent force and an essential resource. If he feels himself under pressure to learn, to meet expectations, he also "becomes," in Allport's sense of the word, as he learns. He begins his life as a helpless organism, and with time and enculturation he becomes man, a knowledgeable participant in the human enterprise.

THE PROTECTIVE AND REGULATORY FUNCTIONS
OF CULTURAL PRESS

Tradition, custom, the knowledge and skills of his society are brought to bear on the growing child, and through his life they remain factors with which he must reckon. But this is not to imply that these factors are largely coercive or constraining. It must not be forgotten that through association and enculturation the child is enabled to survive and to develop his potentialities. Between him and the raw forces of his environment society and culture stand like sheltering screens, providing both protection and the know-how he must have to cope with the physical environment and with other people.

It is easy to understand that culture as a set of skills for exploitation of the physical environment and protection from its violence is a benign force. It is less easy to appreciate the necessity of culture for regulating society. In this function culture provides protection from the violence of men toward one another. Without regulatory patterns human existence would indeed be, as Hobbes observed, "solitary, poor, nasty, brutish, and short."

The difficulty of appreciating this benign aspect of culture is particularly great for "rugged individualists" who have learned from their own culture to deplore and resist its pressures. This paradox is unusually evident among Americans, who tend to be highly ambivalent about the regulatory aspects of their culture, though also remarkably conformist. Over the years observers have commented on the contradictory tendencies of Americans to cluster and to conform, on the one hand, and, on the other, to resist the rules and flout the laws of their own making.

Rules, and the sanctions and mechanisms necessary to make them effective, occur in all societies. Inevitably individuals will come into conflict. "Human society even in its simplest versions is complex enough to require more or less explicit techniques for resolving clashes of interest" (Bennett and Tumin, 1948, p. 532). But between folk societies, and more complex societies too, there is wide variation in the nature and efficiency of regulatory patterns.

Henry has reported on an Indian tribe—the Kaingáng—of Brazil whose regulatory culture is distinctly inadequate. The Kaingáng live in small hunting bands. Within the band they bicker; between bands there are endless, murderous feuds. Henry writes:

> The very lack of fixity of relationships and the multitude of ways of forming them left the Kaingáng with no device for controlling a conflict (between bands). Once a feud arose there was nothing, neither dominating ties of blood nor the voice of chieftainship or government, to stop or limit it. (Henry, 1964, pp. 49–50.)

. . . Among their friends and relatives the Kaingáng were the most ethical people on earth, though to outsiders they were treacherous killers. (*Ibid.*, p. xvi.)

The Pawnee Indians of the United States provide a sharp contrast. Gene Weltfish wrote of their culture as it was in the year 1867. Her long and meticulous study, through elderly informants, convinced Weltfish that Pawnee society had been well-ordered yet remarkably free of coercion or even regulatory mechanisms. She says:

They were a well-disciplined people, maintaining public order under many trying circumstances. And yet they had none of the power mechanisms that we consider essential to a well-ordered life. No orders were ever issued. No assignments for work were ever made nor were over-all plans discussed. There was no code of rules of conduct nor punishment for infraction. There were no commandments nor moralizing proverbs. The only instigator of action was the consenting person. . . . In all his work, both public and private, the Pawnee moved on a totally voluntary basis. Whatever social forms existed were carried within the consciousness of the people, not by others who were in a position to make demands. . . . The Pawnee had chiefs, but these were the focus of consensus, not the wielders of power. (Weltfish, 1965, pp. 5–6.)[1]

Obviously such beautiful order on a wholly voluntary basis does not "just happen." Weltfish explains:

The Pawnee learned this way of living in the earliest beginnings of his life. In the detailed events of everyday living as a child, he began his development as a disciplined and free man or as a woman who felt her dignity and her independence to be inviolate. . . . The kind of voluntarism that the Pawnee practiced . . . is not easily described, for it is implicit in the individual personalities of the people themselves. (*Ibid.*, pp. 6 and 7.)[2]

Pawnee culture must have incorporated enculturation patterns of a highly effective sort. The values of the culture, and the heavy emphasis on religious ceremonials, help to explain Pawnee voluntarism. Nevertheless, the extent to which controls were ap-

---

[1] From *The Lost Universe* by Gene Weltfish, Basic Books, Inc., Publishers, New York, 1965.

[2] *Ibid.*

parently implicit rather than explicit makes the Pawnee an unusual case.

The "yoke of society," as sociologist Émile Durkheim long ago called it, may rest lightly or heavily, but it must be in place if society is to be orderly and the individual secure.

> It is not true . . . that human activity can be released from all restraint. Nothing in the world can enjoy such a privilege. . . . Man's characteristic privilege is that the bond he accepts is not physical but moral; that is, social. (Durkheim, 1951, p. 252.)

Durkheim was fully aware that a base level of interpersonal dependence is prerequisite to the survival of a society and to the satisfaction of most individuals. Interdependence, interpersonal reciprocities, and social order are inextricably linked; the individual accepts their patterned modes at a certain minimum level or he casts himself adrift in *anomie* (rulelessness). Though Durkheim overstates his case and reifies society, yet he propounds a law of human life; regulatory and even coercive aspects of community are to a degree both inevitable and benign. He wrote:

> Law and morality are the totality of ties which bind each of us to society, which make a unitary, coherent aggregate of the mass of individuals. Everything which is a source of solidarity is moral, everything which forces man to take account of other men is moral, everything which forces him to regulate his conduct through something other than the striving of his ego is moral, and morality is as solid as these ties are numerous and strong. We can see how inexact it is to define it, as is often done, through liberty. It rather consists in a state of dependence. (Durkheim, 1960, p. 477.)

The individual's survival and satisfaction with his life are, then, heavily dependent upon social solidarity and the "morality" it engenders. The availability of the police when one's house is being burglarized is an easily recognized and appreciated by-product of social solidarity and morality. But when the same police intervene at other points in his life (e.g., his driving or drinking) the citizen is likely to have a quite different reaction. But on the whole the duly constituted guardians of the social order do have, and must have, the support of popular opinion—i.e., of the culturally patterned values and beliefs. W. E. Abraham makes this point in his analysis of emerging state controls in Ghana. He says:

The possibility of state intervention itself depends on the co-opera-tion of individuals, and this co-operation implies appreciable unity of purpose. Every individual depends for his life and living on the suffer-ance and co-operation of others. . . . Culture is an instrument for mak-ing the sufferance and co-operation natural. . . . By uniting the people in common beliefs and attitudes, or at least, in tolerance for certain beliefs, actions and values, culture fills with order that portion of life which lies beyond the pale of state intervention. (Abraham, 1962, p. 27.)

REGULATORY PATTERNS IN DISORDER, IN FLEXIBILITY, AND IN EXTREME INTEGRATION

If the social bonds are severely disrupted, and customary rules and procedures are disorganized, there sets in a condition of anomie. This principle was stated by Durkheim around the turn of the century. It was inferred from data necessarily limited as to cross-cultural reference, but it has survived the tests of time and of a wider range of data. In explaining anomie and its relation to the incidence of suicide Durkheim said:

. . . When society is disturbed or disorganized, whether by a painful crisis or by a fortunate but too sudden turn of events, it is temporarily incapable of exercising this [restraining] influence upon the individual; and such conditions lead to . . . abrupt rises in the suicide curve. . . . As long as the social forces . . . let loose have not attained a new equilibrium, their relative social values remain indeterminate, and con-sequently all coordination is lacking for a while. People no longer feel sure about what is possible and what is not, what is just and what is unjust, which claims and aspirations are legitimate and which go be-yond the bounds of propriety. As a result, there is nothing to which men do not lay claim. . . . The appetites of men, unrestrained now by a public opinion which has become bewildered and disoriented, no longer know where the bounds are before which they ought to come to a halt. . . . The state of rulelessness (*dereglement*) or *anomie* is further heightened by the fact that human desires are less disciplined at the very moment when they would need a stronger discipline. . . . Effort increases just when it becomes less productive of results. (Durkheim, *op. cit.*, pp. 455–56.)

The suicide rate which so interested Durkheim is but one index of chaos in rule and value systems. Moreover, suicide may have quite another type of significance, e.g., when suicide represents behavior which is under certain circumstances culturally prescribed and valued. In contemporary complex societies there are other indices of chaos which we now label alienation, illness, addiction, delinquency, or crime. The will to live may not languish to the point of extinction, but the satisfaction in living may decline sharply, or the pursuit of ephemeral satisfactions may become an engrossing preoccupation. It seems that a significant proportion of society's members are deeply dissatisfied. But there is little prospect of social stability or slowdown in the rate of cultural change. Clearly man must learn to live with instability, if he is to live at all, and to find a way to avoid anomie while existing in a perpetual state of social disequilibrium.

However, anthropologists have noted vast differences between peoples with respect to their ability to adjust to the shocks of radical change. The Inca culture of Peru disintegrated rapidly after the conquest; many other New World cultures collapsed in much the same way. Presumably these cultures lacked flexibility or adaptability.

Some of the contemporary Africans, notably the Kamba (a Bantu tribe of East Africa), show "a relatively high degree of cultural adaptability." Symmes Oliver reports:

My dominant impression of the Kamba culture is that it is extremely elastic. There is a great deal of give and take in it, and there is a fuzziness and lack of precision about many facets of the culture that goes deeper than the mere existence of alternative ways of doing things. There is something more involved here than the expectable differences between the "rules of the game" and the way the game is actually played. (Oliver, 1965, p. 423.)[3]

---

[3] Symmes Oliver, "Individuality, Freedom of Choice, and Cultural Flexibility of the Kamba," *American Anthropologist*, Vol. 67, No. 2 (April, 1965). (Part of the Culture and Ecology in East Africa Project, sponsored by the University of California, Los Angeles and supported by the National Science Foundation, G-11713, and the National Institute of Mental Health, MH-04097.)

The Kamba "show a strong emphasis on individualism and freedom of choice within broadly defined limits, . . . [and] a shallow cultural commitment on the part of individuals." The "basic structural orientation" of the culture is characterized by a kind of looseness. (*Ibid.*, p. 423.)[4]

To these people change, unless it is coercive, apparently presents no threat; "indeed in many areas, they welcome it." Colonial administrators have commented on what they regarded as the indolence and laissez faire of the Kamba, and also on their "surprising willingness to absorb new ideas.

> . . . The capacity of the Kamba to handle new cultural elements has impressed observers who otherwise found little in Kamba life to admire. . . . The culture has shown great tensile strength. It has yielded, but it has not broken. (*Ibid.*, pp. 424–25.)[5]

And the crucial factor is, it seems, individualism. Yet this is not the individualism of the pastoralist or the pioneer (see Chapter 8, pp. 204–6). The individual in Kamba is free less because freedom is valued than because it is inherent—a by-product of structural "looseness" rather than a goal. There may be, as Symmes Oliver suggests (see Excerpt No. 10), many cultures of this sort, cultures pressing but lightly upon the individual.

Yet the press of culture is, on the whole, less than onerous, and if culture creates problems it does solve problems too. In Bali the clarity and completeness of cultural patterning are by no means highly negative in relation to individual welfare.

> The immutability of all the laws of conduct relieves the individual of any responsibility except that of obeying them. He does not doubt their rightness, since they have always been so. (Belo, 1935, p. 145.)

Conformity is largely a matter of comfortable and comforting habit. When misfortunes occur—illness, flood, famine—the religious concepts make the cause clear, and they supply, too, the remedy. . . .

---

[4] *Ibid.*

[5] *Ibid.*

Although it may seem to us that the Balinese lives in ever present fear of demons and evil spirits, the strain is actually not great because the remedy is known and prescribed. . . . The burden of responsibility is lifted from the offenders [such as a mother who has borne twins] and their fellow-villagers who are affected. Tradition tells them what to do in compensation for the wrong. When it is done, no weight of sin or guilt rests on the individual. He has in such matters, as in all other aspects of his life, no choice, no decisions to be made, only the responsibility to maintain the order which he and his society consider established and proved. (*Ibid.*, p. 145.)

Over time—the long time—the patterns of the traditional culture may become refined to an increasingly excellent fit with one another. There are few loopholes, few contingencies not covered. There can be no case more fully illustrative than the "family pattern" of traditional China (see Excerpt No. 11). As E. O. Reischauer and J. K. Fairbank (1960) observe: "Because of the subordination of the individual to the family, the highest virtues and greatest social satisfactions *naturally* attached to family life." (*Ibid.*, p. 29; italics added.) To the Westerner there is nothing at all "natural" in this outcome. However, it is entirely understandable as outcome of a culture which was to a most unusual degree an internally adjusted and unified whole.

Even so the press of culture, though heavy and pervasive, need not be oppressive nor conducive to mental ill health. In Bali the majority conforms closely "to the scheme laid down by tradition," and the scheme is minutely patterned. Yet the people appear well-mannered, balanced, and relaxed.

The babies do not cry, the small boys do not fight, the young girls bear themselves with decorum, the old men dictate with dignity. Every one carries out his appointed task, with respect for his equals and superiors, and gentleness and consideration for his dependents. The people adhere, apparently with ease, to the laws governing the actions, big and small, of their lives. (Belo, *op. cit.*, p. 141.)

But the folk culture may be, in spite of considerable depth in time, only loosely structured, and its "laws governing . . . actions" may be murky and incomplete. The eastern highlanders of New Guinea appear to be the bearers of a loosely structured culture.

"The range of tolerated variation . . . seems wide enough to include even behavior which is conventionally unacceptable," says Berndt.

> A boy is taught that it is in his own interest to conform, to act on the advice which his elders put forward. . . . [But] the decision is ostensibly left with him, with an opportunity to reject that advice. . . . He is allowed what appears to be a relatively free choice. . . . Pressures are not immediately obvious. (Berndt, 1962, p. 401.)

Among Berndt's New Guineans, by contrast with the Balinese, there is a great deal of emotional tension, a conspicuous absence of "balance" and relaxation. But the striking difference is a function of culturally patterned values, and not of greater or lesser cultural press. The New Guinean hyperemotionality and joy in physical violence are not matters of "individual anxiety, maladjustment, or paranoia." Rather, it is that these people value excessive and vagrant emotional states; "both fear and aggression are deliberately fostered" (*ibid.*, p. 405).

Social space is subject to patterning. It may be sharply delimited, hedged about, and movement in it both prescribed and proscribed.

But can a man at least move freely, feel himself a free agent, in physical space? He cannot; there are boundaries, few or many, which may not be crossed with impunity. It is likely that the house of his neighbor, the territory of another village, tribe, or nation may not be entered on whim, without observance of precautions or regulations. Seating positions—near or far, to the left or to the right of a door, raised dais or ground level—are not openly or equally accessible.

These kinds of space limitations are commonplace and expectable. But there are subtler kinds.

In Bali directional orientation is of crucial importance.

> Every Balinese sleeps with his head either to the North (in North Bali, South . . .) or to the East. He may not even lie down for a moment in the opposite direction, for the feet are dirty and may not be put in the place of the head. To lie in the reversed position is said to be "lying like a dead man." . . . The implication is that only a dead man, who could not help himself, would lie in this dangerously wrong way. (Belo, *op. cit.*, p. 128.)

Because of this and many other Balinese space prescriptions, a child must learn early and never lose sight of the cardinal directions. "When for any reason this sense of direction is temporarily lost, when, as we phrase it, a man feels 'turned around,' he is not only uncomfortable but he is quite unable to function." Belo tells of an eight-year-old who was taken by car to a distant village. "Riding in the car he lost his sense of direction." This was so serious that he was unable to study, even to eat or sleep. In Bali the child's consciousness of position in space develops along with the acquisition of a language in which directional terms figure prominently.

Under conditions of relative cultural simplicity society is likely to be "strongly present to the individuals concerned." The individual is less likely to be without what Durkheim regarded as a "restraining harness." The description is apt if inelegant. Patterning in culture, when clear, strongly mediated, and comprehensible, acts as a limiting or restraining force.

In the context of contemporary Western culture the negative function of this force looms large; modern man is impatient of pattern while fearful without it. Folk culture is conceived as crushing to individuality and "inimical to all originality." The facts, as Alexander Goldenweiser pointed out, are more complex: pattern is at once "limit and model." While "the negative aspect of pattern establishes a taboo, the positive aspect points to a task." Goldenweiser continued:

Modern society teems with equivalent and competing patterns; and imagination, now relatively unleashed, expands this realm still further. So, when a pattern rises to dominance and, like a traffic policeman, checks our progress, we resent it. We are too well aware of the varied possibilities we are forced to forego, because they are beyond our means or social class, are evil or disreputable, or against the Constitution. *It is the awareness of the proscribed that strengthens our reluctance to stick to the prescribed.*

The scene is different among primitives. Here the pattern functions largely as a model, and only quite secondarily as a limit. The alternatives are not here to entice one, nor does the imagination, itself well regimented, readily play with them. Before one is a task: reproduce the pattern. In the absence of a sense of restriction, the pattern has nothing about it of the stern countenance of a taboo, on the contrary, it appears as an inviting and admired exemplar. . . .

The presence of a definite pattern tends to shift emphasis from originality in variation—a feature never quite absent—to quality of execution. To us who have much to choose from, as to doing, and who do most things badly, there is something strange about a culture where each individual is confronted with a set of tasks—under the aegis of pattern—and carries them out well, or very well. But such is the nature of folk cultures.

Primitive society is like a school of the arts of life, where competition is keen, and performance, though uniform in aim, is varied in excellence. There is no drabness in such a life. It has about it all the allurements of personal experience, very much one's own, of competitive skill, of things well done. Even as an animal bends its own instinctive nature to an existence full of excitement and gusto, so does the primitive, while bowing to the pattern, lead a life rich in content and animated in tempo. (Goldenweiser, 1936, pp. 99–104; italics added.)

MIND AND PSYCHE AS BOTH FORMATION AND CAUSE

The individual, "primitive" or civilized, will reflect his culture in his modes of thought, his perceptual and conceptual habits, his motor habits, gestures, and his emotional responses. The extent to which all these functions are culturally shaped is discussed by the anthropologist A. I. Hallowell, who was among the first to recognize and investigate these aspects of cultural influence.

When a concept is firmly patterned, perception will be in accord with it (for many individuals in the society, but probably not for all). This concept-percept relationship, and the cultural patterning of both, is neatly illustrated by a curious conviction prevalent among the Trobriand Islanders of Melanesia. These people insist that they see in the offspring of a pair of parents no resemblance to one another, and none to the mother or her kin. The Trobrianders see the children as properly and actually resembling their father. To suggest anything different is to offend everyone concerned. The physical as well as the social environment, objects as well as people, are subject to perception in accord with the lens of culture through which they are viewed. A people's special interests affect their views; East African cattle-keepers are sensitive to the smallest details of appearance and condition of their animals; Plains Indians and cowboys were equally sensitive to horses. Eskimos perceive the slightest changes in conditions of snow or ice. As Hallowell says, man's attitude toward the features of his environment is a function of their reality as culturally defined. . . .

> The objects of the external world *as meaningfully defined* in a traditional ideology constitute the reality to which the individuals habituated to a particular system of beliefs actually respond.
>
> Different concepts of time and space likewise create varying frameworks of reality as we pass from one cultural tradition to another. The non-quantitative concepts of most aboriginal peoples, for instance, tend to create such an enormous gap between this aspect of their thinking and the quantitative orientation of western thought that it is sometimes difficult or impossible to bridge. (Hallowell, 1949, p. 310.)

It is undoubtedly true too, that

> The cultural patterning of perception . . . is one of the most fundamental aspects of the relation between culture and the individual, since through this process frames of reference are established basic to his relations to other persons and to the objects of the outer world.
>
> Gait, the handling of tools and other motor habits also bear the stamp of cultural patterning and cannot be understood as purely individual modes of behavior. Nor, for that matter, can such commonplace organic functions as breathing. . . . Gestures, too, are subtly patterned forms of bodily movement. . . . (*Ibid.*, pp. 301–3.)

In the matter of emotions there is again ample evidence of cultural influence. Hallowell continues:

> While emotion is often referred to as a "natural response," with the implication that it is one little varied by experience, this is a very inexact concept. "Emotional life," says Landis, "is modified more rigorously in the growth and education of an individual than perhaps any other variety of human experience." . . . As Klineberg points out, . . . "emotions felt by one people may not occur in that same form elsewhere. When a Kwakiutl child dies, the father's emotional experience is a peculiar combination of grief and shame,—grief at the loss of his child, and shame because he has been 'insulted' by the universe, and because his prestige and security have been threatened. It may be that the Kwakiutl father never feels grief without its accompaniment or overtone of shame. . . ." (*Ibid.*, p. 304.)

Emotional states are expressed in culturally patterned ways. This fact Otto Klineberg documented for Chinese culture in a study of emotional expressions as they are described, or prescribed, in literary works. Klineberg reports that "the most extreme degree of patterning of emotional expression is found on the Chinese stage. . . ." A "Treatise on Acting" explains that

> To "draw one leg up and stand on one foot" means surprise. To "raise one hand as high as the face and fan the face with the sleeve" means anger, as does also to "blow the beard to make it fly up." Joy or satisfaction is represented by stretching "the left arm flatly to the left and the right arm to the right." (Klineberg, 1938, p. 518.)

From Chinese novels Klineberg draws further illustrations. "They stretched out their tongues" tells the enculturated reader that "they" were surprised. "He made his two eyes round and stared . . ." means that "he" was angry. "He scratched his ears and cheeks" means happiness, and "he clapped his hands" conveys the fact that "he" was worried or disappointed. Klineberg reminds us that

> Our own literature is of course also rich in these unlabeled expressions. We read, "His jaw dropped"; "He gnashed his teeth"; "His lip curled"; "His eyes almost popped out of his head"; "He clenched his fists"; etc. . . . (Ibid., p. 519.)

Anthropologists have observed that certain emotions, both overtly apparent and actually felt, occur more frequently and in greater intensity among certain peoples than among others. The Assiniboine, for example, were known to early explorers as "The Weepers" because they wept profusely when meeting relatives after considerable absence or even when greeting strangers. Their tears expressed regret that meeting had been so long delayed.

In view of the cross-cultural data we must accept, as Hallowell urges, two very important conclusions:

1. The individual "mind" which learns and creates is not an antecedent and ready-made thing but a *formation*—a *product*. It is a cause only after it has been produced. In infancy and childhood the organization of the native activities into intelligence is heavily dependent upon the presence of others, upon sharing in joint activities, and upon language. The sort of mind capable of develop-

ment through the operation of native endowment in a nonsocial environment is of the moron order, and is practically if not theoretically negligible.

There are extensive data which support this view. Isolated children, and children cut off from communication by sensory defects, are limited to the "moron order." There can be no doubt that full and complete mental maturation is as inseparable from social processes as bodily maturation is from physiological processes.

2. The individual's psyche is no more an antecedent and ready-made thing than is his mind. The psyche too is a formation and a product, and a cause only after it has been produced. It is merely a psychological bias which insists that human emotions must be understood wholly in terms of psychological factors. The psychological explanations in fact are but partial explanations. This has become evident in the errors and naïvetés of psychologies lacking in cultural perspectives.

The influence of culture is evident not only in comparisons between cultures but also in comparison of a given society's rural and urban dwellers. A recent study in Skopje, a city of about 170,000, in Yugoslavia, documents "the transformation from the 'rural personality' to the 'urban personality,' from the family-centered personality to the personality oriented to a wide variety of patterns of behavior and goals in life." (Phillips, 1965, p. 1.) The rural-to-urban shift is, of course, a societal as much as (perhaps more than) a cultural change, but both are importantly involved. Bernard Phillips set out to test "the hypothesis that degree of exposure to heterogeneous experiences is a factor in the development of the urban personality. . . ." (*Ibid.*, p. 5.) He interviewed rural-to-urban migrants in considerable numbers. From their responses he concludes that experience in the urban setting and way of life usually means "improvements in income, housing, general standard of living, opportunities for employment, and formal education for children." But there are other, less immediately evident, but equally important new experiences. The urban way of life

represents a whole new world of people, ideas, activities, and the arts. It provides the kinds of occupational opportunities which are far more challenging than former ones. It provides the type of atmosphere which stimulates the individual to grow intellectually and learn about the new way of life. It generally leads to more leisure so that the individual can take advantage of these things. It provides "vividness" [here Phillips quotes his informants], "heterogeneity," a "lively" atmosphere, a "positive" way of living, "better possibilities for everything," "more experiences in life," and "new attitudes toward life." (*Ibid.*, p. 9.)

Phillips concludes that "exposure to heterogeneous experiences leads to improved knowledge of the self and the environment, which leads to satisfaction as a result of more effective behavior, which leads to a higher level of aspiration and increased value commitment, which leads to increased autonomy. . . ." (*Ibid.*, p. 15.)

This interesting study nicely illustrates the "pull" of culture, i.e., the extent to which culture is, or may be, a major source from which the individual draws both stimulus and material for the enhancement and expansion of the self. The nearly universal lure of cities and of "modernization" must be a result of widespread recognition of self-enhancing possibilities. Note that Phillips' informants were fully aware and most appreciative of the new dimensions their lives had assumed in the urban setting. This was true of most, but not of all, the migrants, however. Some do not "adjust" to the new environment; they suffer from anomie because the "rules" of the urban world are not and do not become their own.

CULTURAL PRESS AND PULL: SOME BASIC PROPOSITIONS

Individuals reared in Western culture (American especially) are inclined to regard the press of culture as onerous, limiting, and frustrating. And so it often is. But human life is social life, and social life without restrictions, with all their frustrations, is impossible. Moreover, social order is essential to the survival as well as the satisfaction and security of the individual.

To the extent that culture patterns the social order and its preservation, culture is a benign force (assuming, of course, that what contributes to the survival of mankind is "good"). This conclusion is inescapable when one takes the large view, over time and space. It is equally inevitable that the individual, concerned with his own little world and its pressures, will be more aware of the limiting and frustrating effects of the social order and its sustaining rules and agencies.

But he cannot live in any comfort without them, nor can the social order survive without the tacit general support of a majority of its constituent individuals. The individual may fall into the directionlessness and despair of anomie, and the society into anarchy and decline, unless the one can rely on the strength of social order and the other on the consent of those ordered.

Cultures vary widely in the extent to which (1) their patterns provide for individual security and the survival of the society, (2) press is exerted explicitly and formally, (3) the patterns of the culture are fully and tightly linked, (4) the content of those patterns is urgently prescriptive and proscriptive. There is wide variation too with respect to the emotional states and the behavior which are culturally valued. Kaingáng, Pawnee, traditional Chinese, Kamba, Balinese, and New Guinean cultures illustrate some of the known extremes with respect to these several variables.

The two faces of culture—its press and its pull—are evident when one considers (with Goldenweiser) that pattern is at once "limit and model." Among the patterns of a culture some are primarily restrictive, others function primarily as stimulus and as invitation, some have both implications. Complex cultures offer an absolutely and relatively large body of pattern possibilities, but the increment in "pattern as model" must be, on the whole, much greater than the increment in "pattern as limit." It is therefore not surprising that "urban personality" has been shown to be richer and more complex than rural. Nor is it surprising that people the world around sense the possibilities inherent in the more complex contexts (in cities and in "modernized" countries) and move toward realizing those possibilities.

Mind and psyche are both formation and cause, in that order. The mind and psyche of the individual develop in society and through culture. They are sustained, impelled, and drawn into "becoming."

EXCERPT NO. 10*

Oliver suggests that the flexibility so striking to him and to other observers of Kamba culture may be less unusual than is generally believed. Nevertheless Kamba does present an instructive example of extreme flexibility, which in this instance means nonspecificity in the patterning, vague and open-ended rules, and a general quality of "diffuseness," all related to individualism. There are exceptions, however; certain aspects of the culture—attitudes toward the clan and toward wealth, for example—are firmly and clearly patterned. Oliver offers a plausible explanation: both the clan and wealth provide islands of security in the sea of Kamba uncertainties. In all cultures, however relatively flexible, it would seem that there must be (as there is in Kamba) "a core of shared understandings and explicit techniques" which prevent social anarchy and disintegration.

It seems reasonable and consistent with general anthropological theory to suggest that cultures may differ significantly with respect to tightness of organization, flexibility, and capacity and readiness for change. It is doubtless true that there are many cultures which are highly structured, relatively rigid, and which call forth strong feelings of allegiance from those who participate in them. It is possible that traditional ethnographic reporting, in which a presumably "typical" segment of a culture is taken as representative and serves as a model for description, with other ways of doing things being relegated to the status of deviations from a supposed norm, has tended to create an impression that cultural systems are more tightly structured than in fact they are. It is also possible that some selection has been made, in terms of tribes chosen for intensive fieldwork and in terms of the usual examples cited in textbooks, in favor of the more dramatic cultures which exhibit a firm kind of unity of the Benedictian sort; this makes for pointed discussion and probably also contributes to a sense of artistic well-being on the part

* From Symmes C. Oliver, "Individuality, Freedom of Choice, and Cultural Flexibility of the Kamba," *American Anthropologist*, Vol. 67, No. 2 (April, 1965), pp. 421–28. (Part of the Culture and Ecology in East Africa Project sponsored by the University of California, Los Angeles, and supported by the National Science Foundation, G-11713, and the National Institute of Mental Health, MH-04097.)

of the ethnographer. Unfortunately, it also has the unintentional effect of leaving the impression that all cultures are organized in this manner.

It is obvious that no culture can be so rigid that alternatives within the system do not exist, and no culture can be so fluid that there is no structure at all. It is further clear that there must be a degree of cultural commitment among all peoples; otherwise the cultural tradition could not continue to operate. I am not suggesting a dichotomy between cultures on an all-or-none basis. Rather, I am suggesting that along the continuum of the culturally possible, some cultures appear to fit with some precision at either end of the continuum, with many others clearly occupying a middle ground. If there are cultures that are tightly organized and relatively resistant to change, there are also cultures which are very loosely structured and susceptible to change. It may be that we have not given sufficient recognition to the latter type. . . .

There seems to be what is almost a conscious avoidance of *specificity* in many of the principles of Kamba culture. The rules are often vague and open-ended. They tend to be quite general, and a person is expected to make his own interpretation of them. The "right thing" to do *should* emerge from argument and discussion, and the argument, though loosely structured, is by no means predetermined. In part, this feature accounts for the diffuseness of much of the Kamba culture.

It must be emphasized that not all of Kamba culture can be so characterized. There are areas of general agreement in the Kamba lifeway, and many situations in which all persons agree on the proper course of well-defined social action. Attitudes toward the clan constitute one such cluster of consistencies, and attitudes toward wealth form another. All Kamba agree on the basic importance of the clan, and all give the same reason for its importance: the clan will help a man if he gets into serious trouble. The clan clearly provides a kind of security in a very fluid system, and here the rules are spelled out with precision. Similarly, virtually all Kamba regard wealth—in land or cattle or both—as a major goal in life. It seems reasonable to suggest that the larger question of security comes into play here as well. In a culture where every man is on his own in many situations, and a poor man is regarded as a foolish person unworthy of help, personal wealth is an understandable concern. There are other similar instances. There is a core of shared understandings and explicit techniques which operates to save the Kamba culture from anarchy and disintegration.

In summation, I have attempted to show that the Kamba culture can be characterized as a system which illustrates a loose structural orientation, a shallow cultural commitment, and a relatively high degree of adaptability. I have suggested that the emphasis on individualism in Kamba culture fits well in this complex, and that other more structured aspects of the culture are probably related to it as well. To those who fall into the habit of thinking of a culture as a kind of strait-jacket, the Kamba are an instructive lesson. The cloak of the Kamba culture does in fact hang together with the appropriate functional stitching, but it is a voluminous and loose-fitting garment indeed.

Such a culture has both advantages, in terms of ready flexibility, and disadvantages, in terms of the real danger that the many divergent points of view may serve to inhibit effective social action. In a broader sense, the Kamba culture, representing one point on a continuum of organizational possibilities, suggests that we take more cognizance of the significance of the many cultures of the world which are not tightly structured, change resistant, and dramatically oriented. It can be argued that the very essence of the phenomenon of culture involves flexibility and the capacity to adapt readily to changing conditions. If this is true, then it follows that cultures analogous to that of the Kamba must be more widespread than we have perhaps assumed. . . .

EXCERPT NO. 11 *

Traditional Chinese society was as tightly organized as Kamba is loosely organized, and as family-centered as Kamba is individualistic. Reischauer and

---

* From E. O. Reischauer and J. K. Fairbank, *East Asia: The Great Tradition* (Boston: Houghton Mifflin Co., 1960), pp. 28–29.

Fairbank comment on the family as the keystone of the economic, political, religious, educational, recreational, and ethical systems of traditional China. The individual saw himself as but a fragment of a kinship unit extending five generations into the past and as many into the future. Within this unit interpersonal relations were both "hierarchic and authoritarian," in accord with cultural patterns of a highly specific sort.

The individual in this society was uncompromisingly subordinated. In it he was constrained to seek, and apparently he quite often found, both security and satisfaction. If he lived long enough, fathered children who survived, and won the esteem of his fellows he could at least exercise personal influence and authority in his old age. For women there was little chance for personal autonomy at any point in the life span before old age.

The Family Pattern

Since ancient times the family, rather than the individual, state or church, has formed the most significant unit in Chinese society. For each individual, the family was the chief source of economic sustenance, security, education, social contact and recreation. Through ancestor worship, it was even his religious focus. The family was also the foundation for political organization. Through the system of mutual responsibility (the so-called *pao-chia* system), individuals were responsible for each other's actions within each household, and families were responsible for one another within a community, much as in Communist China today.

Of the five famous Confucian relationships—between ruler and subject, father and son, husband and wife, elder brother and younger brother, and friend and friend—it is noteworthy that three were determined by kinship. As we shall see, the Confucian virtue of "love" (*jen*) was equivalent to "graded love"—that is, love for others according to one's relationship to them. China's whole ethical system thus tended to be family-centered and particularistic, not universalistic and oriented toward God or the state, as in the West.

The Chinese kinship group was extensive in scope and was conceived as reaching out in each direction to the fifth generation. This meant that an individual's ancestors back to his great-great-grandparents, his descendants down to his great-great-grandchildren, and his contemporaries to his third cousins (descendants of his great-

great-grandparents) were all acknowledged members of his family nexus.

The ideal was to have all the living generations reside in one great household, divided among the various courtyards of a big compound. Actually this was seldom achieved except by the rich. Because of economic necessity and the smallness of farms, most Chinese households seem to have averaged around five persons and were usually limited to close relatives: parents, their unmarried children, their eldest son and his wife, and the latter's children. The typical household was in fact a stem family of a type familiar in the West, rather than the ideal Chinese extended family.

By its very nature the family system was both hierarchic and authoritarian. The status of each person depended on his position by birth or marriage in the family. The gradations of kinship were carefully spelled out. A complex terminology differentiated between paternal and maternal uncles, aunts, cousins, and in-laws, and expressed fine distinctions in senority. In general, authority went by generation and within each generation by sex and by age. Age was respected as a thing worthy in itself and as a source of wisdom. The patriarchal father was the center of authority. He could be autocratic and on occasion even tyrannical. At least in theory he controlled the family property and production of goods. He arranged his children's and grandchildren's marriages. An insubordinate child might be severely punished. In times of stress, parents might even sell their children.

The Subordination of the Individual

Because of the subordination of the individual to the family, the highest virtues and greatest social satisfactions naturally attached to family life. Filial piety was the most admired of virtues. The greatest satisfaction could be derived from the worship of the ancestors and from the birth of a son or grandson to carry on the family line. Few experiences can have been more satisfying than that of the old man whose successful career as head of an extended family was crowned by the affection of his many descendants and the esteem of the community.

The arrangement of marriages, for which a good deal can no doubt be said when wise matchmakers were used, symbolized more clearly than anything else the individual's subordination to his family. Marriage was in fact more of a union of families than of individuals, and family considerations predominated. A family might find it most economical to buy a child bride and rear her within the family for eventual marriage to a son. Such a girl might even be brought into the family before her prospective husband was born, as a "daughter-in-law in anticipation." A rich family might even acquire a bride who would "marry the spirit" of a dead husband.

Women in general were subordinate to men. Traditionally they obeyed their fathers in youth, their husbands in middle life, and their sons in old age. Relationship through the male line took precedence over kinship through the female line. Only sons could carry on the family name and line. As a consequence, baby girls were sacrificed in times of famine, and boys were preserved. Women were expected to be faithful to their husbands and not to remarry if widowed; men on the contrary could take secondary wives and concubines into the household. Except for a dowry, women had no property rights and on marriage entered their husband's families as humble newcomers, often treated little better than servants. Only with age and after she had become a mother-in-law because of her son's marriage did a woman typically becoming a dominating or autocratic figure.

The traditional family pattern seems to have made the individual even more inclined to seek security through conformity than was the case in the less family-bound society of the West.

ADAPTATION NO. 8*

Bernard's discussion of values clarifies their function as cultural pressures toward conforming and "collective" behavior, and emphasizes the ideal pattern ("explicit") vs. behavioral pattern ("implicit") levels of values.

---

* From Jessie Bernard, *American Community Behavior* (New York: Holt, Rinehart and Winston, Inc., 1962), pp. 10–15. Copyright 1949, © 1962 (revised) by Holt, Rinehart and Winston, Inc.

The values most fundamental and pervasive in a culture or subculture are likely to be learned early and to be reinforced throughout the individual's lifetime. They are primary among Allport's forces of "tribalization." They are primary also, as we have noted before, as types of patterns essential to intrasocietal communication and to social order.

In the matter of social order Bernard makes an important point upon which we have touched, but it deserves to be underscored. She notes that conformity to rules and expectations does not necessarily imply coercion; rather, individuals may conform "because they really share the collective values which coordinate group or community behavior." However, coercive power does reside in "collective values," and the individual whose values do not coincide with those of his society (or immediate community) will be under pressure to conform or accept the predictable (patterned) consequences.

Bernard, as a sociologist, takes precisely the point of view of this book when she emphasizes her interest in "values as an explanatory concept." We too are interested in the content and direction conveyed to the individual through his culture, rather than in the intra-person psychological mechanisms through which he is enabled to act.

THE COLLECTIVE VALUE DIMENSION OF COMMUNITY

Values are culturally standardized preference-rejection scales.

Collective values are more than the sum, even the weighted sum, of individual values. Like territorially defined communities or like language—which they resemble in many ways—values seem to have an existence of their own, quite independent of the specific individuals who share them. They have spatial distributions, just as physical phenomena do. Slavery or ethnic values or nationalism, for example, may have clear-cut boundaries. Collective values have life-histories also; they arise, spread, compete, conflict, change and die out, almost as though they were entities in themselves.

People seem to "inhabit" collective values, as they inhabit spatial areas. They may even leave the physical area characterized by certain collective values, as we shall show presently, and still "inhabit" the collective values. Or, figuratively, the boundaries of the collective values stretch to retain them as they move.

Collective values are taken for granted; they are trite, soporific. They may be explicit or implicit. If they are explicit they may be deduced from a study of professed creeds, ideals, and standards, often stated in official documents. Ideals differ from creeds primarily in that they are stated as goals rather than as *faits accomplis*. (Creeds and ideals are sometimes labeled myths; this does not mean that they are not real. They are as real as anything can be. But they are impervious to objective evidence. People who hold them do so quite independently of what they observe about them.) Sometimes values become embodied in standards, which may be defined as ideals stated quantitatively or formulated in scientific terms. Now instead of a belief in a high standard of living, we have standards of nutrition, housing, sanitation; instead of a belief in equal opportunity, we have standards of education. We have standards for working conditions, health care, and business practices. Sometimes we embody these standards in laws. Sometimes they remain outside of the law, but firmly embedded in community customs. Some are national in scope, others are purely local. In either case standards differ from myths in that they can be dealt with operationally. We can determine whether or not we conform to standards.

Implicit values do not appear in public documents or statements. They may never even be put into words; they are implied in behavior. They are operative nevertheless. They can be delineated only by studying the actual behavior of people. What are their goals as revealed in what they do? What do they reward? Competition is one way a community registers its values. The way funds are allocated to competing demands in a tax budget reveals a community's values, as, indeed, the budget of organizations and individuals reveals theirs. Values are revealed in the choices communities make among competing alternatives: for example, closed schools rather than desegregated schools; inadequate schools rather than indebtedness by bonds; lynchings rather than court trials; the family system rather than equality of opportunity.

Explicit and implicit values do not necessarily coincide. They may, in fact, be quite different. But the fact that there is often a wide gap between explicit and implicit values does not mean that explicit values may not exert a compelling influence. Sometimes whatever individuals may feel when a time comes that requires them to stand up and be counted they find they cannot renege on the ideal.

Each individual who shares a collective value acts on the assumption that others will act in accordance with the collective value. Behavior is based on such shared expectations that others will feel, think, and behave in certain ways. People who have shared collective values in this sense build their lives on the premise that they can depend on others to judge people and events according to collective values, whether they approve of these values or not. From this fact flows the ability of collective values to coordinate behavior.

So smooth is such coordination on the basis of collective values that it is often difficult to distinguish behavior resulting from it from organized conspiracy. The organization which goes under the name of "Mafia," for example, depends on such collective values to a large extent; it does not therefore need much formal organization in order to act in a concerted way. The behavior of its members is coordinated by their collective values. It is a case of "everybody" knowing what "everybody" is going to do in a pinch and acting accordingly. The so-called "clannish" behavior of ethnic groups illustrates the same thing. Much of the criticism directed against conformity implies that individuals are being coerced into certain actions; in fact, they may be acting as they do because they really share the collective values which coordinate group or community behavior. For ordinarily collective and individual values do coincide. People accept the values of their community without even thinking about them.

But sometimes they do not. And nothing illustrates better the nature of collective values than these negative cases. Such cases illuminate the power of collective values to coerce individuals.

A southern girl, for example, describes her experience at a party in a northern city at which Negroes were present:

I found it not at all difficult to accept them socially much to my surprise. In that atmosphere it seemed very natural. I talked to them and felt no discomfort at all. Then a girl I had known at [a Southern] college showed up. Everything changed the minute I saw her. Somehow or other we infected one another with prejudice. We became self-conscious about the Negroes and couldn't talk to them as social equals again.

Collective values, then, may be coercive, often even overriding individual values in the sense of making it costly to defy them. People do things they would prefer not to do and would not do in another setting. Actually, however, the likelihood is that collective values are accepted by the individuals whose behavior is shaped by them, that they are approved of as well as consented to.

VALUES AS AN EXPLANATORY CONCEPT

Values help explain behavior. Psychological concepts like motivation, drive, and tension tells us what the mechanisms are that activate individuals. But they do not tell us the direction this activity will take (form-content distinction). The sociologist takes it for granted that the individual has certain psychological equipment, that is, he can be motivated, he will be active. What the sociologist is interested in, however, is the organization and channeling of this motivation. One could study inherited reflexes or other individual mechanisms of motivation and learning forever and never understand asceticism, martyrdom, or other valued forms of behavior.

VALUES IN AMERICAN COMMUNITY LIFE

Over a period of 150 years several thousand foreign commentators have attempted to distill the essence of American values. Scores of social scientists spend their lives researching and interpreting them, and community leaders often try their hand at formulating them also. The results do not always agree, although, as one foreign observer noted, despite the heterogeneity of values of different ethnic and racial, occupational and class groups in our society, there is "a strong unity . . . and a basic homogeneity and stability in its valuations." The seeming chaos of American life fell into order for him when he viewed it in the light of a common creed.

Americans of all national origins, classes, regions, creeds, and colors have something in common: a social *ethos*, a political creed. It is difficult to avoid the judgment that this "American Creed" is the cement in the structure of this great and disparate nation. . . . There is no doubt that these ideals . . . of the essential dignity of the individual human being, of the fundamental equality of all men, and of certain inalienable rights to freedom, justice, and a fair opportunity . . . are active realities. . . .

Unless one has actually scrutinized the literature on American society it is difficult to realize the preoccupation with the conditions of freedom and equality which it reveals.

CHAPTER 8

The Uniqueness and Thrust
of the Individual

The individual utilizes the milieu's elements in order to transcend them.

Clausse (paraphrased)

There are levels of individuality ranging between universal and idiosyncratic (a matter discussed in Chapter 3). It is the universal component in each of us to which reference is made in the statement: "each man is in certain respects like *every* other man." But Kluckhohn and Mowrer (1944) added, referring to the intermediate levels of individuality: "each man is in certain respects like *some* other men." And finally, identifying the idiosyncratic level: "each man is in certain respects like *no* other man."

Individual idiosyncrasy, like male-female differences in physical strength, is a fact of human life. Folk societies, though relatively homogeneous, show that the individual is never completely submerged. In every society individuals vary in temperament, aptitudes, and intelligence. A few can be counted upon to thrust themselves vigorously, or even violently, into unconventional roles, to disturb the patterned rounds of life, to innovate or even desecrate. Most individuals at least occasionally toy with such impulses; some act on them now and then, a few distinguish themselves by the frequency or the extremity of their unpatterned thrusts.

That we are unique, each of us, is inevitable. Even identical twins, whose genetic endowments are the same, begin to lead their separate lives, hence to have somewhat different experiences, at birth (and in a sense, before birth). Earlier in this book we have touched upon the logic of uniqueness and upon some of its implications (e.g., with respect to innovation).

HUMAN RESTLESSNESS AND CULTURAL CHANGE

Culture is cumulative; most of it is the result of very small increments over many generations of nameless individuals. A culture seems almost to have a life of its own because individuals come and go, yet the culture goes on, seldom perceptibly modified by the lifetime of a given individual.

Yet a culture constantly changes, and perhaps nothing else about it is truly constant. It changes, and not solely in response to environmental changes or outside influences. There is, more importantly, the cumulative effect of many individuals each restlessly testing, revising, re-combining cultural elements, and of the rare few who do so with significant and lasting effect.

Why does the individual so often tinker with the received culture? Why does he incline to rattle and worry what he often perceives as the bars of a cultural cage?

One fundamental reason seems to be a built-in quality of the animal—its restlessness. Man is restless in the presence of the known and the unknown, he is restless when circumscribed by boundaries and he thrashes about trying to locate them when he is not. Given stability and security he seeks variety and the spice of hazards; if his world is in flux he cries for certainties and surcease from the anxieties that beset him among uncertainties.

Yet none of this could happen if the creature were not so generously endowed with the capacity for thought, for awareness and reflection. It may be a mixed blessing, this capacity, but it is also a marvel and the source of all that we call culture. Man is often lazy, apathetic, inert. Under the goad of survival, he may rise to tremendous exertions. But sometimes his exertions are great when there is no such generator at work; nothing drives him but his insatiable curiosity, his avidity for something newly created, created preferably by himself. He endlessly improvises and elaborates. To do so is in the nature of man, and deeply rooted in his biological heritage. As Linton said:

> The bulk of all cultures consists of what are, from the practical point of view, embroideries upon the fabric of existence. . . .
> This tendency toward unnecessary and in some cases even injurious elaboration of culture is one of the most significant phenomena of human life. It proves that the development of culture has become an end in itself. Man may be a rational being, but he certainly is not a utilitarian one. The constant revision and expansion of his social heredity is a result of some inner drive, not of outer necessity.
> It seems that man enjoys playing with both his mind and his muscles. The skilled craftsman is not content with endless repetitions. He takes delight in setting and solving for himself new problems of creation. The thinker derives pleasure from speculating about all sorts of things which are of no practical importance. . . . It seems probable that the human capacity for being bored, rather than man's social or natural needs, lies at the root of man's cultural advance. (Linton, 1936, p. 90.)

All this is true in the long and large view of man and his history. But that history shows also, for given cultures, periods of quiescence, of slumberous unchange and compulsive repetition, some of them centuries long. Like the infant hypnotically entranced with reproducing a sound or a gesture again and again, a whole society may perseverate for generations. The traditionalism of the folk culture is of this order.

INDIVIDUALITY IN FOLK SOCIETIES

Anthropologists long have been aware that individuals differ from one another in folk as they do in more sophisticated societies. In an essay published in 1936 Goldenweiser wrote:

> Anthropologists are no longer surprised when new evidence is brought forth of the existence of full-fledged individuality among primitives. In the heydey of folk theory it was glibly assumed that the primitive individual was literally submerged, that no room was left for personality or self-expression in a society ridden by tradition, dominated by established habits and dogmas, shot through with inflexible patterns.

No one any longer believes this. We know now that the very uniformity of primitive patterns should not be taken literally. After all, variation is not completely spirited away; in art, craft, storytelling, dancing, social behavior, there is difference between performance and performance, difference in skill, in details of form, in facility of execution. So also in religion, as Radin and others have pointed out, some lead, others follow, some originate, others imitate, some throw themselves body and soul into supernatural participation, others offer little more than lip service to the divine. Again, the prevalence of hard and fast matrimonial regulations does not preclude occasional divagations, including elopements with a "wrong" mate, or even, in some few instances, suicides over romantic frustrations.

We learn from Malinowski that the Melanesian standards of beauty differ materially from our own, but also that, within these culturally conditioned limits, individual taste will have its sway. So also with crime; it may remain true that among primitives practice agrees with legal or customary regulation a little more closely than it does with us, but this does not preclude breaches of customs and taboos, secular or sacred. In brief, cultural uniformity as a feature of primitiveness must be accepted in a relative, not an absolute, sense. . . . Anthropological field records agree in representing primitives as leading a lusty, animated, exciting existence. (Goldenweiser, 1936, p. 99.)

Goldenweiser went on to discuss in some detail the varying possibilities, and even necessities, for individuality in the folk society (see Excerpt No. 12). And he added an interesting comment; i.e., the individual's behavior is always, for him, a "personal experience." "Whether [it is] wholly conventional, or truly original, or a bit of each, . . . [it] *is one's own*"; no one else lives it or can experience what goes on inside one's own skin. In this sense all of the behavior of each individual is unique.

Statements about culture and its patterns are generalizations; they are abstractions from the infinity of unique experiences in a given society over time. Anthropologists, though they are aware of this fact, often seem not to be, because they report primarily in terms of patterns. It is through life histories that one is able best to glimpse what life is like as the individual lives it in a given context. Margaret Lantis makes a pointedly relevant comment in her collection of Nunivak Eskimo biographies and genealogies. She says:

The old culture appears less heroic when one sees it in actual cases rather than in generalization. The boy's first seal catch might not be harpooned out among the ice floes but might easily be a seal pup caught on shore. The young hunter required to fast during the Bladder Festival recalls this not as a spiritual experience but as an occasion when he had a headache and felt bad. . . . (Lantis, 1960, p. 170.)

INDIVIDUALITY IN CONFORMITY

Man shows remarkable ingenuity in finding ways to express individuality, even within conformity. Goldenweiser commented upon a peculiar and striking form sometimes taken by this phenomenon: "involution." Where cultural pressures set sharp limits to creative excursions, the creative urge may find expression in re-combinations of conventional elements. A very few "unit elements" may be subjected to the most elaborate and imaginative interworkings, so that the effect is of something "different" though what has in fact been created is not new elements but new relations between elements.

Involution occurs especially in the arts and in rituals. It is limited neither to folkish cultures nor to cultures of what might be called "high press." The Bach fugue, for example, is an involutional form. The creation of such a form may represent, as it presumably does in the case of Bach, nothing more than the preferences and skills of the individual artist. Or it may represent the artist's ingenuity in finding a way to create novelty while remaining within culturally prescribed forms.

INDIVIDUALITY IN FLEXIBLE, PERMISSIVE, AND SUPPORTIVE CONTEXTS

The prescribed forms within which involution develops are of the sharp and specific sorts. But cultural patterning may be, as we have noted (and seen illustrated in Kamba culture), remarkably flexible and diffuse. It may also be permissive and inviting toward idiosyncrasy. In any of these cases the patterning is conducive to it. Even religion, an aspect of culture not notable for permissiveness, may be conducive to individuality. Among the major faiths

Buddhism is notable in this respect. Writing on "Buddhism and the Burmese," Burling comments:

> With no gods, there is no one toward whom prayers can be directed, and although Buddhists chant and bow low before statues of the Buddha, these are, in principle not prayers, but aids to contemplation and insight. Of course, the chants and verbal formulae that humble men recite may seem to differ little, even to the worshippers, from mechanically repeated Christian prayers, but to the truly thoughtful worshipper the difference is a profound one. With no gods and no prayer, but simply a theory of the universe and an explanation for man's sorry state, each man becomes responsible for his own salvation. Every man can meditate by himself; . . . (Burling, 1965, p. 82.)

It is probably in values and the theme-ethos-world view aspects of cultures that individuality is most supported and encouraged (or the reverse). Certain cultures are famed, and with good reason, for the independence of spirit shown by the bearers of that culture. The French are a notable example. Laurence Wylie, writing of changes in a village in southern France during the decade 1951 to 1961, says:

> Probably the element of life in Peyrane that will change last is the most basic element in French civilization—the sense of the dignity of the individual that impels a man to humanize the world about him and that permits him to participate in a sophisticated culture but still maintain a ferociously independent personality. (Wylie, 1964, p. 370.)

The "ferociously independent personality" turns up in other societies too, whether with support of the culture or in defiance of it. Its appearance in the United States is not surprising, in spite of the prevalence of conformity as a behavioral pattern. On the ideal pattern level Americans love individuality and like to see it strongly, if symbolically, expressed. Indeed they love it so much that they are happy to pay well to see it exhibited in commercialized, professionalized competitions (e.g., boxing, auto racing). They are heartened to see one strong man dare another, and even more to see him take on "the establishment." The case of Ralph Nader v. the automobile industry (in 1965 and 1966) is a handy example. The American response to Nader's challenge (car manufacturers could and should build safer cars; they are morally responsible for much of the highway carnage) has been perceptively analyzed by Henry Brandon writing in *Saturday Review*. Mr. Brandon says:

> To anyone who has lost faith in the power of the individual and his ability to assert himself in the world of industrial giants, the story of Ralph Nader is a reassuring one. For two years now he has been a one-man protest movement in defense of the civil rights of the automobile user. He has helped to force such shining symbols of American industrial success as General Motors and Ford to admit what they have never admitted before; that they share a greater responsibility for preventing death on the road and for bearing the burden of proof—until now borne by the consumer—that a car is unsafe.
>
> Part of his success Mr. Nader attributes to the fact that Americans are "starving for acts of the individual in a conflict situation outside the sports arena." The public response to his crusade attests to that. (Brandon, 1966, p. 9.)

WILLFUL, AGGRESSIVE, THRUSTFUL INDIVIDUALS: VARIABLE INCIDENCE AND RESPONSES TO THEM

The fact that Americans are "starving for acts of the individual in a conflict situation . . ." reflects more than their culture. There is, we believe, a universal factor involved. We have noted before (Chapter 1) man's willfulness, as well as his intelligence, and a wide range of variation between individuals in both respects. The man who is both highly willful and highly intelligent has a great advantage over his fellows, a head start in whatever competitions may be important in his society. Those of his fellows who are close to him, close in the sense of social space, that is, and so placed as to be his actual or potential rivals, may take no joy in his triumphs. But those to whom he is no personal threat, and to whom he is remote and the more heroic for it, will likely see him as a model. Identifying with him, they can take very personal pleasure in his triumphs.

The extent to which individuals will strive aggressively for competitive advantage is highly variable as between societies and between individuals in a given society. It is variable too as between aspects of a given sociocultural system. But such striving is in any case a matter of individualism, which may be culturally (or sub-culturally) patterned, or idiosyncratic, or both. The "naturally aggressive" individual, he who seems to have been so from infancy, probably appears at least occasionally in all societies. Norbeck found one such in the Japanese fishing village of Takashima, a sociocultural setting distinctly not conducive to such types. (Norbeck, 1954.) But David Ausubel reports that New Zealanders are typically bland and unstriving though the context in which they operate is modern and urban-industrial, hence conducive (or generally thought to be) to striving-aggressive types.

The New Zealand situation also illustrates how patterning toward striving-aggressive behavior varies between aspects of a given sociocultural system. Ausubel says:

> . . . The New Zealander's attitude towards work generates less drive and eagerness to get ahead and advance in his job than is typical of Americans. . . . [The New Zealander is] less disposed to continue striving in the face of adversity and to practice self-denial for the sake of attaining long-term occupational goals. . . . Self-denial, of course, is by no means foreign to the New Zealand character structure, but it manifests itself principally in areas unconnected with vocational matters. (Ausubel, 1965, p. 36.)[1]

Whatever the culture, strongly independent, striving, aggressive, or thrustful individuals do turn up more or less frequently. Idiosyncratic thrust of considerable strength and consistency appears in persons of three different types. There are: (1) those who are temperamentally unsuited for the cultures in which they find themselves; (2) sociopaths—those who are unsuited for satisfactory functioning in any context; and (3) the under-enculturated—those who have somehow grown up without acquiring the values characteristic of the "good citizen" in the given society.

Ruth Benedict (see Excerpt No. 13) deals with Type 1. She assumed, apparently, that there were no other types. It may be that inadequate enculturation, conducive to Type 3, is a commonplace in complex sociocultural contexts and rare in folk contexts. It may

---

[1] From *The Fern and the Tiki* by David P. Ausubel. Copyright © 1960 by David P. Ausubel. Holt, Rinehart and Winston, Inc., Publishers.

be too that the survival of the sociopath is more likely in the complex setting, where anonymity may save him from severe sanctions, and the vast range of alternatives may allow him to find a survival role. The three types are, however, different and distinguishable.

We are not concerned here with those highly exceptional cases which probably turn up in every society—the sociopaths. They are, presumably, constitutional cripples, i.e., individuals unfitted for social life by some genetic inadequacy. They fall outside the range of normalcy, hence outside the range of this discussion. The true sociopath may be sometimes nearly indistinguishable from the equally aberrant individual whose deviance is not so much constitutional as social-cultural. The grossly under-enculturated may closely approximate the sociopath. Madé, the young Balinese described by Belo (see Excerpt No. 14), may be a true sociopath, but we cannot be sure.

In structure and in content cultures vary with respect to opportunity for and tolerance of personal impulse. Folk or traditional cultures are, on the whole, low on the opportunity-tolerance scale. But there are three kinds of exceptions: (1) the unusually "flexible" culture; (2) the culture in which there is provision for periodic moratoria, times when the usual rules are suspended; and (3) the culture in which certain individual attributes—unusual strength of person or personality, for example—confer at least qualified license.

Documentation for an unusually flexible culture has been provided by Margaret Mead (1928), based on her observations of the people of Manu'a Archipelago in the Samoan Islands. "The Manu'an culture presents such a striking picture of flexibility, rapid slight changes, easy acceptance of innovation and deviation, that it would seem to give each gifted individual a particularly open field for the exercise of his peculiar talents" (Mead, 1928, p. 481).

Among these people social prestige is a prime preoccupation. One's status in the prestige system is identified by the titles he has achieved. "It is only as the holder of a title, the accession to which has been validated by large distributions of property," that the individual is "honoured and obeyed."

Selection for a title is based on two major considerations—personal qualifications of strength, charm, leadership, integrity; and the possession of special abilities: skill as a carpenter, orator, or fisherman. (*Ibid.*, p. 482.)

There are limitations on free access to achieved status, especially age and sex limitations. These Samoans are tolerant of slow personal development but highly intolerant of precocity; a boy must not talk "above his age." A woman, regardless of age, may not do or achieve like a man.

Nevertheless children are free to exercise personal choice in a number of ways. "The selection of a residence," for example is

very much in the children's hands. Any child over five or six is an economic asset; little truants are welcomed by any relative, and a ten-year-old may change his or her residence two or three times before settling down. This freedom of choice actually serves as a powerful deterrent of specific adult tyrannies, and the child is often content to remain in one household, serene in the reflection that he can always run away if he wishes.

The selection of tutors is also left to the young people themselves, with the exception of children of high chiefs. . . . Freedom is permitted in the matter of personal names. . . . Also, for all the young people, except the daughters of houses of rank, there is comparative freedom of choice of partners in sex-experience (though not in marriage). (*Ibid.*, pp. 486–87.)

There is in this flexible culture, which "looks so favourable to the display of individuality, . . . a powerful conservative force" (*ibid.*, p. 495). Innovations introduced by individuals are not copied by others, hence preserved to accumulate so that the culture evolves significantly over time.

Moratoria-providing cultures allow for impulse-release, sometimes on a mass scale. During a moratorium "individuals who feel the need of it may break almost all the rules of decorum." (Belo, 1935, p. 142.)

. . . Just as . . . joyous occasions [celebrations, religious festivals, dramatic presentations] punctuate the dreary round of everyday life, so do the occasions of wild frenzy break into it, affording the individual a necessary release. If it were not for these organized departures from the habitual tempo, it would not be possible for the individual to conform, at all other times, to the rigid order of behavior which is exacted from him. *(Ibid.,* p. 144.)

Eastern highlanders of New Guinea provide dramatic illustration of the extent to which strength and aggressiveness may open the way for impulse gratification with impunity. But under pressure from a sophisticate culture this source of immunity is being reduced. Berndt (1962) reports:

Traditionally, the rights and rules upheld and sanctioned by public opinion and sentiment . . . could be contravened on occasion according to the "strength" of the persons concerned. With the introduction of the informal court these rights and rules have become more tightly defined and more strictly enforced. . . . Nevertheless, the traditional theme of strength-through-aggression has not been seriously curtailed but only diverted into new channels. . . . (Berndt, 1962 p. 406.)

Individual self-assertiveness was, indeed, an ideal among these people. It was expressed especially in sorcery, fighting, and sex. Ingroup cohesion was low, as might be expected, and ingroup/outgroup relations marked by endlessly recurring violence. ". . . conflict has been institutionalized; . . . hereditary leadership is . . . almost negligible, and authority is highly personalized. *(Ibid.,* pp. 410 and 416.) Leadership is achieved, authority validated, in displays of aggression and strength.

Cultural patterning, as it affects the assertive or innovating individual, is itself affected by physical environment and subsistence patterns. Among nonindustrial peoples it is with pastoral nomadism that we are most likely to find both opportunity and tolerance for individual thrust (see Ekvall, Excerpt No. 15). Survival of the group demands, however, that there be limits and techniques for enforcing them.

Among the Tibetan nomads the "law of tradition or custom" is the "law of reprisal . . . characterized by retaliation in kind. . . ." (Ekvall, 1964, p. 1110.) The body of Tibetan law (before Chinese control in 1959) was an amalgam of this customary law with "canon" (Buddhistic) and "royal" (decrees of the ruler) law.

But it was the basic mobility—the power and pattern of movement —inherent in the concept and practice of nomadism which enabled each nomadic community to evade, with marked success, the imposition of royal law. . . . Mediation was the process by which antisocial behavior within a community was contained to prevent fragmentation of the community. . . . The difficulties of mediation between self-willed nomads, who held to their right of dissent, were many and great, but there were inherent pressures which operated to aid such mediation. . . . At some point . . . the interest of the group as a whole—the well being of all its members—would be weighed against personal and individual interest and intransigeance, and pressure would begin to build up to induce him to seek or accept mediation. (*Ibid.*, pp. 1112–13.)

That herders and farmers differ, the world around, has never been doubted by anthropologists. However, their impression has been verified in an African study (The Culture and Ecology in East Africa Project, as reported by Goldschmidt and others in the *American Anthropologist* of April, 1965).

Goldschmidt comments on the distinctive characteristics of pastoralists, e.g.: (1) their independence and self-reliance, induced by living in small isolated groups whose survival depends on the strength and sagacity of one or a few men; (2) their "high status mobility," which reflects the fact that "cattle are a volatile form of wealth"; these conditions are conducive to independent striving and to achieved leadership; (3) their militarism and aggressiveness, related to the facts that cattle are a form of wealth quite readily stolen, and that group territorial boundaries are difficult to define and preserve.

The personality attributes of the ideal pastoralist may be summarized as follows: a high degree of independence of action; a willingness to take chances; a readiness to act, and a capacity for action; self-containment and control, especially in the face of danger; bravery, fortitude, and the ability to withstand pain and hardship; arrogance, sexuality, and a realistic appraisal of the world (Goldschmidt, 1965, pp. 404–5.)

Among pastoralists "ritual life will tend toward greater emphasis upon rites of passage,

which focus on the individual and his status, rather than on rites of intensification, which reinforce group solidarity and, in so doing, tend to submerge the individual within the community. (*Ibid.*, p. 405.)

After careful comparison of farming and herding societies (four of each) in East Africa, Robert Edgerton concludes that "the more pastoral the economy the more that society will maximize and value independence of action for its male members." (Edgerton, 1965, p. 446.)

In Western sophisticate culture there may be a parallel to pastoralism. The celebrated "rugged individualism" associated with pioneering—pioneering both territorially and economically—rests on a set of conditions not unlike the conditions of pastoralism. Group smallness and isolation, volatile forms of wealth—in cash and other fluid assets, movable boundaries, high status mobility, achieved leadership, aggressiveness, militancy—all these were features of the "expanding frontier" phase in American society.

THRUSTFULNESS IN RELATION TO SUPPORTING AND BOUNDARY CONDITIONS

We may conclude, then, that individual thrustfulness varies with (1) personal factors—constitution and enculturation particularly; (2) with cultural factors—opportunity and tolerance particularly; (3) with physical environment and subsistence conditions—especially degrees of mobility, self-dependency, and status achievement opportunity. These are major among supporting and boundary conditions.

There is a further relevant consideration: to what extent is thrustfulness more likely in the complex urban-industrial context? At least two major aspects of this context are conducive: social individuation and cultural richness. Thrust is facilitated by the detachment of the individual from a close and confining social nexus. It is facilitated by richness of cultural resources, which provide manifold possibilities, and tend to stimulate innovation and improvisation.

Both the detachment and the richness factor are apparent in recent developments in Japan.

Vast suburban apartment houses (*danchi*) have mushroomed in that country since World War II, and they are extremely popular. The chronic housing shortage is but a part of the reason.

A large majority of families living in danchi are nuclear families simply because the smallness of units . . . does not permit the large extended family to live together in the same apartment. . . . [This provides] the couples with a good excuse for living away from the husbands' [sometimes the wives'] families. (Hoshino, 1964, p. 313.)

In traditional Japan, housing arrangements simply did not permit such segmentation of the family, and such privacy for a young couple and their children. Nor were segmentation and privacy valued—on the ideal pattern level, at any rate. The language has no equivalent for the English "privacy." But

. . . an awareness of and a need for privacy have increased in recent years as the result of postwar education which stresses individualism as a value, and in the absence of a proper translation, the English word "privacy" is borrowed increasingly by the Japanese mass media. (*Ibid.*, p. 314.)

However, some Japanese scholars (e.g., Shogo Koyano) believe that change in family patterns has been more a matter of structure than of attitudes and values. But child-rearing practices are clearly affected by *danchi* living; young mothers are relatively free from the advice and supervision of the older women in the family.

Dr. Spock and other modern sources of child rearing advice have begun to be followed by Japanese families. As in the United States, pediatricians offer advice, and magazines and books are available as sources of information. . . . The "scientific" sources are more frequently consulted in urban than in rural communities. (Koyano, 1964, p. 155.)

For young mothers, more than for fathers, physically detached living allows scope for individual decision and choice. Mass media, as well as the urban accessibility of specialists and experts, provides new richness of resources from which to choose. Today's individual mother, the *danchi* dweller especially, enjoys degrees of freedom far beyond those known to her own mother.

EXCERPT NO. 12*

Alexander Goldenweiser (1880–1940) belongs to "the classical period in anthropology, 1900–1920." (Mead and Bunzel, 1960). Ruth Bunzel says that he was "described by one of his contemporaries as 'the most philosophical of American anthropologists; . . . [he] was less interested in exploring new problems than in ordering systematically and coherently the vast body of ethnographic data.' " (Ibid., p. 508.)

Being more philosopher than fieldworker Goldenweiser bent his efforts toward extracting principles from the data, and they have stood the test of time. The principle of "involution," largely ignored for many years, has been rediscovered and is being re-applied by young scholars. Its applicability as an explanatory device may be much wider than yet has been appreciated.

Of even greater interest, for our purposes, is Goldenweiser's highly perceptive statement concerning the ownness of personal experience. Like Allport, Goldenweiser was sensitive to those private worlds inside which each of us lives and has experiences which are "one's own. . . . Envisaged as experiences, all situations are individual, and as such, unique, personal, historical. . . . Man, not being a robot, lives—as an individual."

Consider, first, this. The customary or prescribed routine does not weigh evenly over the whole expanse of the cultural scene. The sacred things and acts come first here; in this domain the past, habitual, prescribed, has full sway at the cost of the individual and variable. Next come the social things and acts, sanctified by the divine only vicariously, such as etiquette, socioeconomic relations, the cooperative aspects of industry. Here individual variation, though still limited, has freer play. Finally, we have the wide range of activities which, in their very nature, are individual, such as hunting, fishing, fighting, the technical aspects of craft and art, and certain specialized pursuits, matter of fact at least to a degree, such as medicine. It has been shown at another place that in these domains the relative objectivity of outlook forced upon the mind by the concreteness of experience and the strictly pragmatic nature of objectives, paves the way for dispassionate observation, accumulation of valid knowledge, and invention. Patently, the individual here is no longer a slave to the social. Rules, to be sure, there are

---

* From Alexander A. Goldenweiser, "Loose Ends of Theory . . . ," *Essays in Anthropology*, R. H. Lowie (ed.) (Berkeley: University of California Press, 1936), pp. 99–104.

in plenty here also, but here—in contrast to the socioreligious and the narrowly social realms—these rules cannot do more than set up a framework for experience and behavior within which ample opportunity is offered to think, act, and react in one's own way. But this is not all. In such matters as fighting, hunting, or craftmanship prescriptions can at best be only regulative. What is or can be prescribed is to act in such and such a way *if* and when so and so happens. But what will happen or when, exactly, can neither be prescribed nor foreseen nor controlled; it remains conjectural. Time, place, and event are immersed in the capricious flow of history. What is involved here is the difference between knowing how a pot is made and how to make a pot, this particular pot which has not dried quite sufficiently, bulges out so and so, must be a little larger than its predecessor which has proved a bit small, and should be fashioned with especial care to show the neighboring potter where he comes off; the difference between knowing how a lion is speared and how to spear a lion, this particular fellow, yonder not so far off, wounded but full of vim, a little too distant for a sure spear thrust but too near for taking a chance at a charge, the very lion, moreover, which carried off a fair-sized youngster from camp yesterday and devoured him. In all such situations—and their name is legion—the primitive is confronted with experience in its tridimensional capacity; or shall I say four-dimensional, including time? There is a thrill in such episodes, and a uniqueness, quite beyond the reach of customary regulations.

The final point carries us fully into the psychological domain. Personal experience is nonsubstitutive, noninterchangeable. It is *one's own*, and there the matter ends. What may be the content of such experience, whether wholly conventional, or truly original, or a bit of each, is an entirely different problem. *Whatever* the content it *is one's own*, and counts as such. However narrowly limited acts, thoughts, skills may be, however objectively similar as between one man and the next, to each one, as he acts, performs, thinks, dreams, dances, sings, or prays, each of these episodes counts as one rung in the ladder of his life, as something he identifies himself with, something his own effort has gone into, an experience to be remembered, with pride, joy, or horror. Nor is there, from this angle, any significant difference between religious, narrowly social, or mainly personal situations. Envisaged as experiences, all situations are individual, and as such, unique, personal, historical. Society apart, man, not being a robot, lives—as an individual. . . .

INVOLUTION

The application of the pattern concept to a cultural feature in the process of development provides, I think, a way of explaining one peculiarity of primitive cultures. The primary effect of pattern, is, of course, to check development, or at least to limit it. As soon as the pattern form is reached further change is inhibited by the tenacity of the pattern. While characteristic of all things cultural, especially in primitiveness, this aspect of pattern is particularly conspicuous in rituals and the forms of religious objects, where the tenacity of pattern is enhanced by social inertia or a sacred halo. But there are also other instances where pattern merely sets a limit, a frame, as it were, within which further change is permitted if not invited. Take, for instance, the decorative art of the Maori, distinguished by its complexity, elaborateness, and the extent to which the entire decorated object is pervaded by the decoration. On analysis the unit elements of the design are found to be few in number; in some instances, in fact, the complex design is brought about through a multiplicity of spatial arrangements of one and the same unit. What we have here is a pattern plus continued development. The pattern precludes the use of another unit or of other units, but it is not inimical to play with the unit or units. The inevitable result is progressive complication, variety within uniformity, virtuosity within monotony. This is *involution*.

A parallel instance, in later periods of history, is provided by what is called ornateness in art, as in the late Gothic. The basic forms of the art have reached finality, the structural features are fixed beyond variation, inventive originality is exhausted. Still development goes on. Being hemmed in on all sides by crystallized pattern, it takes the function of elaboration. Expansive creativeness having dried up at the source, a special kind of virtuosity takes its place, a sort of technical hairsplitting. No longer capable of genuine procreation, art here, like a seedless orange, breeds within itself,

crowding its inner structure with the pale specters of unborn generations.

Anyone familiar with primitive cultures will think of similar
instances in other cultural domains; for example, in ceremonial,
whether that of the Toda dairies, or that of the Plains Sun Dance, or
that of the Australian *intichiuma*. In detailed content these ceremonies are, of course, quite different, but in one respect there is a
common feature; in each case we are overwhelmed, almost shocked,
often bored, by what seems an excessive heaping up of unit elements
—whether in form, rhythm, or dance-step—with a total effect of
enormous, to the novice bewildering, complexity. Similarly, in
ceremonial etiquette as described, for instance, by Malinowski
with reference to the interminable exchanges of presents and the
like which precede, accompany, and follow the conclusion of matrimonial unions. The patterns of behavior here implied are few, as
Malinowski points out, yet the actual procedure is enormously
complex. Does not the reason lie in the fact that what we have here
is a narrow pattern of behavior plus a possibility of further change
within the pattern? If the pattern were less narrow, or if there
were no pattern, the change might have been an unfoldment. Within
the narrow possibilities determined by pattern, the change can only
be an elaboration, leading, as an ultimate limit, to seemingly insane
complexity.[2]

It may be true—I think it is—that involution characterizes primitive society, on account of the dominance of pattern in primitive
conditions. Still, if the principle is correctly formulated, it should
apply to conditions other than primitive, in otherwise similar circumstances. This, indeed, seems to be the case. Under this heading

---

[2] It must not be assumed, of course, that *all* complexity is reducible to
this factor, involution. Ordered complexity has its own appeal, especially to
the sophisticated; and in such things as ritual or decorative art many primitives are sophisticates. Even disordered complexity, an infinitely variegated
or multicolored chaos, may have a positive appeal. Such situations, then, if
desirable as consummations, may become causal in guiding development in
the corresponding direction. All that the formulation of the text should be
understood to imply is that pattern plus development within the pattern limits
must and does lead to involution, that is, a tendency toward elaborateness
or complexity, consisting of a combination, repetition, or juxtaposition of
relatively uniform elements.

I have already referred to ornateness in art. A good further illustration is provided by the music of Bach, his fugues particularly. We have here a deliberate limitation of invention in so far as the basic melodic elements are concerned. On the other hand, invention, development goes on, only it takes the form of playing with these elements, repeating, combining and recombining. The result is a highly complex musical texture; so complex, in fact, as frequently to confuse the ear, unless unusually musical or experienced. This feature stands out in bald relief especially when compared, say, with Beethoven, where elaboration or combination of basic melodic elements is not abandoned but supplemented by continued melodic invention. The resulting effect is relative simplicity and freshness.

Psychopathology provides another example. In neurosis, so often associated with introversion, the individual's relations to outside people or things are queered, in one way or another. The possibility of a workable understanding, on an objective level, being eliminated, an adjustment, if one is reached at all, is worked out on a subjective level; the "pleasure principle" supplants the "reality principle." Being cut off from a large number of possible external accommodations, the mind of the individual turns upon itself, unceasingly it crosses and recrosses its own tracks, like a mouse in a maze, beating desperately at times against the inner wall of the frontier of the ego, beyond which it may not go. The mind of the introverted neurotic is limited but complex—it is involuted.[3]

EXCERPT NO. 13*

Though her emphasis was heavily on the side of cultural determinism, even Benedict recognized that an individual's "set" toward a particular type of behavior may prevail against the press and pull of culture. This recognition, and her hypothesis that there are temperament types "of universal recurrence,"

---

[3] It will be observed that, from one angle, the principle of involution represents a special case of the principle of limited possibilities. The limitation here is in range, or form, or the number of basic elements. Granted that development continues, it must, under such conditions, lead to complexity. Complexity, then, elaboration or elaborateness, repetitiousness, are earmarks of involution.

* From Ruth Fulton Benedict, "Anthropology and the Abnormal," *The Journal of General Psychology*, Vol. 10 (1934), pp. 59–80.

is entirely in accord with data accumulated over the thirty years elapsed since she wrote. There now can be no question whether the unique genetic endowment of the individual includes factors having to do with temperament. Nor is there substantial reason to doubt that the individual's readiness to "adapt himself to society" is a function of inherent temperament, plus inherent talent (e.g., creativity) and intelligence as well. We do not accept Benedict's view that the deviant necessarily is he who is merely unable to adapt; he may be one who simply chooses not to adapt, either in certain respects or quite generally.

I have spoken of individuals as having sets toward certain types of behavior, and of these sets as running sometimes counter to the types of behavior which are institutionalized in the culture to which they belong. From all that we know of contrasting cultures, it seems clear that differences of temperament occur in every society. The matter has never been made the subject of investigation, but from the available material it would appear that these temperament types are very likely of universal recurrence. That is, there is an ascertainable range of human behavior that is found wherever a sufficiently large series of individuals is observed. But the proportion in which behavior types stand to one another in different societies is not universal. The vast majority of the individuals in any group are shaped to the fashion of that culture. In other words, most individuals are plastic to the moulding force of the society into which they are born. In a society that values trance, as in India, they will have supernormal experience. In a society that institutionalizes homosexuality, they will be homosexual. In a society that sets the gathering of possessions as the chief human objective, they will amass property. The deviants, whatever the type of behavior the culture has institutionalized, will remain few in number, and there seems no more difficulty in moulding the vast malleable majority to the "normality" of what we consider an aberrant trait, such as delusions of reference, than to the normality of such accepted behavior patterns as acquisitiveness. The small proportion of the number of the deviants in any culture is not a function of the sure instinct with which that society has built itself upon the fundamental sanities, but of the universal fact that, happily, the majority of mankind quite readily take any shape that is presented to them.

The relativity of normality is not an academic issue. In the first place, it suggests that the apparent weakness of the aberrant is most often and in great measure illusory. It springs not from the fact that he is lacking in necessary vigor, but that he is an individual upon whom that culture has put more than the usual strain. His inability to adapt himself to society is a reflection of the fact that that adaptation involves a conflict in him that it does not in the so-called normal.

EXCERPT NO. 14*

Belo documents, from Bali, a wide range of temperaments, and the occurrence of individual assertiveness in a closely patterned, tightly structured context. Even in this efficiently ordered society an occasional individual steers his course against the currents and without regard for the approved ways or for the opinions of his fellows.

There are in all societies occasional individuals who "will not stick to the rules of the game." They demonstrate convincingly that culture is by no means the determinant of behavior; such individuals are both selective and rejective of what is available in their cultural milieu. They use the selected elements in the process of rejecting other elements. They chart their course on the idiosyncratic level to greater degree than does the average man. In them the idiosyncratic level of individuality is a thicker stratum, as it were, than in the majority of the society's members.

. . . In such a social scheme (i.e., the Balinese) each individual has his place, and he has only to do what is expected of him to fit with nicety into the life of the group. But there are occasions when an individual finds it impossible to conform, and at these times disturbance and maladjustment appear. Certain temperaments, for instance, are not amenable to the national habit of submissive obedience. Women with fiery dispositions may run away from their husbands, taking shelter with their own families, and refusing to return, or departing with a lover. A small boy of eight told the following story of his rebellion against his father's authority, the events described having occurred when he was no more than six or seven:

---

* From Jane Belo, "The Balinese Temper," in *Character and Personality*, Vol. 4 (1935), pp. 120–46. (Italics added.)

"My father beat my mother too hard, and I became too angry. Then my father beat me very hard. I followed him when he went out to work in the rice fields. I took money from the pocket of his jacket which he had laid down on the edge of the fields. I ran away. For a month I did not go home.

"With the money I bought rice in the market, and I stayed out all day in the rice fields, and I never saw my father and my mother. At night I would go into the house of one of my other fathers (uncles) and sleep with the children. My father and mother did not know where I was. Then one day my mother saw me. She wept, and begged me to come home. I went home.

"My father was only silent."

In this encounter, since the father did not beat him on his return, the child seems to have triumphed over the man.

Another deviant is Madé, who rebelled not so much against paternal authority as against the prescribed rules of tradition. He is a young man of impulsive temperament, with ways unusually quick and nervous in a Balinese, quick to laugh and quick to be angered, extremely efficient when engaged in tasks which interest him, lazy and unreliable at all other tasks. Born in a small hamlet far from the town, and several miles' distance from the motor road, he decided when still a boy to become a chauffeur. He left his farmer parents, and went to live with relatives in town. There he attended school, learned to speak Malay, and began to pick up from the older boys the knowledge of his chosen trade. He served his apprenticeship with them, receiving their teaching in return for the performance of menial duties. When he had sufficient knowledge, he in turn got a job as chauffeur, and was able to marry, buying with the money he earned the rice which he had not been able to raise on his family land. (So strong is the farming background in Balinese life that any man who has had employment and loses it automatically goes back to tilling the land until he can find new work.) Although Madé is skillful as a driver and mechanic, he is not very successful. The very qualities which made him turn from the environment and occupation to which he was born, and to which his forebears had for generations conformed, impede his progress as a chauffeur. He refuses to carry out orders unless it pleases him. He is impatient with any part of his work which is not mechanical. He will drive tirelessly for several hundred miles, and cheerfully apply himself to any necessary repairs in a breakdown. But if after a short journey he is asked to lift out a parcel from the car, he calls another to do it for him—a very unusual thing in Balinese who are not of high caste, as they are universally reluctant to ask their equals to serve them. Another unusual quality is his lack of the sense of relaxation common to most Balinese. Generally they will sit for hours without impatience, waiting for something to happen, and they seem to find pleasant the state of doing nothing. Often they drop off to sleep. But Madé could not be left alone for ten minutes in a car; he would be off on some errand of his own, to bargain for coconuts or to flirt with some pretty girl at a market stall. He took rebukes from his masters with ill grace, flaring up in insolence, or sulking and glowering to himself. To cover up his impetuosity and his shirking of explicit orders, he developed habits of dishonesty. All these things caused him to make an unsatisfactory chauffeur, and he repeatedly lost his position, whether he worked for Europeans, or for Chinese or Arab car owners. He is an impulsive spender, vain about his costume and the prestige afforded him by his possessions. The money that he earns is soon gone, and he will probably never save enough, as many of the young men do, to buy a secondhand car of his own. This is the case of an unusually ill-adapted Balinese. It is curious to note that such a type cannot adjust itself to the new order any more than to the old. He makes many friends and many enemies among the Balinese. Men and women respond to his spontaneous charm, his vivacity and gayety as a companion. But in his friendly relations he is always getting into trouble, for *he will not stick to the rules of the game.*

EXCERPT NO. 15*

The conditions of life for pastoralist and agriculturalist, and the relative independence available to the former, are generally as Ekvall describes them. But one feature of Tibetan nomadism is unusual: the "population hunger" of the

* From Robert B. Ekvall, "Law and the Individual among the Tibetan Nomads," *American Anthropologist*, Vol. 66 (October, 1964), pp. 1113–14.

nomadic communities, and their eagerness to accept new manpower.

Pastoralists, like peoples of other nonindustrial subsistence technologies, are seldom so hospitable. To leave one's own group, or to be cast out, is often tantamount to a death sentence. The Tibetan nomad was indeed "fortified," in his inclination to follow "his own will and purpose," in the sure knowledge of acceptance by another if he abandoned his own group.

Under these circumstances the "contest between community consensus and pressure" and the individual was markedly unequal. Ordinarily the matter is not so simple, though the individual may "win" (i.e., survive in his own group in spite of persistent self-assertion in face of community consensus and pressure), unless he flouts a pattern or patterns sustained on penalty of death.

The individual's response to the pressure of community consensus, impelling him to submit to traditional law and accept mediation, was somewhat different in a nomadic community from what it was in a sedentary community. The sedentary agriculturalist was tied to his immovable house and equally immovable fields. If, pressured beyond what he was willing to bear, he were to choose flight and alienation from his community, he would have to leave house and fields behind him and could hope to get away with the barest minimum of personal wealth. With such alternatives before him he was much like a prisoner, and the pressure on him to conform was very great.

The nomadic pastoralist, on the other hand, was comparatively free. Individually he was highly mobile within his mobile society. His tent could be packed on two yaks and easily moved with all the rest of his possessions, and what might be called his fields-on-the-hoof in the cycle of production could move with equal ease and speed. This mobility gave him the power of moving out of his community with no diminishment of his resources and having to leave nothing behind. He had nothing in pawn and thus was in a position to resist the pressures of community consensus and, in turn, to extract from that community the maximum of consideration and deference to his views and desires. With great finality he retained the right of effective dissent. In his mind, and in the minds of all concerned, was sure foreknowledge that, if he found the pressures unacceptable and the group loyalty fickle or lacking, or if he considered his community's treatment of him lacking in fairness and unjust, he had the capability of moving to another community and of taking all his wealth with him.

The problem of acceptance into another community was a minor one or did not exist, for Tibetan nomadic communities were— what might be called—"population hungry" to a marked degree. Accretions of manpower were everywhere welcome. In the individual's resistance to community pressure and in every contest-of-wills situation, one final threat was common knowledge. The menace lay in the fact that the place where a refugee would find the warmest welcome would be in a hostile community, for it was there, if enmity were ever expressed in action, that he, as the committed renegade, would be most valued for his first-hand knowledge of terrain, habits of movement and capabilities and vulnerabilities of the community from which he had broken away.

Although never exactly easy, in any such move the actual getaway did not pose insurmountable difficulties. The pattern of constant and somewhat confused movement, which is nomadic existence, afforded many opportunities of escape, and any effective blocking of such escape was difficult. The well planned getaway included the arrival, on a prearranged schedule, of a welcoming and rescue party from the new home community; to meet the new recruit early in the course of his flight; to forestall any attempts at hindrance; and to take over protection of him and his family and possessions. Pursuit—fearful of ambush—stopped when the rescue party hove in sight (Ekvall, 1952:89–90).

In the contest between community consensus and pressure and his own will and purpose, the Tibetan nomadic pastoralist was fortified by the realization of all these possibilities. He knew, too, that everyone else involved was equally aware of these advantages which he possessed and could use, to preserve intact his final right of dissent, and to maintain his own bristling, individualistic independence.

CHAPTER 9

The Nature and
Conditions of Autonomy

It is in society that the individual gradually acquires his autonomy.

Chombard de Lauwe

Autonomy I take to mean the exercise of choice, performed largely with deliberation and intent. It is that dimension of self which lies "beyond conformity" (to borrow an apt phrase from Winston White, 1961). It is at once a formation made possible by society and culture, and an achievement of transcendence.

This is not, however, to equate autonomy with the "authenticity" of existentialist philosophy, in which all acts are equally acceptable so long as they qualify as authentic. Apparently authenticity characterizes such of the existentialist's choices as he believes reflect his uniqueness, and not the culturally patterned values of his society. These patterned elements he is likely to reject, as a matter of principle. Autonomy, on the other hand, is emphatically not a matter of either acceptance or rejection as a matter of principle—a process which has more in common with conformity. Autonomy rather reflects reasoned, judicious, flexible selectivity or uncoerced creativity and innovation.

Coercion toward conformity may have its principal source in society or in the individual himself. The distinction is in a sense

219

an analytical artifact, since one can resist the pressures exerted by society, if they fall short of overpowering physical force or the societal equivalent of blackmail. But resistance may be a demonstration of autonomy; the nonautonomous man is so much at one with the prevailing opinion, so fearful of it, or so lacking in ideas of his own that it may not even occur to him to resist. In that case he is self-coerced, in that he and society are, for such reasons, largely one.

AUTONOMY AND INDIVIDUALISM

But the autonomy with which we are concerned is not merely a matter of "rugged individualism." This latter variety of freedom is a phenomenon of aspirations and energies unfettered, with variable results. As Herbert Muller says, in his analysis of *Freedom in the Ancient World:* "the individualism of the Greeks was . . . likely to become reckless and lawless, or simply selfish, because it was neither sanctioned nor disciplined by any explicit democratic or religious principle.

It was rooted in the Homeric tradition of personal fame and glory and was nourished by habitual competition, as much in art and athletics as in business. . . . (Muller, 1961, p. 202.)

Individualism of a less than "rugged" variety is supportive of autonomy too, and in the cross-cultural record it is no great novelty. It appears in cultures of a quite folkish sort, as well as in the sophisticate cultures of the Occidental, individual-oriented, tradition. One might not expect to find individualism among Malay villagers of South Thailand, but it is there. Fraser reports:

Within the nuclear family there is a minimum of subordination of individual members to the family group. Women are accorded respect on the basis of their accomplishments almost commensurate with men. Even children are given consideration as individuals rather than as simply members of a group. . . . Within the limits set by one's relations with others (e.g., avoidance of trouble to others), competition is an important element in economic pursuits. (Fraser, 1966, p. 87.)

Individualism is conducive to autonomy, but persons strongly inclined toward autonomy sometimes arise where individualism is not a patterned value, and where values, and conditions generally, are not notably conducive. The sophisticate culture provides for the potentially autonomous man a favoring climate, yet in it individuals are most unequally responsive.

AUTONOMY AND CULTURAL MILIEU

Autonomy is not conformity, yet it is not anticonformity. It is, rather, an ability to transcend the milieu, to stand detached, critical, speculative, and thoughtful, in making choices and in acting on them. The individual exercises autonomy through his reason and his will.

Nor is autonomy an either—or. Few individuals in any society are autonomous in any general sense, but in some societies a good many may exercise a limited autonomy.

And there is one more dimension of autonomy of which we should take note: it may be either cultural—a patterned expectation met by the individual in his own (idiosyncratic) way, or supracultural—a matter of idea systems generated by the individual, exercising his own reason and will in reworking cultural "givens," in improvising and innovating beyond and possibly in defiance of them. A given individual may be autonomous in both these ways (cultural or supra-cultural), combining them in a given activity or in a sequence of activities over time.

Autonomy in accord with patterned expectation is not a contradiction in terms, since the expectation is general and the autonomy specific. "Individualism" as an ideal pattern is a prime example. The pattern calls for individuals who are in certain respects independent, self-determining, and even assertive. Other patterns set certain limits to the expression of individualism (e.g., rules and laws against ingroup murder, against marrying one's parallel cousin), but there is cultural "pull" toward it. There are also ideal patterns of a less generalized sort which are conducive to autonomy in certain of life's activities. E. A. Kennard (1937) comments on Hopi concepts concerning the power of will, and the individual's duty to concentrate his will upon achieving important goals, i.e., "upon keeping happy, healthy, and arriving at old age."

The Hopi word "oqa'la" is translated "strong," but it refers to strength of will, mind, or spirit, and is never used in reference to physical characteristics alone. A strong man always gets his wish and is able to set aside all trouble, and concentrate upon following his road in this life to the end. (Kennard, 1937, p. 493.)

Untimely death is regarded as evidence of lack of will to live; the Hopi believe that one can will his own death, and much more. The fact that an eagle nested close (conveniently close) to the village of Shipaulovi was attributed to the prayers of a former village chief who had greatly desired it. The people said: "He was really strong in those things" (*ibid.*, p. 494).

Not uncommonly, it is in accord with the culture that the individual's thoughts, and his expression of them, be valued in deliberations affecting the tribe. In his role as full-fledged member of the society (a role often limited to men) the individual may be expected to show thoughtfulness, even some inventiveness. But often the pattern is as it was in the Akan society (Ghana): "the time to express one's eccentricity was in the period of deliberation."

To persist in one's individual opinion, when this deviated from the public opinion deliberately arrived at and publicized, was a piece of malice. The unity principle was very strongly cherished. . . . The value of the freedom of expression lay for them [the Akans] in the possible aspect of the truth which it might reveal. But if action is to be taken at all, then there is a point where discussion must end. (Abraham, 1962, pp. 75–76.)

Autonomy of the supra-cultural sort is manifest in innovation, whether the departure be approved, ignored, or disapproved. Independence of mind and strength of will are the essence of autonomy. They will lead, if exercised in culturally proscribed ways, to social disapproval if the innovation is known and believed by the innovator's fellows to be of some consequence. Where the press toward conformity is heavy, and the sanctions upon nonconformity severe, the exercise of autonomy will be inhibited, concealed, or scorned, but by no means eliminated. Donald Levine (1965) provides an example from the traditional Amhara culture of Ethiopia.

. . . Variation and the development of personal styles [in music and dance] are not encouraged. Innovation, particularly in religious forms, is likely to meet strong resistance. . . . Like music and dance, Amhara design provides little scope for the free play of imagination. . . . Painting provides a richer medium, but here again individuality is carefully constricted. (*Ibid.*, p. 267.)

Under these conditions conformity is the rule, but there is no "want of inventiveness on the part of Amhara artists." Hundreds of strictly unconventional drawings have been collected, Levine says, but the collector (one Marcel Griaule) reports:

. . . "these drawings are scorned by the people, who pay scarcely any attention to them, and by the artists themselves, who regard them as a sort of pastime of no importance, or as an activity reserved primarily for apprentices." (*Ibid.*, p. 268.)

Even the written literature of Ethiopia has provided "little scope for individuality."

The effect of this literature has not been, as David Riesman suggests is true of the written word generally, an individualizing one. . . . It has served rather to buttress conformity, by rekindling identification with the sacred symbols of society. . . . [But] a good deal of original expression and personalized commentary may be found [in the *oral* literature]. (*Ibid.*, pp. 268–69.)

AUTONOMY AND CULTURAL COMPLEXITY

Looking across the complexity continuum one concludes that opportunities, even inducements toward autonomy increase fairly regularly with complexity. Yet the qualifier—"fairly"—must be noted. Value systems do not conform neatly to the complexity continuum, and they function to support or to inhibit individual inclinations toward autonomy. They affect, as well, the ways and the activities through which it is expressed.

We have suggested that deliberation and the exercise of reason, will, and creativity all are elements in autonomy. These elements are not limited to "civilized" (i.e., to urban dwelling) man, nor to men of industrialized societies, nor to modern man. Redfield (1953) says:

> In primitive as in civilized societies some people live unreflective and matter-of-fact lives, while a few others are disposed to speculation; and these latter accomplish some critical and even creative thought on problems of existence and conduct.
>
> I see no reason to deny the probability that this much creative thinking took place before the first cities were built among some food producers, and even among some food-collecting "savages." The presence of some leisure seems a necessary condition. . . . Systematization and skepticism—these two fruits of the speculative mind are to be found in many a study of the history of thought in the ancient civilizations. . . .
>
> [But among] the folk only a few people are able to ask the great questions, or can look with doubt and intellectual challenge at what is for most men all of the time taken for granted; and, without writing, what these few minds accomplish leaves little residue. But the first cities bring a literate elite and a new freedom of the mind to criticize and to record. Then the moral order, though it is shaken by civilization, is also, in civilization, taken by reason into charge. (Redfield, 1953, pp. 117–19.)[1]

Recalling the Amhara, among whom we noted that the written word has been put to use largely in the service of conformity, we have an apt illustration of values acting to deflect the impact of a large increment in complexity. The case shows that what is usually true is not necessarily true; the more complex culture is not necessarily the more supportive of autonomy. As S. N. Eisenstadt (1956) points out, there are striking differences with respect to value orientations (individual-oriented vs. collectivity-oriented) even between societies all of which are in the European culture area and tradition. He cites the highly "organized and institutionalized age groups" of Soviet Russia, Israel, and (formerly) Germany and Italy, as expressions of the values of societies marked by "a very explicit community orientation. . . ." And by contrast:

---

[1] Robert Redfield, *The Primitive World and Its Transformation* (Ithaca, N.Y.: Cornell University Press). Copyright 1953, Cornell University. Used by permission of Cornell University Press.

The peer and adolescent groups of Western Europe and the United States societies in which individualistic orientation is stronger, are looser in their composition and less institutionalized. (Eisenstadt, 1956, p. 241.)

However, many observers conclude that conformity runs high precisely in these loosely structured, uninstitutionalized peer groups of Western Europe and the United States. The fact that it is voluntary conformity, a matter of self-coercion, means merely that it is a function of values consensus rather than of coercive structure. Winston White (1961) complains that American and European intellectuals who worry about conformity are tilting with windmills; he assures us that we are in fact moving "beyond conformity," mainly as a result of advanced technology and the "structural differentiation" it brings in train.

The resources of personality . . . have been emancipated from ascriptive ties in significantly new ways. Durable consumers' goods in the home and automation in the factory and office liberate human effort from tasks of a mere physical nature. Upgrading the levels of performance requires greater skills on the job and in more complex interpersonal relationships.

The current preoccupation on the American scene with education is, of course, the most salient symptom of this shift. Education, moreover, is not solely a matter of job-training or "catching up with the Russians." It is also a matter of enlarging the individual's understanding . . . of the complex world he lives in. . . .

The impact of the current change . . . must be confronted by the individual independently. It cannot be absorbed *for* the individual by the family, the church, a class, or an economic or political interest. . . . He is, indeed, forced to be free. . . .

But he does *not* arrive at such independence without the resources that society and its culture make possible. (White, 1961, pp. 163–64.)

Taking the long and large view we may conclude that what makes for social and cultural complexity makes also for conditions favorable to individual autonomy. But a powerful intervening factor—i.e., values—is at work, with the result that though the complexity-autonomy relationship holds in general, exceptions are not uncommon. Complex cultures vary both between one and another and—to a striking degree—internally. Of complexity elements the following are features of high complexity, and features generally *supportive* of autonomy, though by no means ensuring it:

— *Society large* (population in tens of thousands or in millions).
— *Culture extremely bulky* as to total content (vast reservoir of skills, knowledge, and ideas available to the individual).
— *High longevity; low morbidity rate* (health and living conditions at high average level).
— *Social order maintained* (large-scale violent disturbances rare; violent expressions of interpersonal aggression controlled and penalized).
— *Cultural press medium to light;* cultural pull strong.
— *Literacy widely disseminated* through the society.
— *Urbanism* (large proportion, if not majority, of population lives in cities, experiences high frequency and varied interpersonal contacts, develops "urban personality").
— *Heterogeneity*—social and cultural (patterns, roles, contacts, stimuli extremely numerous and highly diversified).
— *Advanced technology* (reflecting and requiring enormous knowledge of natural phenomena, organizational skills, and extreme structural differentiation in systems for producing and distributing goods and services).
— *Formal enculturation* extended and intensive (reflecting cultural bulk, social system complexity, advanced technology, etc., and required by these conditions).
— *Leisure* (large majority of population directly engaged in occupational roles—some 40 or 50 hours per week; many less fully engaged).

AUTONOMY WITHIN THE COMPLEX SOCIETY

Certain of these complexity conditions will be unevenly distributed through a very large and internally diversified society. This unevenness is theoretically largely avoidable. It has in fact been significantly reduced in the most highly complex societies. However, even in those same societies there are segments—the uneducated, the very poor, the despised minorities (who are likely to be both uneducated and poor), the constitutionally handicapped—bearing impoverished variants of the richly elaborated complex culture.

The values most relevant to autonomy are likely also to be unevenly spread through societies which are very large and internally differentiated by class or caste. Lower classes and castes may live in cities but they are likely to be isolated, to a significant degree, from the mainstream of city life. They are likely to be minimally aware of the mainstream, and only partially and inadequately enculturated. With respect to the value system this is strikingly true (see Figure 4). With respect to "moral norms" Robert Angell (1958) writes:

The moralization both of children and immigrants is hampered in modern democratic societies by the tendency . . . for the less educated and less prosperous elements of the population to be "morally uncovered." . . . The sliding apart of social classes in large cities has left the lower classes exposed. . . . When they were integral parts of villages and towns they benefiited from the leadership and cohesion of the whole community. (*Ibid.*, p. 62 and p. 60.)[2]

AUTONOMY AND VALUES

In listing "values affecting autonomy" (Figure 4) we do not aspire to a comprehensive statement. However, the four pairs listed are almost certainly those of most immediate relevance and greatest force. In each pair the member listed first (member [a]) is conducive to autonomy; member (b) does not rule out the possibility, but it does not encourage autonomy (it exerts no pull toward autonomy).

In fact the anthropological record seems to indicate quite clearly that autonomy is never entirely out of the question. Whatever the combination of conditions, including values, the individual can and sometimes does choose to transcend his milieu, if only in limited ways. His unique expression of autonomy may leave no perceptible mark on culture, it may have no apparent effect on his fellows. Yet for him, in terms of his personal satisfaction and zest for living, it may be of crucial import.

THE AUTONOMOUS MAN

We shift now from the macroscopic view—individual in context —to the microscopic—a focus on the individual himself. The ques-

---

[2] Robert Angell, *Free Society and Moral Crisis* (Ann Arbor: University of Michigan Press). Copyright 1958, University of Michigan. Used by permission of the University of Michigan Press.

tion is now: what are the marks of the highly autonomous man, and how does he develop?

Autonomy, like most aspects of unique individuals, is no either—or phenomenon. It is rather a matter of degree. We shall focus on the high-degree individual, his attributes, and their probable sources and genesis.

FIGURE 4
Values Affecting Autonomy

		FOLK CULTURE	SOPHISTICATE CULTURE
1.	*a.* Individual-oriented	Occasional	Predominant (in Occidental culture areas)
	b. Collectivity-oriented	Usual	Predominant (in Oriental culture areas)
2.	*a.* Reasoning-oriented (speculative; skeptical; deliberative; education and idea-oriented)	Rare	Predominant (in urban-educated segments of societies)
	b. Tradition-oriented (uncritical acceptance; minimal awareness, or conscious inspection of milieu)	Predominant	Usual (in isolated—physically and/or culturally—segments of societies)

FIGURE 4 (continued)

Values Affecting Autonomy

	FOLK CULTURE	SOPHISTICATE CULTURE
3. a. Creativity-oriented (innovation, novelty, "fresh views," originality) . . Rare		Predominant (in urban-educated segments of societies)
b. Conservation-oriented (reproduce pattern; avoid change) . . . Predominant		Usual (in isolated segments of societies)
4. a. Cosmopolitan-oriented (learn about, compare, own and "foreign" cultures) . . . Rare		Predominant (in urban-educated segments of societies)
b. Ethnocentrism-oriented (own culture, in traditional form, beyond question or criticism) . . . Predominant		Usual (in isolated segments)

Autonomy is achievable because ideological diversity is not only achievable but, in the long view, inevitable. Levinson (1964) argues:

Many social scientists have been so impressed with the number and pervasiveness of the mechanisms of ideological control . . . that they have made rather generous assumptions about the degree of ideological uniformity achieved among the members of any given society.

They have tended also to assume that such uniformities as do exist are brought about directly by social pressures. . . . My position . . . is that (a) the degree of ideological diversity in most social systems is greater than most social scientists have recognized, and (b) personality influences ideology formation in all societies, whether the ideological diversity among their members is small or great. (*Ibid.*, p. 307.)

Levinson rejects, as "simplistic and dreadfully limiting," what he calls "sponge" theory, i.e., the view that "people acquire their opinions and values by absorbing, in a more or less automatic fashion, those ideas which their environment presents most often and with the greatest pressure." Sponge theory undervalues the "role of reason and the more complex conceptual-imaginative processes" (*ibid.*, p. 308). Stanley Diamond makes the same point in criticizing Kroeber's belief that the individual is free only as he is able to choose between culturally given alternatives. This view is "too restricted because it does not give sufficient weight to the human decisions which create the alternatives that are open to choice . . . and it gives no credence to the capacity of the human mind to stand outside of its particular tradition, to be skeptical, or perhaps to be passionate. . . .

Even the familiar argument about the "inevitability" of a language relative to its individual speakers becomes ambiguous on closer inspection. Any given language may be spoken with great flexibility; words, idioms and dialects are constantly being invented at varying rates of speed, and lost. Each speaker shapes the language in a subtly personal way; rhythm, volume, pitch, juxtaposition of words, style, vary widely and significantly from person to person. All they share in common is a code that appears the grosser, the more closely we scrutinize it. Speech is not only a broadly societal but a familiar and personal series of experiences and symbols. Language itself is an invention; what could be more arbitrary, more *decisive* than the association of a particular sound with a particular thing or event. Such an invention, such a group of specific correlations is the very opposite of an accident; it is hardly inevitable. (Diamond, 1964, p. 33.)

Ideological diversities relate to, and must partly depend upon, diversities of other sorts. Joseph Church emphasizes "feeling states," "future orientations," and the idiosyncratic "logic of action." He writes:

Let us make clear that we are not embracing a transcendental teleology. Yet it is perfectly obvious . . . that people do define goals and work to achieve them. . . . A number of people, it is true, live lives of stimulus-bondage, prisoners of their routines and of their surroundings. . . . But these reservations do not alter the basic datum that some people regulate their current activities in accordance with anticipated future events. . . . It is clear that self-control and self-direction vary directly with cognitive maturity, and especially with the ability to manipulate situations symbolically, to anticipate consequences, to weigh, to judge, and to decide. . . . The normal individual past early childhood lives with an integral schema of self within which his motives can be his own and in terms of which he can regulate his own behavior. (Church, 1961, pp. 208-10.)

A. H. Maslow's study of "self-actualizing" persons provides evidence in support of these views. He regards autonomy as one of the fifteen salient characteristics of self-actualizing men. Autonomy, as Maslow defines it, is measurable in behavior which requires both independence, vis-à-vis context, and stability. He writes:

Since they are propelled by growth motivation rather than by deficiency motivation, self-actualizing people are not dependent for their main satisfactions on the real world, or other people or culture or means to ends or, in general, on extrinsic satisfactions. . . .

This independence of environment means a relative stability in the face of hard knocks, blows, deprivations, frustrations, and the like. These people can maintain a relative serenity and happiness in the midst of circumstances that would drive other people to suicide. . . .

Deficiency-motivated people *must* have other people available, since most of their main need gratifications (love, safety, respect, prestige, belongingness) can come only from other human beings. But growth-motivated people may actually be *hampered* by others. The determinants of satisfaction and of the good life are for them now inner-individual and *not* social. They have become strong enough to be independent of the good opinion of other people, or even of their affection. The honors, the status, the rewards, the prestige, and the love they can bestow must have become less important than self-development and inner growth. (Maslow, 1954, pp. 213–14; italics in original.)

Perhaps highly autonomous persons are also highly self-actualizing. This seems probable, though it is not to say that the autonomous man must show all fifteen of the salient characteristics of self-actualizers. (For these characteristics, see Adaptation No. 9.)

GENESIS OF AUTONOMOUS MAN

About the genesis of the autonomous man we know little. However, as we have noted, certain types and conditions of society and culture, much more than others, will be conducive to his development. And there can be little doubt that individual biological antecedents are highly relevant.

Constitutional differences in individuals generate preferences among ways of relating to self, and to culture and to the world. . . . [Both] biological data and theories and self-actualization theories . . . show than an organ system presses to express itself. . . . The muscular person likes to use his muscles, indeed, *has* to use them in order to self-actualize and to achieve the subjective feeling of harmonious, uninhibited, satisfying functioning. . . . People with intelligence must use their intelligence, people with eyes must use their eyes, people with the capacity to love have the *impulse* to love and the *need* to love in order to feel healthy. Capacities clamor to be used, and cease their clamor only when they are used sufficiently. That is to say, capacities are needs, and therefore are intrinsic values as well. To the extent that capacities differ, so will values also differ. (Maslow, 1959, p. 122.)

No doubt individual capacities "are" needs, and therefore intrinsic values, but we cannot accept this generalization without reference to enculturation. Enough now is known about development in the very early years of childhood to show how individual capacities can be radically stunted, altered, or oriented in these years.

Cognitive capacities are peculiarly susceptible to early stunting. Children in the culturally "isolated" segments of large and complex societies are seriously affected. J. McV. Hunt has described the developmental sequence under these circumstances.

The intellectual inferiority apparent among so many children of parents of low educational and socioeconomic status, regardless of race, is already evident by the time they begin kindergarten or first grade at age 5 or 6. Such children are apt to have various linguistic liabilities: limited vocabularies, poor articulation, and syntactical deficiencies that are revealed in the tendency to rely on unusually short sentences with faulty grammar. They also show perceptual deficiencies in the sense that they recognize fewer objects and situations than do most middle-class children. And, perhaps more important, they usually have fewer interests than do the middle-class children who are the pace setters in the schools. Moreover, the objects recognized by and the interests of children typical of the lower class differ from those of children of the middle class. These deficiencies give such children the poor start which so commonly handicaps them ever after in scholastic competition. . . .

. . . Late in his second or early in his third year, after he has developed a number of pseudo-words and achieved the "learning set" that "things have names," the child in a crowded, poverty-stricken family probably meets another obstacle: His questions too seldom bring suitable answers, and too often bring punishment that inhibits further questioning. Moreover, the conditions [e.g., crowding] that originally provided a rich variety of input for the very young infant now supply a paucity of suitable playthings and models for imitation. . . .

The effects of a lower-class environment on a child's development [become serious late in his second or early in his third year, and] may become even more serious during his fourth and fifth years. Furthermore, the longer these conditions continue, the more likely the effects are to be lasting. Evidence from animal studies supports this. . . .

Counteracting cultural deprivation at this stage of development might best be accomplished by giving the child the opportunity to encounter a wide variety of objects, pictures, and appropriate behavioral models, and by giving him social approval for appropriate behavior. The setting should encourage him to indulge his inclinations to scrutinize and manipulate the new objects as long as he is interested and should provide him with appropriate answers to his questions. Such varied experiences would foster the development of representative imagery which could then be the referents for spoken words and later for written language. (Hunt, 1964, pp. 83-91.)

The development of character is also greatly affected by the child's very early experiences. Research has been focused on social pathology. There is ample evidence in support of the conclusion that antisocial character components can be identified by age six. High predictive accuracy (*c.* 90%) has been verified, in tests conducted in France, Japan, and the United States. The predictive scale used in these tests was developed in the United States by Sheldon and Eleanor Glueck (1950, 1956, 1962). The Gluecks have demonstrated that "there are many sociocultural aspects of family life that have a bearing on the propulsion of children in the direction of delinquency." Exposure to "delinquency subculture" and to certain aspects of the "general culture" may also play a part in shaping a delinquency-prone character (Glueck and Glueck, 1962, p. 163).

The young child is likely to be both plastic and helpless in the face of the environment in which he lives—he knows no other—and he can be directly affected by the pressure and demands of the environment. (Bloom, 1964, p. 196.)

In view of such research findings it is clear that the individual's constitutional "givens" may or may not be actualized. Strong pressures external to the person may prevent or retard the development of a character "natural" to him. Yet "we do regard it as possible for a few individuals to be sufficiently powerful to alter or at least effect some modification in the environment" (*ibid.*, p. 196).

Benjamin Bloom believes that such successful resistance is unlikely unless the individual is "older" and has had "experience with other environments." Perhaps a successful thrust of this sort is likely to be fully apparent only when the individual is beyond childhood. But the thrust too may have its roots, not necessarily in some "other environment," but in early childhood.

A study of nearly 400 "eminent" men and women of the 20th century—" 'eminent' . . . because they became important enough to their contemporaries to have books [at least two] written about them" provides important insights. The authors (Victor and Mildred Goertzel) made their selection of subjects on a basis of the objective criterion noted above. The subjects therefore included "men who have been as eminently wicked [e.g., Hitler] as others [e.g., Gandhi] have been productive of good" (Goertzel, 1962, p. vii). The point is important; the highly autonomous man (which we assume many, though not all, of these eminent people to have been) is not necessarily also the "good" man, as judged against standards of his own culture or against widely held "humanitarian" standards.

What were these eminent people like as children? The Goertzels report:

Many of the children of the past who were to become eminent, like the intellectually gifted children of today, tended to possess superior ability in reasoning and in recognizing relationships. They showed intellectual curiosity, had a wide range of interests, did effective work independently. They showed their greatest superiority in reading ability; many read at the age of four. Almost all were early readers of good books. They were original thinkers and had scant patience with drill and routine. They were likely to be rejected by their playmates and had parents who valued learning. The majority of them came from middle-class business and professional homes. Their brothers and sisters were capable. Most of those children who became eminent would probably have tested high on today's intelligence tests. . . .

We have ourselves seen a number of intellectually gifted youngsters grow up and fit themselves competently into suitable and remunerative positions which offer them little intellectual stimulation or deep satisfaction. These same children had financial and emotional security in their childhood homes and received the best of schooling. When we turn to biographies and autobiographies, we find exciting, experimental, creative men and women who in their childhood experienced trauma, deprivations, frustrations and conflicts of the kind commonly thought to predispose one to mental illness or delinquency. . . . (Ibid., pp. x and xii.)

The authors of this study remind us of much evidence that creativity (which we take to be an element in autonomy) is not neatly correlated with intelligence (measured intelligence, at any rate). This is not to say that there is evidence of low intelligence coupled with high creativity, but there is ample evidence of average intelligence with high creativity, and high intelligence with low creativity. (*Ibid.*, pp. 277–80.) And their study has "raised a whole new series of uncomfortable queries" (*ibid.*, p. xiv), concerning the relations between factors long believed essential in the genesis of healthy (i.e., nonneurotic or psychotic; nondelinquent or criminal) individuals. Security and emotional stability in the childhood milieu are, it seems, not essential. Access to the intellectual tools which the culture's store of knowledge and skills provides apparently *is* essential to the development of high-level autonomy. The Goertzel study serves, on the whole, as documentation of the fact that in some individuals a "demand for autonomy" (Allport) is an inherent and overriding dimension of the self.

THE DEMAND FOR AUTONOMY

In all individuals this demand apparently exists, though in highly variable degrees. Allport says:

If the demand for autonomy were not a major force we could not explain the prominence of negativistic behavior in childhood. The crying, rejecting, and anger of a young infant as well as the negativistic behavior of the two-year-old are primitive indications of *a being bent on asserting* itself. All his life long this being will be attempting to reconcile . . . two modes of becoming, the tribal and the personal: the one that makes him into a mirror, and the other that lights the lamp of individuality within.

The truth of the matter . . . is that the moral sense and life-styles of most people reach far beyond the confines of domestic and community mores in which they were first fashioned. If we look into ourselves we observe that our tribal morality seems to us somehow peripheral to our personal integrity. True, we obey conventions of modesty, decorum, and self-control, and have many habits that fashion us in part as mirror-images of our home, class, and cultural ways of living. But we know that we have selected, reshaped, and transcended these ways to a marked degree. (Allport, 1955, pp. 34–35.)

As Allport says, "if we look into ourselves . . . we know . . ." something about what remains unique, individual, and personally precious in spite of all the tribalizing. The sense of freedom, like the sense of individuality, "cannot be debated but only experienced" (Golding, 1960, p. 5). Individuality too is a subjective reality; in the nature of man it is a necessity as well.

The imp of individuality in everyone continually asserts itself—not out of vanity but out of necessity. We may be of planetary insignificance but we cannot live by such long views; we may have needs in common and perhaps should behave accordingly, but we insist that our eccentricities be reckoned in. Our individuality may be a fiction, but it is necessary to act as if it were fact.

And so each of us is engaged in a continual process of isolating, discovering and asserting his individuality. It may be our destiny to be drawn into the flames, but at least we can beat our wings: individuals are we. We cry out our uniqueness, though, being social animals, we do so discreetly. Our claims are modest. We say only that no one else has quite the same intermingling of experience and feeling as we; no one else has seen precisely what I have seen, even if it is not very much; has thought all that I have thought, though I may not be very wise; or feels exactly as I feel. (Griffith, 1959, pp. 7–8.)

THE SENSE OF AUTONOMY; ITS FEEDBACK

Whatever its sources the individual's sense of uniqueness is a crucial fact of life; "the way a man defines his situation constitutes for him its reality" (Allport, *op. cit.*, p. 84). No doubt the actor usually is unable to view himself and his actions in time-space perspective, or with much detachment. The important point is that his sense of reality, his definition of situation, carries with it a conviction that "he is working within a frame of choice, not of destiny" (*ibid.*). The conviction moves and sustains him in action.

In contexts which undermine this conviction, the motive power will be undermined too. Confidence and zest must underlie a strong and strongly motivating conviction. "To the extent that a man feels powerless to control his future, he will not learn as well what he needs to know to affect it" (Seeman, 1966, p. 38). Melvin Seeman asks: "What kinds of knowledge can dispel feelings of isolation and helplessness (alienation)?" His answer (based on studies in the U.S., Sweden, and France) is:

A person's feelings of self-reliance and power are tied up with whether he belongs to an organization that has some control over his occupational destiny, [and] . . . whether he has some control over *its* destiny. . . .

The ability to learn and retain knowledge which has some connection with control over an individual's future [politics, parole, or health information] is also directly affected by belonging to a union or other relevant organization. . . . (*Ibid.*, p. 39.)

COGNITIVE THEORY: THE COMPLEXITIES OF DECISION MAKING

But, organization or no, the individual's reasoning faculties and habits remain the principal vehicle through which he defines his situation and makes his choices. We have noted earlier (Chapter 6) that a cognitive theory of behavior and development is in the making, a fact evident in research interests and in recent pronouncements by psychologists whose earlier views were different. O. H. Mowrer (1964, p. 11), for example, says: "We have dropped the reflex as the model for behavior and rediscovered *reason*." (Italics original.)

Philosophers too are re-examining reason. They tell us that making choices involves deliberation, or "reasoning about what to do . . . [and] the conclusion of deliberation is usually called decision" (Morgenbesser and Walsh, 1962, pp. 2–3). We make decisions "on the basis of principle; often we are called upon to make a decision *of* principle." Kolenda (1964) continues:

Of course, decisions are ours; we are prepared to claim them as ours and to accept responsibility for them. Thus we assert and manifest our freedom. . . . As a bearer of rationality, each person ought to feel responsible for the ways in which this rationality will manifest itself. . . . Any rational decision ought to be not only consonant with all important convictions of the agent, it must also be in harmony with the conviction of other rational agents." (Kolenda, 1964, pp. 75–76.)

But there's the rub! In complex, and even in not-so-complex settings actual and logical incompatibilities swarm like hornets around the decision maker. He chooses this course and offends his best friend; that course and he may lose his ladylove; another and he may wind up a soldier when he never meant to be, yet neither did he ever mean to be thought anything short of a brave and true citizen. So complicated does the matter become that mathematicians, economists, and psychologists bring to bear upon it great batteries of statistical, systems research, and psychometric techniques.

A recent thick volume entitled *Human Judgments and Optimality* by M. W. Shelly and G. L. Bryan (eds.) (1964) is a case in point. In this formidable tome a chapter (by R. N. Shephard) is devoted to the problems of "subjectively optimum selection among multiattribute alternatives." Shephard tells us what we all know too well: the choice one made yesterday, full of confidence and certainty, often looks silly today, even to oneself. The difficulty (stated in impeccable scientese is that:

> Many practical decision problems require that a choice be made among alternatives, each of which consists of a number of subjectively disparate attributes. But, after a choice of this kind has been made, the decision maker sometimes comes to the realization that his particular choice was not the best one even by his own subjective standards. One source of the subjective nonoptimality of such decisions seems to be man's demonstrable inability to take proper account, simultaneously, of the various component attributes of the alternatives. . . . (*Ibid.*, p. 257.)

Shephard concludes that "a more detailed knowledge of the underlying psychological processes actually used in human decision making would probably be helpful in any attempt to achieve a closer approach to subjective optimality." (*Ibid.*, p. 278.) There will undoubtedly be much more study of this and of many other facets of decision making. Some of the mechanics must yield to such study, but the essence of autonomy lies precisely in its stubborn, elusive, indeterminacy.

THE REALITY AND SIGNIFICANCE OF AUTONOMY

It is no mean achievement, on the part of a variety of students of human behavior, to have recognized that autonomy is real, that it remains a potent factor in the modern world, and a shaper of the future.

Autonomy is in the nature of man. A distinguished biologist concludes:

Man is a creature who can choose, eliminate, decide, and thereby create. . . . To decide, to choose and decide, this is truly the operation of man. . . . (Dubos, 1966, p. 64.)

And autonomy is in the nature of civilization. Historian Herbert J. Muller writes:

The interdependence of civilized life by no means prohibits independence of spirit, but requires more of it. . . . As Whitehead said, civilization comes down to a program for discontent. But its justification comes down to the only possible reasons why it is better to be a man than an oyster, an intelligent man than a moron, an educated man than an illiterate, a free man than a slave. It lies in the expansion, refinement, and enrichment of man's distinctive consciousness, the realization of his distinctive capacities for knowing, feeling, striving and creating. (Muller, 1961, p. 36.)

ADAPTATION NO. 9*

Maslow's "self-actualizing people" are strongly endowed with a sense of and a demand for autonomy and individuality. They are unusually competent, and they are notable for these characteristics:

Creativeness; a certain attitude, a certain spirit that arises out of the nature of the character of the person performing the act.

A greater than common freshness, penetration, and efficiency of perception. These people seem to see the true and the real more easily.

These individuals are less inhibited, less constricted, less bound, less enculturated, more spontaneous, more natural.

Self-actualizing people are not well adjusted (in the naïve sense of approval of and identification with the culture). They get along with the culture in various ways, but of all of them it may be said that in a certain profound and meaningful sense they resist encul-

* From Abraham H. Maslow, "Self-Actualization: a Study in Psychological Health," in W. Wolff (ed.), *Symposia on Topical Issues*, Vol. I, "Values in Personality Research" (New York: Grune & Stratton, 1950), pp. 11–34. Used by permission.

turation and maintain a certain inner detachment from the culture in which they are immersed.

These people fall well within the limits of apparent conventionality in choice of clothes, of language, of food, of ways of doing things in our culture. And yet they are not *really* conventional.

The inner attitude is that it is ordinarily of no great consequence which folkways are used. The general tendency of these people is simply to accept most states of affairs that they consider unimportant or unchangeable or not of primary concern to them as individuals.

This tolerant acceptance is not warm approval with identification. Their yielding to convention is apt to be rather casual and perfunctory, with cutting of corners in favor of directness, honesty, saving of energy, etc. In the pinches, when yielding to convention is too annoying or too expensive, the apparent conventionality reveals itself for the superficial thing that it is, and is tossed off as easily as a cloak.

Hardly any of these people can be called authority rebels in the adolescent or hot sense. Their calm, long-time concern with the improvement of culture seems to imply an acceptance of slowness of change along with the unquestioned desirability and necessity of such change.

This is by no means a lack of fight. When quick change is possible or when resolution and courage are needed, it is available in these people. Although they are not radical in the ordinary sense, they easily *could* be. This is primarily an intellectual group, most of whom already have a mission and feel that they are doing something important to improve the world. They are a realistic group and seem to be unwilling to make great but useless sacrifices. They are not against fighting but only against ineffective fighting.

They have had their episodes of fighting, impatience, and eagerness in youth, and in most cases have learned that their optimism about quick change was unwarranted. What they settled down to as a group was an accepting, calm, good-humored everyday effort to improve the culture, usually from within, rather than to reject it and fight it from without.

An inner feeing of detachment from the culture is not necessarily conscious but is displayed by almost all, particularly in discussions of American culture. They weigh it, assay it, taste it, and then make their own decisions.

This is certainly very different from the ordinary sort of passive yielding to cultural shaping displayed for instance by the ethnocentric subjects of the many studies of authoritarian personalities.

Detachment from the culture is probably also reflected in our self-actualizing subjects' detachment from people and their liking for privacy, which has been described above, as also in their lesser than average need for and liking for the familiar and customary.

They are autonomous; they are ruled by the laws of their own character rather than by the rules of society. It is in this sense that they are not only or merely Americans, but also to a greater degree than others, members at large of the human species. To say that they are above or beyond the American culture would be misleading if interpreted strictly, for after all they speak American, act American, have American characters, etc.

Yet if we compare them with the oversocialized, the robotized, or the ethnocentric, we are irresistibly tempted to hypothesize that this group is not simply another subcultural group, but rather less enculturated, less flattened out, less molded. This implies *degree*, and placing on a continuum that ranges from relative acceptance of the culture to relative detachment from it.

The perennial question: Is it possible to be a good or healthy man in an imperfect culture? has been answered by the observation that it *is* possible for relatively healthy people to develop in the American culture. They manage to get along by a complex combination of inner autonomy and outer acceptance that of course will be possible only so long as the culture remains tolerant of this kind of detached withholding from complete cultural identification.

EPILOGUE

Epilogue

Man's accumulated knowledge is enormous, yet, says Margaret Mead, he has still to develop "an image of the future that is capable of inspiring the man of today to become an active and responsible participant in the world of tomorrow." (Mead, 1964, p. 240.) Knowledge brings power, and man's knowledge of himself is already great enough to allow his control of his own destiny.

Curiously enough, it is at just this juncture that men in the most powerful societies are seized by a crisis of confidence. Perhaps it is, as Mead suggests, that they would willingly evade the responsibilities of power.

We began with the question: to what extent can man determine his own destiny? It is a big question; it has been asked again and again over man's centuries, and answered again and again by the very wise and the not-so-wise. I lay no claim to personal wisdom, but it is my hope that this drawing together of many facts and ideas, from many sources, may meet a need which has come sharply to the fore with the crisis of confidence.

Speaking frankly, and, I believe, autonomously, it is my conclusion that most men exercise more control over their own destinies than they know, that many exercise more control than they like to believe, and that most could exercise still more if they would. It is, of course, comforting to be assured, about our unfortunate or unpleasant behavior, that it is "an accident," "the hand of fate," "an act of God," or that "you just couldn't help it." Many aspects of one's life are of course beyond one's control. But many are not, and those that are not can make a vast difference to oneself, to one's contemporaries, perhaps even to men of the future.

Kolenda says that man's freedom is a consequence of reason, and I agree. But the formula requires, for completeness, another element: man's freedom is a consequence of reason, and responsibility is a correlate of freedom.

BIBLIOGRAPHY

Bibliography

ABRAHAM, W. E. *The Mind of Africa*. Chicago: The University of Chicago Press, 1962.

ADLER, ALFRED. *Superiority and Social Interest* (ed. HEINZ L. ANSBACHER, AND ROWENA R. ANSBACHER). Evanston, Ill., Northwestern University Press, 1964.

ALBERT, ETHEL M. "Women of Burundi: A Study of Social Values," *Women of Tropical Africa* (ed. DENISE PAULME). Berkeley: University of California Press, 1963.

ALLPORT, GORDON W. *Personality:—A Psychological Interpretation*. New York: Henry Holt & Company Inc., 1937.

———. *The Nature of Personality: Selected Papers*. Reading, Mass.: Addison-Wesley Publishing Company, Inc., 1950.

———. *The Nature of Prejudice*. Reading, Mass.: Addison-Wesley Publishing Company, Inc., 1954.

———. *Becoming*. New Haven: Yale University Press, 1955.

———. *Pattern and Growth in Personality*. New York: Holt, Rinehart & Winston, Inc., 1961.

ANGELL, ROBERT COOLEY. *Free Society and Moral Crisis*. Ann Arbor: University of Michigan Press, 1965. (First publication, 1958.)

AUSUBEL, DAVID P. *The Fern and the Tiki*. New York: Holt, Rinehart & Winston, Inc., 1965.

BARNETT, H. G. *Innovation: the Basis of Cultural Change*. New York: McGraw-Hill Book Co., 1953.

BARNOUW, VICTOR. *Culture and Personality*. Homewood, Ill.: The Dorsey Press, 1963.

BELO, JANE. "The Balinese Temper," *Character and Personality*, Vol. 4 (1935), pp. 120–46.

BENEDICT, RUTH FULTON. "Anthropology and the Abnormal," *The Journal of General Psychology*, Vol. 10 (1934), pp. 59–80.

BENNETT, JOHN W. "The Interpretation of Pueblo Culture: A Question of Values," *Personal Character and Cultural Milieu* (ed. DOUGLAS G. HARING). Syracuse, N.Y.: Syracuse University Press, 1956.

BENNETT, JOHN W., AND TUMIN, MELVIN M. *Social Life*. New York: Alfred A. Knopf, Inc., 1948.

BERNARD, JESSIE. *American Community Behavior.* New York: Holt, Rinehart & Winston, Inc., 1962.

BERNDT, RONALD M. *Excess and Restraint: Social Control among a New Guinea Mountain People.* Chicago: University of Chicago Press, 1962.

BLITSTEN, DOROTHY R. *The World of the Family.* New York: Random House, Inc., 1963.

BLOOM, BENJAMIN S. *Stability and Change in Human Characteristics.* New York: John Wiley & Sons, Inc., 1964.

BRANDON, HENRY. "One Man Who Mattered," *Saturday Review* (May 28, 1966), pp. 9–10.

BROWN, WILLIAM. *Science and Personality.* New Haven: Yale University Press, 1929.

BRUNER, EDWARD M. "Urbanization and Ethnic Identity in North Sumatra," *American Anthropologist,* Vol. 63 (June, 1961), pp. 508–21.

BURLING, ROBBINS. *Hill Farms and Padi Fields: Life in Mainland Southeast Asia.* Englewood Cliffs, N.J.: Prentice-Hall, Inc., 1965.

CHAPPLE, E. D., AND COON, C. S. *Principles of Anthropology.* Copyright 1942 by Holt, Rinehart and Winston, Inc. Used by permission of the publisher.

CHILDE, V. GORDON. *Man Makes Himself.* New York: Mentor Book, New American Library of World Literature, Inc., 1951. (Paperback.)

CHURCH, JOSEPH. *Language and the Discovery of Reality.* New York: Random House, Inc., 1961. © Copyright 1961 by Joseph Church. Reprinted by permission of Random House, Inc.

COOLEY, C. H. *Social Organization.* New York: Charles Scribner's Sons, 1909.

COON, C. S. (ed.). *Reader in General Anthropology.* New York: Henry Holt & Company, Inc., 1948.

DAVIS, KINGSLEY. *Human Society.* New York: The Macmillan Company, 1949.

DE LAGUNA, G. A. "Culture and Rationality," *American Anthropologist,* Vol. 51, No. 3 (July, 1949), pp. 379–91.

DENNIS, WAYNE. *The Hopi Child.* New York: John Wiley and Sons, Inc. 1965. (Paperback)

DEUTSCH, MARTIN. "Nursery Education: The Influence of Social Programming on Early Development," *The Journal of Nursery Education,* Vol. 18, No. 3 (April, 1963), pp. 191–97.

DIAMOND, STANLEY. "What History Is," *Process and Pattern in Culture* (ed. R. A. MANNERS). Chicago: Aldine Publishing Company, 1964.

DUBOS, RENÉ J. "Man Adapting: Using All Our Genes," *Current* (January, 1966), pp. 61–64.

DURKHEIM, ÉMILE. *Suicide.* Trans. JOHN A. SPAULDING and GEORGE SIMPSON (ed. GEORGE SIMPSON). New York: The Free Press, 1951.

———. "On Anomie," trans. W. C. BRADBURY, JR., *University Observer* (Winter, 1947).

EDGERTON, ROBERT B. "Cultural vs. Ecological Factors in the Expression of Values, Attitudes, and Personality Characteristics," *American Anthropologist*, Vol. 67 (April, 1965), pp. 442–47.

EISENSTADT, S. N. *From Generation to Generation.* New York: The Free Press, 1956.

EKVALL, R. B. *Tibetan Sky Lines.* New York: Farrar, Straus & Young, Inc., 1952.

———. "Law and the Individual among the Tibetan Nomads," *American Anthropologist*, Vol. 66 (October, 1964), pp. 1110–15.

FARON, L. C. *Hawks of the Sun: Mapuche Morality and Its Ritual Attributes.* Pittsburgh: University of Pittsburgh Press, 1964.

FISCHER, JOHN L., AND FISCHER, ANN. "The New Englanders of Orchard Town, U.S.A.," *Six Cultures: Studies of Child Rearing* (ed. B. WHITING). New York: John Wiley & Sons, Inc., 1963.

FORD, C. S., AND BEACH, F. A. *Patterns of Sexual Behavior.* New York: Harper & Row, Publishers, 1951.

FRASER, THOMAS M., JR. *Fishermen of South Thailand, The Malay Villagers.* New York: Holt, Rinehart & Winston, Inc., 1966.

FREEMAN, LINTON C., AND WINCH, ROBERT F. "Societal Complexity: An Empirical Test of a Typology of Societies," *American Journal of Sociology*, Vol. LXII (1957), pp. 461–66.

FREUD, SIGMUND. *The Problem of Anxiety.* New York: W. W. Norton, Inc., 1927.

FRIEDL, ERNESTINE. *Vasilika: A Village in Modern Greece.* New York: Holt, Rinehart & Winston, Inc., 1962.

FROMM, ERICH. *The Art of Loving.* New York: Harper & Row, Publishers, 1956.

———. *The Heart of Man.* New York: Harper & Row, Publishers, 1964.

GANZ, MADELAINE. *The Psychology of Alfred Adler and the Development of the Child.* London: Routledge & Kegan Paul, Ltd., 1953.

GILLIN, JOHN. *The Ways of Men*. New York: Appleton-Century-Crofts, 1948.

GLUECK, SHELDON, AND GLUECK, ELEANOR. *Family Environment and Delinquency*. Boston: Houghton Mifflin Company, 1962.

GOERTZEL, VICTOR, AND GOERTZEL, MILDRED GEORGE. *Cradles of Eminence*. Boston: Little, Brown and Company, 1962. Copyright © 1962, by Victor and Mildred Goertzel. Reprinted with permission of Little, Brown and Company.

GOLDENWEISER, ALEXANDER A. "Loose Ends of Theory on the Individual, Pattern, and Involution in Primitive Society," *Essays in Anthropology* (ed. R. H. LOWIE). Berkeley: University of California Press, 1936.

GOLDING, WILLIAM. *Free Fall*. New York: Harcourt, Brace & World, Inc., 1960.

GOLDSCHMIDT, WALTER. *Man's Way*. New York: Holt, Rinehart & Winston, Inc., 1959.

GOLDSCHMIDT, WALTER, AND OTHERS. "Variation and Adaptability of Culture: A Symposium" and "Theory and Strategy in the Study of Cultural Adaptability," *American Anthropologist*, Vol. 67 (April, 1965), pp. 402–8.

GOODMAN, MARY ELLEN. *Race Awareness in Young Children*. New York: Collier Books, 1964.

GOODMAN, MARY ELLEN, AND COCKRELL, DURA-LOUISE. "Emergent Citizenship—A Study of Four-Year-Olds." (Mimeograph), 1958.

GOODMAN, MARY ELLEN; HUZIOKA, Y.; AND MATSUURA, H. (with the assistance of KISAKA, K., AND KUMAGAI, S.). "Social Awareness in Young Children; A Study of Japanese Five-Year-Olds." (Mimeograph), 1956.

GORER, G. *The Peoples of Great Russia*. New York: Chanticleer Press, Inc., 1950.

GRIFFITH, THOMAS. *The Waist-High Culture*. New York: Harper & Row, Publishers, 1959.

HALL, EDWARD T. *The Silent Language*. New York: Doubleday & Company, Inc., 1959.

HALLOWELL, A. IRVING. "Psychological Leads for Ethnological Field Workers," *Personal Character and Cultural Milieu* (ed. DOUGLAS G. HARING). Syracuse, N.Y.: Syracuse University Press, 1956.

HARING, DOUGLAS G. (ed.). *Personal Character and Cultural Milieu*. Syracuse, N.Y.: Syracuse University Press, 1956.

HENRY, JULES. "The Personal Community and Its Invariant Properties," *American Anthropologist*, Vol. 60, No. 5 (October, 1958), pp. 827–31.

————. *Jungle People*. New York: Vintage Books, Inc., Random House, 1964.

HOBART, CHARLES W. "Commitment, Value Conflict and the Future of the American Family," *Journal of Marriage and Family Living*, Vol. 25 (November, 1963), pp. 405–12.

HOBBES, THOMAS. *Leviathan*. Everyman's Library. New York: E. P. Dutton & Co., Inc., 1950.

HOEBEL, E. ADAMSON. *Man in the Primitive World*. 2nd ed. New York: McGraw-Hill Book Co., 1958.

HOSHINO, IKUMI. "Apartment Life in Japan," *Journal of Marriage and the Family*, Vol. 26, No. 3 (August, 1964), pp. 312–17.

HSU, F. L. K. *Americans and Chinese: Two Ways of Life*. New York: Henry Schuman, Inc., 1953.

————. *Clan, Caste, and Club*. Princeton, N.J.: D. Van Nostrand Company, Inc., 1963.

HUNT, J. McVICKER. "How Children Develop Intellectually," *Children*, Vol. 11, No. 3 U.S. Department of Health, Education and Welfare, Welfare Administration, Children's Bureau, Washington, D.C. (May-June, 1964), pp. 83–91.

ISHWARAN, K. *Family Life in the Netherlands*. The Hague, 1959.

JACOBS, MELVILLE. *Pattern in Cultural Anthropology*. Homewood, Ill.: The Dorsey Press, 1964.

KENNARD, E. A. "Hopi Reactions to Death," *American Anthropologist*, Vol. 39, No. 3 (July-September, 1937), pp. 491–96.

KLINEBERG, OTTO. "Emotional Expression in Chinese Literature," *The Journal of Abnormal and Social Psychology* (October, 1938), pp. 517–20.

KLUCKHOHN, CLYDE. *Mirror for Man*. New York: McGraw-Hill Book Co., 1949.

KLUCKHOHN, CLYDE, AND KELLY, WILLIAM H. "The Concept of Culture," *Culture and Behavior* (ed. RICHARD KLUCKHOHN). New York: The Free Press, 1962.

KLUCKHOHN, CLYDE, AND KROEBER, A. L. *Culture: A Critical Review of Concepts and Definitions*. New York: Vintage Books, Inc., Random House, 1963.

KLUCKHOHN, CLYDE, AND MOWRER, O. H. "'Culture and Personality': a Conceptual Scheme," *American Anthropologist*, Vol. 46 (January, 1944), pp. 1–29.

KLUCKHOHN, CLYDE, AND MURRAY, H. A. (eds.). *Personality in Nature, Society, and Culture*. New York: Alfred A. Knopf, Inc., 1948.

KROEBER, ALFRED L. *Anthropology*. New York: Harcourt, Brace & Company, Inc., 1948.

KROEBER, ALFRED L., AND KLUCKHOHN, CLYDE. *Culture: A Critical Review of Concepts and Definitions*. New York: Vintage Books, Inc., Random House, 1963.

KOLENDA, KONSTANTIN. *The Freedom of Reason*. San Antonio, Tex.: Principia Press of Trinity University, 1964.

KOYANO, SHOGO. "Changing Family Behavior in Four Japanese Communities," *Journal of Marriage and the Family*, Vol. 26, No. 2 (May, 1964), pp. 149–59.

LANTIS, MARGARET (ed.). *Eskimo Childhood and Interpersonal Relationships*. Seattle: University of Washington Press, 1960.

LEE, DOROTHY. *Freedom and Culture*. Englewood Cliffs, N.J.: Prentice-Hall, Inc., 1959.

LEVINE, DONALD N. *Wax and Gold; Tradition and Innovation in Ethiopian Culture*. Chicago: University of Chicago Press, 1965.

LEVINSON, DANIEL J. "Idea Systems in the Individual and in Society," *Explorations in Social Change* (eds. GEORGE K. ZOLLSCHAN AND WALTER HIRSCH). Boston: Houghton Mifflin Co., 1964.

LINTON, RALPH. *The Study of Man*. New York: Appleton-Century-Crofts, 1936.

———. "Present World Conditions in Cultural Perspective," *The Science of Man in the World Crisis* (ed. R. LINTON). New York: Columbia University Press, 1945.

MARTIN, WILLIAM. "Rediscovering the Mind of the Child: A Significant Trend in Research in Child Development," *Merrill-Palmer Quarterly*, Vol. 6 (1960), pp. 67–76.

MASLOW, ABRAHAM H. *Motivation and Personality*. New York: Harper & Row, Publishers, 1954.

———. "Psychological Data and Value Theory," *New Knowledge in Human Values* (ed. A. H. MASLOW). New York: Harper & Row, Publishers, 1959.

———. "Self-Actualization: a Study in Psychological Health," *Symposia on Topical Issues* (ed. by W. WOLFF), Vol. I, "Values in Personality Research." New York: Grune & Stratton, Inc., 1950.

MEAD, MARGARET. "The Role of the Individual in Samoan Culture," *The Journal of the Royal Anthropological Institute of Great Britain and Ireland*, Vol. LVIII (1928), pp. 481–95.

———. "An Investigation of the Thought of Primitive Children with Special Reference to Animism," *Journal of the Royal Anthropological Institute*, Vol. LXII (1932), pp. 173–90.

———— (ed.). *Cooperation and Competition among Primitive Peoples.* New York: McGraw-Hill Book Co., 1937.

————. *Continuities in Cultural Evolution.* New Haven: Yale University Press, 1964.

————. "Continuities in Cultural Evolution," an Author's Précis (of the book of the same title), *Current Anthropology*, Vol. 7 (February, 1966), pp. 67–68.

MEAD, MARGARET, AND BUNZEL, RUTH L. (eds.). *The Golden Age of American Anthropology.* New York: George Braziller, Inc., 1960.

MINER, HORACE. *The Primitive City of Timbuctoo.* Rev. ed. New York: Doubleday & Company, Inc., 1965.

MISHKIN, BERNARD. "Contemporary Quechua," *Handbook of South American Indians* (ed. JULIAN H. STEWARD), Vol. II. New York: Cooper Square Publishers, Inc., 1963.

MORGENBESSER, SIDNEY, AND WALSH, JAMES (eds.). *The Free Will.* Englewood Cliffs, N.J.; Prentice-Hall, Inc., 1962.

MOWRER, O. HOBART. *The New Group Therapy.* Princeton, N.J.: D. Van Nostrand Company, Inc., 1964.

MULLER, HERBERT J. *Freedom in the Ancient World.* New York: Harper & Row, Publishers, Inc., 1961.

NIZER, LOUIS. *My Life in Court.* New York: Pyramid Books, Inc., 1963. (Paperback.)

NEWMAN, PHILIP L. "Wild Man Behavior in a New Guinea Highlands Community," *American Anthropologist*, Vol. 66, No. 1 (February, 1964), pp. 1–19.

NORBECK, EDWARD. *Takashima.* Salt Lake City: University of Utah Press, 1954.

————. *Changing Japan.* Case Studies in Anthropology. New York: Holt, Rinehart & Winston, Inc., 1965.

OLIVER, SYMMES C. "Individuality, Freedom of Choice, and Cultural Flexibility of the Kamba," *American Anthropologist*, Vol. 67, No. 2, April, 1965), pp. 421–28.

OPLER, MORRIS. "Themes as Dynamic Forces in Culture," *American Journal of Sociology*, Vol. LI (1945), pp. 198–206.

————. "Rejoinder," *American Journal of Sociology*, Vol. LII, No. 1 (July, 1946), p. 43.

————. "The Human Being in Culture Theory," *American Anthropologist*, Vol. 66, No. 3, Part I (June, 1964), pp. 507–28.

PARSONS, TALCOTT. *The Social System.* New York: The Free Press, 1951.

PHELPS, ROBERT. "On Being Middle Class," (review of *Bourgeois Anonymous*, MORRIS PHILIPSON), *New Republic*, Vol. 152 (June 19, 1965), p. 25.

PHILLIPS, BARBARA. "Critique," (student paper prepared for Anthropology 370, The Individual and Culture, Rice University), 1965.

PHILLIPS, BERNARD S. "The Urban Personality and the Rural Personality in Skopje, Yugoslavia." Milwaukee: University of Wisconsin, Dept. of Sociology, Clearinghouse for Sociological Literature, 1965.

RANK, OTTO. *Art and Artist: Creative Urge and Personality Development*. Trans. CHARLES F. ATKINSON. New York: Tudor Publishing Co., 1932.

————. *Will Therapy; and, Truth and Reality*. Trans. and with a Preface and Introduction by JESSIE TAFT. New York: Alfred A. Knopf, Inc., 1945.

RAY, VERNE F. *Primitive Pragmatists*. Seattle: University of Washington Press, 1963.

READ, MARGARET. *Children of Their Fathers*. New Haven: Yale University Press, 1960.

REDFIELD, ROBERT. "The Folk Society," *American Journal of Sociology*, Vol. 52 (1947), pp. 293–308. Reprinted by permission of the University of Chicago Press.

————. *The Primitive World and Its Transformations*. Ithaca, N.Y.: Cornell University Press, 1953 (first publication). (Cornell paperback, 1965.)

REISCHAUER, E. O., AND FAIRBANK, J. K. *East Asia: The Great Tradition*. Boston: Houghton Mifflin Co., 1960.

RIESMAN, DAVID. *Individualism Reconsidered*. New York: The Free Press, 1964.

SEEMAN, MELVIN. "Antidote to Alienation—Learning to Belong," *Trans-Action* (May-June, 1966), pp. 35–39.

SHELLY, M. W., AND BRYAN, G. L. (eds.). *Human Judgments and Optimality*. New York: John Wiley & Sons, Inc., 1964.

SHEN, TSUNG-LIEN, AND LIU, SHEN-CHI. *Tibet and the Tibetans*. Stanford, Cal.: Stanford University Press, 1953.

SHEPARD, ROGER N. "On Subjectively Optimum Selection Among Multiattribute Alternatives," *Human Judgments and Optimality* (eds. M. W. SHELLY AND G. L. BRYAN). New York: John Wiley & Sons, Inc., 1964.

SHUB, BORIS. "Soviets Expose American Baby," *New Leader*, Vol. XXXIII, No. 24 (June, 1950), pp. 11–12.

SKINNER, B. F. *Walden Two*. New York: The Macmillan Co., 1948.

———. *Science and Human Behavior*. New York: The Macmillan Co., 1953.

SLOTKIN, J. S. *Social Anthropology*. New York: The Macmillan Co., 1950.

SOROKIN, PITIRIM A. *Altruistic Love: A Study of American Good Neighbors and Christian Saints*. Boston: The Beacon Press, Inc., 1950.

———. *The Ways and Power of Love*. Boston: The Beacon Press, Inc., 1954.

STRAUSS, ANSELM (ed.). *George Herbert Mead on Social Psychology, Selected Papers*. Chicago: Phoenix Books, The University of Chicago Press, 1964. (Paperback.)

SUMNER, WILLIAM G. *Folkways*. Boston: Ginn & Company, 1907.

THOMAS, ALEXANDER; BIRCH, HERBERT G.; CHESS, STELLA; HERTZIG, MARGARET E., AND KORN, SAM. *Behavioral Individuality in Early Childhood*. New York: New York University Press, 1963.

TURNBULL, COLIN M. *The Forest People*. New York: Simon and Schuster, Inc., 1961.

TURNER, RALPH. *The Great Cultural Traditions*. New York: Mc-Graw-Hill Book Company, 1941.

UCHENDU, VICTOR. *The Igbo of Southeast Nigeria*. New York: Holt, Rinehart & Winston, Inc., 1965.

VON MERING, OTTO. *A Grammar of Human Values*. Pittsburgh: University of Pittsburgh Press, 1961.

VOGEL, EZRA F. *Japan's New Middle Class*. Berkeley: University of California Press, 1963.

WELTFISH, GENE. *The Lost Universe*. New York: Basic Books, Inc., 1965.

WHITE, LESLIE A. "Man's Control over Civilization: An Anthropocentric Illusion," *The Scientific Monthly*, Vol. LXVI, No. 3 (March, 1948), pp. 235–47.

WHITE, WINSTON. *Beyond Conformity*. New York: The Free Press, 1961.

WHITEFORD, ANDREW HUNTER. *Two Cities of Latin America*. New York: Anchor Books, Doubleday & Company, Inc., 1964. (Paperback.)

WHITING, JOHN W. M. *Becoming a Kwoma*. New Haven: Yale University Press, 1941.

WIRTH, LOUIS.   "Urbanism as a Way of Life," *American Journal of Sociology*, Vol. XLIV (July, 1938), pp. 1–24.

WYLIE, LAURENCE.   *Village in the Vaucluse*. New York: Harper Colophon Books, Harper & Row, Publishers, 1964. (Paperback.)

INDEX

Index

A

Abraham, W. E., 171, 222
Adler, Alfred, 14, 15–17
Africa, 48, 64–71, 77, 119, 177, 205, 206
  Congo pygmies, 92, 106–7
  Ethiopia, 223, 224
  Ghana, 171, 222
  Igbo, 135
  Kamba, 172–73, 182, 183–85, 198
  Mano, 92
  Ngoni, 80, 113–16, 117
Albert, Ethel M., 43, 62, 64–71
Allport, Gordon W., 2, 6–10, 13, 14, 17, 19–21, 129, 146, 167, 236, 237
Altruism, 14, 21
Amhara, 223, 224
Andaman Islanders, 83, 92, 103
Angell, Robert, 227
Anomie, 170, 171–72, 181
Ansbacher, Heinz L. and Rowena R., 17
Arapesh, 120
Athenians, 83, 93
Australians, 80, 92, 103, 211
Ausubel, David P., 201
Autonomy, 2, 3, 4, 14, 19–20, 181, 219–42
Aztecs, 77, 83, 93

B

Bali, 143, 173–74, 175–76, 182, 202, 214–16
Barnett, H. G., 50–53, 62, 88, 96–97
Barnouw, Victor, 3
Beach, F. A., 49
Bedouin, Ruwalla, 83, 92

Beliefs, 44–46
Belo, Jane, 143, 173–74, 175–76, 202, 203–4, 214–16
Benedict, Ruth, 201, 212–14
Bennett, John W., 88, 97–100, 168
Bernard, Jessie, 188–93
Berndt, 132, 175, 204
Biological antecedents and influences, 55, 56, 57, 60–61, 62, 64, 79, 81
Blitsten, Dorothy, 85–86, 88, 111, 122–27
Bloom, Benjamin, 138–39, 234
Brandon, Henry, 200
Brown, William, 8n.
Bruner, Edward, 109
Bryan, G. L., 239
Buddhism, 199
Bunzel, Ruth, 208
Burling, Robbins, 133, 143–44, 199
Burmese, 199
Burundi, 62, 64–71

C

Chapple, E. D., 88, 103–4
Childe, V. Gordon, 75
Children, 80, 126, 127, 128–64, 167, 203, 235
  American, 138, 162–64
  race awareness in, 139–40
China, 33, 119, 135, 142–43, 144–45, 174, 178–79, 182, 185–88
Church, Joseph, 231
Clausse, 194
Cognition, 4, 238–39
Collectivity-oriented cultures, 228
Compadrazgo, 121
Conservation-oriented cultures, 229
Cooley, Charles H., 105

Coon, C. S., 82–84, 88, 89–93, 102–4, 106, 122
Cosmopolitan-oriented cultures, 229
Creative "I", 14–15
Creativity, 4, 5, 14, 17–19, 21, 25, 86, 229, 235–36, 240
Creativity-oriented cultures, 229
Culture
  as antecedent and influence, 55, 56, 57–58, 61, 64
  bulk of, 226
  change, 195–96
  complexity of
    and autonomy, 223–29
    and enculturation, 130–34
    and individual, 75–100
    and innovation, 96–97
    and social relations, 102–7, 109
  definition of, 32, 36, 60
  generic features of, 48–50
  levels of complexity, 83–84, 89–93
  nature of, 32–53
  and personality, 3, 37, 57
  press of, 3, 5, 167–93, 226
  pull of, 5, 167–93, 226
  simple-complex continuum, 5, 81–84
  variable complexity of, 75, 88–89
Cultures, diversity of, 32–34

D

Darwin, Charles, 20
Davis, Kingsley, 112
de Laguna, Grace, 37–38
De Lauwe, Chombard, 219
Dennis, Wayne, 108–9, 131
Determinism, cultural, 1–2, 34–35
Deutsch, Martin, 129
Diamond, Stanley, 35, 230–31
Dubos, Rene, 239–40
Durkheim, Émile, 102, 170, 171–72, 176

E

Edgerton, Robert, 206
Eisenstadt, S. N., 224–25
Ekvall, R. B., 204–5, 216–18
Enculturation, 5, 102, 113–16, 117, 128–64, 169, 226, 240–41

Eskimo, 90, 92, 102, 177, 197–98
Ethics and morals, 76–81
Ethnocentrism-oriented cultures, 229
Europe, 123, 225

F

Fairbank, J. K., 174, 185–88
Family, 108–16, 117, 120, 122–27, 186–87
Far East, 123
Faron, L. C., 79
Fischer, John and Ann, 140–41, 162–64
Folk cultures, 228–29
Folk society, bias toward, 97–100
Ford, C. S., 49
France, 234, 237
Fraser, Thomas, 220
Freedom, 22–23, 76
  and ethical-moral systems, 76–81
  illusion of, 1
  and patterning of space, 175–76
  problem of, vs. determinism, 6–10
  and security, 113–14, 117
  as value vs. structural element, 173, 183–85
Freeman, Linton C., 89
Freud, S., 9n., 13, 16, 17, 20
Friedl, Ernestine, 111, 152–56
Fromm, Erich, 14, 22–23

G

Ganz, Madelaine, 15, 16
Germany, 224
Gillin, John, 167
Glueck, Sheldon and Eleanor, 234
Goertzel, Victor and Mildred, 235–36
Goldenweiser, A., 176–77, 182, 196–97, 198, 208–12
Goldring, William, 237
Goldschmidt, Walter, 80, 81, 205–6
Gorer, G., 58, 148
Griaule, Marcel, 223
Griffith, Thomas, 237
Groenman, S., 112
Gururumba, 27–31

H

Hall, Edward T., 40
Hallowell, A. I., 129, 136, 177–78, 179
Haring, Douglas, 3, 33, 40, 41, 97
Harris, Z. S., 37
Henry, Jules, 82, 108–10, 118–22, 168–69
Heterogeneity, 226
Hobart, Charles W., 113
Hobbes, Thomas, 168
Hoebel, E. Adamson, 77–79
Hopi; *see* Indians, Hopi
Hoshino, Ikumi, 207
Hsu, F. L. K., 142–43, 144–45, 146
Human Relations Area Files, 49
Hunt, J. McV., 233–34

I

Ifugao, 77–79
Inca, 172
India, 93, 119, 120, 121–22
Indians
 Great Basin, 92, 102
 Hopi, 98–100, 108–9, 119, 121, 131, 221–22
 Maidu, 92
 Modoc, 111, 148–51
 Pawnee, 169–70, 182
 Plains, 121, 177
Individual
 antecedents of and influences on, 3, 4, 55–58, 62, 64
 as cause, 17–18
 in context, 26–27, 36, 50, 54–71, 75
 ideal types, 23–25
 as microcosm, 37–38
 nature and development of, 13–31
 psychology (Adler), 14, 15–17
 specialization of, 85, 89–90, 103–4, 117
 subordination of, 187–88
 thrust of, 3, 5, 194–218
 uniqueness of, 54–71, 130, 194–218
 variability of, 27–31, 130
  and innovation, 50–53, 62
Individual-oriented cultures, 228

Individualism, 76, 168, 173, 200–201, 206, 220–21
Individuality
 in conformity, 198
 levels of, 55–57, 61, 62, 64
 in various contexts, 198–200
Individuation, 129, 145
Inferiority complex, 15–17
Innovation, 4, 5, 50–53, 222
Institutions
 complexity of, 89, 91–93, 102–3
 number of, 89, 91
Intentions, 14, 19–20
Involution, 198, 210–12
Ishwaran, K., 112–13
Israel, 224
Italy, 224

J

Jacobs, Melville, 86
James, William, 9
Japan, 109, 110, 136–38, 146–48, 201, 206–7, 234

K

Kaingáng, 168–69, 182
Kamba, 172–73, 182, 183–85, 198
Kennard, E. A., 221–22
Kinsey Reports, 42
Klineberg, Otto, 178–79
Kluckhohn, Clyde, 33, 36, 38, 39, 40, 47, 48, 49, 54–57, 59, 61, 130, 194
Kolenda, Konstantin, 3, 238, 246
Koyano, Shogo, 207
Kroeber, Alfred L., 36, 38, 39, 40, 59–60, 230
Kwoma, 134, 156–62

L

La Barre, W., 148
Language, 230–31
Lantis, Margaret, 197–98
Lapps, 83, 90, 92
Lee, Dorothy, 3
Leisure, 226
Levine, Donald, 223
Levinson, Daniel, 140, 146, 230
Linton, Ralph, 50, 84–85, 87, 196
Literacy, 226

Liu, Shên-Chi, 34
Loving, 14, 22

M

Maidu, 92
Malinowski, B., 197, 211
Mano (Liberia), 92
Manus, 135, 136
Maori, 210
Mapuche, 79
Martin, William, 129–30
Maslow, Abraham H., 14, 24–26,
    27, 46, 231–32, 240–42
McDougall, W., 20
Mead, George Herbert, 14–15
Mead, Margaret, 38–39, 135, 136,
    202–3, 208, 245
Merton, Robert, 14
Mesopotamia, 87
Middle East, 123
Miner, Horace, 105, 107
Mishkin, B., 115–16
Modoc Indians, 111, 148–51
Moral
    norms, 227
    order, 79–80
Morgenbesser, S., 238
Moslems, 85–86
Mowrer, O. H., 54–57, 61, 130,
    194, 238
Muller, Herbert J., 3, 220, 240

N

Nader, Ralph, 199–200
National character, 58
Navaho, 44–45, 47
New Guinea, 27–31, 33, 34, 132,
    174–75, 182, 204
    Arapesh, 120
    Kwoma, 134, 156–62
New Zealand, 201
Newman, Philip L., 27–31
Ngoni, 80, 113–16, 117
Nizer, Louis, 110
Norbeck, Edward, 109, 110, 146–
    48, 201

O

Oliver, Symmes, 172–73, 183–85
Opler, Morris, 32, 47, 50
Orwell, George, 167

P

Parsons, Talcott, 14, 44, 60, 105
Pattern, as limit and as model, 176–
    77, 182
Patterning
    and assertive or innovating indi-
        vidual, 204–6
    of concepts and precepts, 177–78
    of emotional states, 178–79
    of social order, 181
Patterns, 39–43
    explicit and implicit, 39–40, 43
    ideal and behavioral, 42–43
Paulme, Denise, 64
Pawnee, 169–70, 182
Permissiveness, 26
Personal community, 5, 82, 108–9,
    111, 117, 118–22
Phillips, Barbara, 55, 56
Phillips, Bernard S., 180–81
Physical environment, influences on
    individual, 55, 56, 57, 60–61,
    62
Pinot, R., 128
Prejudice, 20, 42
Primary reaction pattern, 130
Pygmies, Congo, 92, 106–7

Q

Quechua (Peru), 115–16

R

Radin, Paul, 197
Rank, Otto, 14, 17–19
Ray, Verne, 148–51
Read, Margaret, 80, 113–15, 117
Reasoning-oriented cultures, 228
Redfield, Robert, 79–80, 82, 88,
    93–96, 98, 131, 224
Reischauer, E. O., 174, 185–88
Relationships
    family, 108–16
    in folk society, 95–96
    and the individual, 116–17
    lack of fixity, 168
    types of, 101–7
Religion, 79, 91–92, 209
    shamans, 89–90
Rickman, J., 58
Riesman, David, 35
Romans, 93
Russia, Soviet, 224

S

Samoa, 202–3
Sapir, Edward, 37
Schopenhauer, Arthur, 20
Seeman, Melvin, 237–38
Self
  -actualizing, 14, 24–26, 231–32,
    240–42
  -appraisal, 15–16
  -awareness, 14, 22–23
  -determination, 1, 2, 23–24
  -direction, 17
  -insight, 7
Sexual behavior, 42, 49
Shamans, 89, 90
Shelly, M. W., 239
Shen, Tsung-Lien, 34
Shephard, R. N., 239
Shub, Boris, 58
Siberia, 33
Skinner, B. F., 1
Slotkin, J. S., 101
Social order, 226
Social relations, primary vs. sec-
    ondary, 101, 105, 107
Societal antecedents and influences,
    55, 56, 57–60, 61, 62, 63–64
Society
  definition of, 32, 58–60
  folk, 93–96, 98, 102, 106, 117,
    196–98
  size of, 226
  solidarity of, and values, 170–71
Sophisticate cultures, 228–29
Sorokin, Pitirim A., 14, 21, 22
Strauss, Anselm, 14–15
Subsistence needs, 80–81
Sumner, William Graham, 47
Sweden, 237
Symbols, 44–46

T

Taft, Jessie, 18
Tagore, Sir Rabindranath, 1
Technical order, 79
Technology, 75–76, 82–86, 88, 103,
    107, 226
Temperament, types of, 212–16
Thai, 133, 143–44, 220
Themes (cultural) and world views,
    46–48

Thomas, Alexander, 130
Tibet, 33, 204–5, 216–18
Tierra del Fuegians, 92
Timbuctoo, 107
Toda, 211
Tolerance, 14
  and empathy, 19–21, 27
Trade, 89–91
Tradition–oriented cultures, 228
Tribalism, 129, 145
Trobrianders, 83, 92, 177
Tumin, M., 168
Turnbull, Colin M., 106–7
Turner, Ralph, 87

U

Uchendu, Victor, 135
United States, 234, 237
Urban personality, 180–81, 182
Urbanism, 226

V

Values, 44–46, 81, 113–15, 173,
    175, 188–93, 224, 225, 226–
    27, 228–29
Vasilika, 111, 152–56
Vikings, 93
Vogel, Ezra, 109
Von Mering, Otto, 4

W

Walsh, J., 238
Weltfish, Gene, 169–70
White, Leslie A., 1–2
White, Winston, 219, 225
Whiteford, Andrew Hunter, 62,
    63–64
Whiting, John, 134, 156–62
"Wild Man", 27–31
Will, 14, 15, 16, 17–19, 20, 23
Winch, Robert F., 89
Wirth, Louis, 101–2
Witchcraft, 44–45
Women, 64–71, 78, 104–5, 115,
    125, 188, 203
Writing and literacy, 75–76, 86–88
Wylie, Laurence, 199

Y

Yugoslavia, 180–81

This book has been set in 10 point Times Roman, leaded 3 points; and 9 point Times Roman, leaded 2 points. The part numbers are in 18 point Spartan Heavy italic caps. The chapter numbers have the word "Chapter" in 10 point Spartan Medium caps, followed by an 18 point Spartan Heavy arabic number. The chapter titles are in 18 point Spartan Heavy.